TOOLS AND TECHNIQUES OF LEADERSHIP AND MANAGEMENT

Many of today's books on the tools and techniques of leadership and management provide descriptions of long lists for use in decision-making, leading, coaching and project management. This book takes a completely different approach. It contests the claims that the tools and techniques are based on evidence and explains why human activities of leading and managing are simply not amenable to scientific proof and, consequently, why the long-term futures of organizations are unpredictable.

The book undertakes a critical exploration of just what these tools and techniques are about, showing that while they may lead to competent performance, they cannot go further to expert performance because expertise involves going beyond rules and procedures. Ralph Stacey investigates the many questions that are thrown up as a result of this new approach, such as:

- How do we apply this new way of thinking?
- What are the practical tools and techniques it gives us?
- What is the role of leaders in an unpredictable world?
- How does complexity affect the way organizations are structured and function?

This book will be relevant to students on courses and modules that deal with leadership, decision-making, and organizational development and behaviour, as well as professional leaders and managers who want to develop their own understanding and techniques.

Ralph Stacey is Professor of Management and founding member of, and currently supervisor on, an innovative Master and Doctoral programme in complexity, leadership and organizational change at the Business School of the University of Hertfordshire in the UK. He is also a member of the Institute of Group Analysis. Ralph has published numerous titles, many of them with Routledge, and is co-editor of Routledge's series on *Complexity as the Experience of Organizing*.

TOOLS AND TECHNIQUES OF LEADERSHIP AND MANAGEMENT

Meeting the challenge of complexity

Ralph Stacey

Routledge
Taylor & Francis Group

LONDON AND NEW YORK

First published 2012
by Routledge
2 Park Square, Milton Park, Abingdon, Oxon OX14 4RN

Simultaneously published in the USA and Canada
by Routledge
711 Third Avenue, New York, NY 10017

Routledge is an imprint of the Taylor & Francis Group, an informa business

British Library Cataloguing in Publication Data
A catalogue record for this book is available from the British Library

Library of Congress Cataloging in Publication Data
Stacey, Ralph D.
Tools and techniques of leadership and management: meeting the challenge of
complexity / Ralph Stacey.
p. cm.
Includes bibliographical references and index.
ISBN 978-0-415-53117-7 (hardback)–ISBN 978-0-415-53118-4 (pbk.)–ISBN
978-0-203-11589-3 (ebook) 1. Leadership. 2. Management. I. Title.
HD57.7.S7133 2012
658.4'092–dc23
2011049078

ISBN: 978-0-415-53117-7 (hbk)
ISBN: 978-0-415-53118-4 (pbk)
ISBN: 978-0-203-11589-3 (ebk)

Typeset in Bembo
by Taylor & Francis Books

CONTENTS

PREFACE

Colleagues and I take up insights from the complexity sciences to argue that organization-wide stability and change emerges in many, many local interactions between members of the organization and between them and members of other organizations such as suppliers, consumers, competitors, regulators and governments. Organizations are patterns of interaction between human beings and these patterns emerge in the interplay of the intentions, plans, choices and actions of all involved. To say that organization-wide patterns emerge in this interplay is to say that these organizational patterns are unpredictable. So what the new sciences of uncertainty, the sciences of complexity, make clear is that long-term futures are in a very important sense unpredictable. Since they have to confront uncertain futures, that is, since they cannot predict the long-term consequences of their actions, and since they cannot control the interplay of intentions, it follows that leaders and managers cannot choose the future of their organizations, no matter how much planning and envisioning they do. The view we have been expressing problematizes the dominant discourse built on the notion that, in one way or another, the powerful can determine what will happen; indeed it problematizes all the tools and techniques of the dominant discourse. However, if they cannot achieve what they want simply by planning, then what are they and everyone else doing to accomplish whatever it is that they accomplish? This question directs our attention to what people in organizations actually do rather than what they say they do or what academics and consultants claim they should do. With this focus on what people actually do, it becomes clear that they accomplish their work in ambiguous and uncertain situations through ongoing conversation with each other in which they establish patterns of power relations that reflect their ideologies, which are also reflected in the choices they make. Whenever I present this view in conference addresses, seminars and workshops, I am pressed to provide the alternative set of tools and techniques to replace the ones I claim do not work. I immediately explain that the view I am presenting invites reflection on what people are already doing. Reflecting on what we are already doing cannot yield in an uncertain world the kinds of generalities appropriate for all contexts that can only apply to a certain world. This explanation does nothing to diminish the pressure.

Recently, at the suggestion of one of our staff group, we started blogging. It was striking how any blog on tools and techniques attracted a lot of attention and led to sometimes lengthy exchanges of view. Similar pressures to those described above were exerted in the blog conversation. It was these pressures which attracted me to writing this book, in which I will try to explain what the problem is with the conventional tools and techniques of leadership and management, and where I will also try to point to the kind of 'techniques' that are available for sustaining and developing the expertise of leaders and managers.

I am very fortunate in having belonged, and continuing to belong, to a group of very insightful colleagues. I express my great thanks to them for their contributions to what we are together doing and for their comments on this book. I am also grateful to the members and graduates of the Doctor of Management programme who constantly point to new areas of interest. Finally, I want to say thank you to colleagues at the University of Hertfordshire who have made it possible for me to do what I do.

Ralph Stacey
London, October 2011

1

INTRODUCTION

In a number of books published since 2000,[1] colleagues and I have together developed a way of thinking about organizations as patterns of interaction between human beings. In our various ways we all became dissatisfied with the dominant discourse on organizations and their leadership and management because those taking part in this discourse present an abstract notion of what an organization is, namely, a system in which the ordinary, lived reality of human beings who are actually 'the organization' disappears from view. The dominant management discourse on organizations is reflected in how managers usually talk together about the nature of their managerial activity. It is also reflected in the kind of organizational research that attracts funding from research bodies, the kind of papers that prestigious research journals will publish, the kind of courses taught at business schools and in the textbooks they use, as well as in organizational training and development activities. According to the dominant discourse on organizations, leaders, managers and powerful coalitions of them are supposed to objectively observe their organizations and use the tools of rational analysis to select appropriate objectives, targets and strategic visions for their organizations. They are then supposed to formulate strategies of macro change and design organizational structures and procedures to implement actions to achieve the targets, objectives and visions. They are supposed to adopt rational monitoring procedures to secure control over the movement of their organizations into the future. Powerful coalitions of managers are supposed to know what is happening through environmental scanning and internal resource analyses, on the basis of which they are supposed to choose the outcomes for their organization and design the systems, including learning systems, which will enable them to be in control of the strategic direction of their organization so as to improve. One only has to think of the 2008 financial crisis, now in 2011 being experienced as the sovereign debt crisis, for it to become undeniably clear that leaders and managers are either not doing what they are supposed to be doing or that the advice is totally unrealistic. I am convinced that it is the latter which is the case.

Thinking in terms of the dominant discourse simply does not resonate with our lived experience of activities of organizing, leading and managing. In the books we have published since 2000, colleagues and I have proposed an alternative way of thinking about organizations which we have called the theory of complex responsive processes. This theory problematizes taken-for-granted notions in the dominant discourse such as control, planning, prescriptions, tools and techniques. It points to how little control anyone has over outcomes, but this does not mean lack of control. Control is achieved through the constraints of power, through ideology, through the social background all are socialized into, and through the control of human bodies using the techniques of disciplinary power. No one can control outcomes but the powerful can control human bodies to a considerable degree, although this control will usually be limited as people practise the arts of resistance. The theory, then, has a different notion of what is practical and of management techniques compared to the dominant discourse.

I was prompted to write this book by the experience of presenting this view to leaders and managers. That experience is one of being frequently and insistently asked a number of questions at lectures, seminars and workshops, or when people in organizations contact me. What I want to try to do in this book is address those questions. The questions, repeated over and over again, are always along the following lines:

- How do we apply the theory of complex responsive processes?
- What are the practical tools and techniques the theory gives us so that we may improve our organizations?
- You say that we cannot forecast what the outcomes of our action will be and this problematizes planning. But surely we must plan?
- If everything emerges, is there any need for managers and leaders?
- What is the role of leaders in an unpredictable world?
- How does complexity affect the way organizations are structured and function?
- Which real world organizations have used your thinking and achieved success?
- What are some examples of organizations that deal with complexity the best? What are some common characteristics of these organizations? What are some common characteristics of their leaders?
- What are the relationships between managing complexity well and supporting innovation in an organization?
- What examples are there of organizations that have dealt with the complexity of rapidly changing business requirements? How did they meet that challenge effectively? Are there any important guiding principles of management practice for leaders in this type of organization?

If organizations are thought to change when powerful coalitions of leaders and managers change the macro designs, rules, procedures, structures and visions for the organization as a whole, then it makes unquestionable sense to ask what particular tools, techniques, competences, organizational structures, cultures, social networks and so on, lead to success. It seems to be pure common sense to look for the best practices conducted in successful organizations as a guide to what leaders and managers should be doing in their own organization; to establish benchmarks to judge their organization's performance; and to ask for the evidence that any proposed approach to leadership and management actually works in practice. However, a move to thinking in terms of complex responsive processes shifts the focus of attention from the long-term, big-picture, macro level to the details of the micro interactions taking place in the present between living humans in organizations. Instead of abstracting from and covering over the micro processes of organizational dynamics, such organizational dynamics become the route to understanding how organizations are being both sustained and changed at the same time and what part the activities of leading and managing play in this paradox of stability (continuity) and instability (change). From this point of view, the repeated questions of the kind given above do not make all that much sense. They are questions framed in one paradigm, the dominant discourse, and then taken up in a completely different paradigm, the alternative discourse. It is a quite understandable attempt to comprehend the alternative in terms of the dominant discourse and of course this cannot be done without completely neutering the alternative.

The aim of this book, therefore, is to explore why the frequently asked questions are problematical from the perspective of complex responsive processes. The exploration will involve coming to understand why the instrumentally rational tools and techniques of leadership and management are so limited and how they actually amount to a form of discipline rather than the direct cause of organizational stability and change. The exploration in this book will move from the rules and step-by-step procedures of the dominant view of leadership and management tools and techniques to consider how we might understand the practical judgment exercised by expert leaders and managers who have left the rules behind in order to deal with unique and uncertain situations. But first, are leaders and managers the same? If they are different, one would expect to find, in the dominant discourse, different tools and techniques for each. The next section looks at this question.

The split between managers and leaders

The words 'leadership' and 'management' both appeared at about the same time in the nineteenth century as descriptions of what business leaders and managers, as well as politicians, actually did, namely, the politics of guiding and influencing the opinions and actions of others using persuasion and domination. The words described rather different activities, one elevated and the other rather lowly. However, by 1925 'leadership' and 'management' were being used synonymously and related very much to roles in the modern commercial and industrial corporations in which leader-managers were thought to choose what an organization should be and do. In the period after the Second World War, management practice focused on the scientific manager who was supposed to design and manipulate systems, involving the use of models and analytical techniques to make decisions. Since the 1970s managers have come to be regarded as mere technicians, taking rational decisions using clearly defined routines and implementing strategies.[2] To compensate for this downgrading of managers, consultancies and business schools elevated the notion of leader as one who chose the direction while managers implemented the choice. It was now the leaders rather than the managers who were the professionals. In 1977 Zaleznik published a paper drawing a distinction between managers and leaders. According to Zaleznik,[3] managers differ in motivation from leaders and in how they think and act – they emphasize rationality, control, problem solving, goals and targets. Managers coordinate and balance conflicting views and get people to accept solutions. They are tactical and bureaucratic. Leaders work in an opposite way. Instead of limiting choices, they develop fresh approaches and open up new issues. They project their ideas into images that excite people. They formulate visions and inspire others to follow them. It is also generally thought to be the role of an organization's leaders to shape its values or culture, understood to be the deep-seated assumptions governing the behaviour of the individual members of an organization.[4]

However, this distinction between managers as traditional and rational while true leaders are charismatic is clearly an idealization and a rather simplistic one at that. In reality, leaders do find that they have to attend to often mundane administrative tasks and managers do have to lead those who report to them if they are to get anything done. For me, leadership and management are aspects of a legitimate power role in an organization and they cannot be separated. Throughout this book I will, therefore, usually use the term 'leaders and managers' as inseparable descriptors of an organizational role. Where I do use only one of the terms, I still mean both.

Outline of the book

Chapters 2 and *3* present a short summary of key aspects of the theory of complex responsive processes as the basis for the discussion of tools and techniques through the rest of the book. Drawing on the modern natural sciences of complexity as source domains for analogies with organizations, the complex responsive processes way of thinking about organizations and their management places the choices, designs and learning activities of people, including leaders, managers and powerful coalitions of them, in one organization in the context of similar activities by people in other organizations. It becomes understood that both continuity and change in all organizations are emerging in the many, many local communicative, political and ideologically based choices of all members of all the interdependent organizations, including the disproportionately influential choices of leaders and powerful coalitions of managers. What happens to an organization is not simply the consequence of choices made by powerful people in that organization. Instead, what happens to any one organization is the consequence of the interplay between the many choices and actions of all involved across many connected, interdependent organizations. Instead of thinking of organizations as the realization of a macro design chosen by the most powerful members of those organizations, we come to understand organizations as perpetually constructed macro or global patterns emerging across an organization in many, many local interactions. Continuity and change arise in local interactions, not simply in macro plans. This mode of thinking turns the dominant discourse on its head. According to the dominant discourse, organizational outcomes are chosen by powerful managers and then implemented, while from the complex responsive processes perspective organizational outcomes emerge in a way not simply determined by central choices but arising in the ongoing local interaction of many, many people, where that interaction can be understood as the interplay of many different intentions, choices and strategies. The two modes of thinking contradict each other and this means that we cannot say that mode one works in some situations while mode two is more appropriate in other situations – this attempt to have your cake and eat it simply blocks the radically different nature of the alternative thinking. If one mode of thinking resonates with, and makes sense of, our experience, then the other will not.

Chapter 4 describes the tools of instrumental rationality and explores the nature of these tools and techniques. In my experience, many people in organizations talk about management tools and techniques in a rather loose and taken-for-granted way as if we all know exactly what is meant by such tools or techniques. This chapter, therefore, sets out a long but by no means exhaustive list of what people normally mean when they talk about the tools and techniques of leadership and management. The tools and techniques are prescribed in the belief that they will enable leaders and managers to choose an improved future for their organizations and to control movement towards that future. This belief is based on a taken-for-granted underlying assumption of efficient causality. The prescriptions all take the form: *if* you apply tool M, *then* you will get result X. It is only if organizational life takes the form of taking an action which produces a predictable outcome that we can apply the tools as recommended. This chapter argues that the inevitably uncertain and ambiguous processes of interaction between people, which produce an organization, do not take a linear form and efficient causality does not apply. The claim that the use of particular tools and techniques will enable leaders and managers to choose and control future direction simply cannot be sustained in any rational argument. This conclusion is reinforced when it is understood that the tools and techniques of instrumental rationality are actually second-order abstractions from lived experience in organizations. Such abstractions have to be made particular in particular contingent situations characterized by some degree of uniqueness. What the tools or techniques actually mean will depend upon how they are taken up in contingent local interaction. The effect of attempting to apply the tool or technique will therefore be characterized by considerable uncertainty. Finally, the tools and techniques take the form of rules and procedures, and it is clear that following a rule is a complex matter depending on the nature of the society that those attempting to follow the rule live in. This chapter, then, seriously problematizes the whole notion of instrumentally rational leadership and management tools and techniques as direct causes of stability and change.

Chapter 5 continues with the analysis of the instrumentally rational tools and techniques of leadership and management. There is a well-known argument that those who are proficient in and expert at performing an activity do not use rules or tools at all. Following rules seems relevant when moving from novice to competent actor, but to go further than competence requires going beyond the rules. Insistence on following rules traps people at the level of competent performer and blocks the development of expertise. The expert and the merely competent actually display different forms of knowing. This chapter looks at the work underlying this conclusion. It then provides a general critique of the tools and techniques of instrumental rationality and concludes with a consideration of tools and techniques in relation to leadership. For the reasons given in the previous chapter, the tools and techniques of instrumental rationality cannot be the cause of change or improvement; on the contrary, they can sometimes, as we see in this chapter, be harmful in restricting spontaneity and blocking the development of practical judgment. However, many of them are essential in modern organizations and societies where some degree of control has to be exercised from a distance, and this use has to depend on practical judgment if it is to be beneficial rather than harmful. So, if the tools and techniques are used, but not actually for their proclaimed purpose, what are they actually used for? The next chapter considers how the tools and techniques of instrumental rationality are, in reality, the techniques of disciplinary power.

Chapter 6 explores the work of the French philosopher Michel Foucault,[5] who argues that discipline is a specific form of power which operates through the use of simple instruments of hierarchical observation, normalizing judgments and examination. This chapter explores how modern leadership and management practices employ these specific instruments of disciplinary power, and it will make the point that the tools and techniques of instrumental rationality discussed in the last two chapters are indeed the same as the instruments of disciplinary power. The aim of disciplinary power is that of controlling the bodies of people in a group, organization or society and the actions of those bodies. So, while the tools and techniques of technical rationality cannot achieve their stated purpose, namely, setting and controlling future outcomes, they do succeed in providing the means leaders and managers use to control the bodies and activities of those they supervise, even though this is not what they are claimed to be used for. However, modern organizations and societies could not exist without the techniques of disciplinary power, although it is, of course, as we will see in the next chapter, possible to practise them in ways which become highly dictatorial and ultimately, at the extreme, fascist. The tools and techniques of instrumental rationality are in practice the techniques of the exercise of disciplinary power in which embodied human persons are supervised by managers in a hierarchy, by those reporting to them in this hierarchy and by colleagues. These are social processes from which no one escapes – the supervisors are themselves perpetually supervised. However, when the techniques of disciplinary power are simply applied in unreflexive ways, they create the potential for bullying and domination, in the extreme taking the form of fascist and totalitarian organizations and societies. Of course, reflexivity can never be a guarantee that bullying and totalitarianism will be avoided because some may simply use the technique of reflexivity for more skilful domination of others.

Chapter 7 is a consideration of another technique defined by American management academic Edgar Schein as coercive persuasion.[6] Schein, well known for his view of the leader's role as essentially one of defining and changing an organization's culture, also claims that all such culture change must involve coercive persuasion, or brainwashing, since people will naturally resist suggestions that they change fundamental aspects of how they think. Leaders then become instigators and organizers of coercive persuasion. I argue that there is a fundamental distinction between the techniques of disciplinary power, discussed in the last chapter, and those of coercive persuasion. The former are aimed at controlling the bodies of people in a group, organization or society and the actions of those bodies. Whether the techniques of disciplinary power are ethical or not will depend on the particular circumstances in which they are used and on what the consequences for people and their work are. Coercive persuasion has a completely different aim – it is targeted at very specific activities of bodies, namely, minds. It seeks to foster dependency and, by definition, block questioning and reflexive thinking. It is, therefore, inimical to learning. The techniques of discipline, however, could create conditions in which learning is possible, just as Foucault argues, although they could also be used in unreflective ways to produce fascist environments that block learning. The aim of coercive persuasion is to break down the personalities of people and reconstruct them in ways that are chosen by the most powerful. For me, this can never be ethical and I cannot see how it can have any legitimate place in organizational life.

Chapter 8 explores how organizations reflect the wider institutions of society; indeed, they are expressions of various institutions such as the law, property rights and professional bodies. Wider institutional settings, therefore, impact on what leaders and managers can and cannot do in organizations. The purpose of this chapter is to explore the nature of institutions and how they enable and constrain the activities of leaders and managers. In particular, this chapter is an inquiry into the link between institutions and the organizational techniques of management and leadership. The inquiry starts by considering what the economics and organizational literatures have to say about institutions and how they change, pointing to how the central concern is with habits, rules and routines, as well as laws, rights, obligations, norms, customs, traditions and codes of conduct. Next, the literature on power and the social nature of institutions is briefly explored, before looking at the differences between the literature on institutions and the theory of complex responsive processes. Then there is a consideration of how the theory of complex responsive processes understands institutions as patterns of interaction between people, making power and ideology central to institutions. The chapter ends with a brief indication of what institutions mean for our understanding of the techniques of leadership and management.

Chapter 9 asks whether there are any 'techniques' of practical judgment. Since leaders and managers can only become experts through experience, it follows that some form of mentoring is a very important way in which to foster the development of leadership and management expertise. It also follows that some form of ongoing or periodic supervision would be highly important in sustaining and further developing this expertise. Coaching as a form of mentoring could thus be a very important technique with regard to the exercise of practical judgment. However, a distinction should be drawn between the kind of instrumentally rational, step-following forms of coaching which focus on goals and tasks in a narrow way and the kind of more discursive and exploratory forms that coaching, understood as a kind of work therapy, might take. The rest of this chapter looks at how we might think about 'techniques' that foster and sustain the capacity for practical judgment. First, practical judgment requires ongoing reflection on the judgments made and the consequences they produce. Mindless action does not yield practical judgment; instead, mindful action is required in which the actors reflexively think together about how they are thinking about what they are doing. I think, then, that we can understand the first requirement of ongoing practical judgment to be an ongoing inquiry, one that takes narrative, reflexive forms. Second, practical judgment relies on ongoing participation in the conversational life of an organization in ways that widen and deepen communication. Third, practical judgment involves some degree of spontaneity and improvisation, and there are 'techniques' which can make people more aware of this. Fourth, practical judgment is essentially the ordinary politics of everyday life where the techniques of rhetoric play a part and the matter of ethics assumes major importance.

Chapter 10 concludes the book with further consideration of the kinds of question presented in Chapter 1:

- Which organizations have taken up complex responsive processes and what has been the outcome?
- How can one use the insights of complex responsive processes? What does one say to those who claim that there are some easily recognizable laws or principles that could generate a better atmosphere and therefore better outcomes?
- Can organizations which foster healthier social environments, a matter of quality, be identified? Do they produce better outcomes? What fosters something positive amongst the people? Why are some organizations better able to produce good outcomes?
- Is the theory of complex responsive processes postmodern?
- As a manager, what could one do with the insight that strategies are emergent patterns of action arising in the interplay of choices made by many different groups of people? Surely there is more to it than just thinking? Surely there are tools and techniques for bringing about improvement?

In the *Appendix*, given the emphasis I have placed on reflexive inquiry, it seems right that I undertake such an inquiry myself. The Appendix presents an account of how I have come to think in the way I have and how this is reflected in the changes running through the books I have written over the past 20 years as well as the way I work.

2

THE THEORY OF COMPLEX RESPONSIVE PROCESSES

Understanding organizations as patterns of interaction between people

Introduction

Before taking up a lectureship at what became the University of Hertfordshire, I spent a number of years in industry, the last few of these as Manager of the Corporate Planning department of a large, international construction company. Because of this experience it was natural that I should teach the course on Strategic Management on the Business School's new MBA. As a strategist in industry I had not read much of the literature on strategy or planning, although at various conferences I heard about techniques such as the Boston Grid. I recall coming back from one of these conferences thinking that I would do a paper for the executive directors of the company analysing the subsidiary companies into Stars, Question Marks, Cash Cows or Dogs, as required by the Boston Grid. I presented the analysis to the executive directors, who treated it with some scorn, asking what I thought they could do with it. Well, the prescription is to milk the Cash Cows and use the cash generated to invest in Stars, while carefully monitoring Question Marks and closing down Dogs. This only increased the scorn poured on the analysis, which was dismissed as simplistic and mechanistic. Also, the directors were clearly more than scornful; some were quite annoyed. Those labelled Stars did not complain, but naturally those labelled Dogs and Question Marks were far from happy. Most annoyed, though, was the director of the largest subsidiary in the company, which generated a very significant part of the profits and cash flow, when his business was labelled a Cash Cow. What the analysis did lead to was a rather testy and quite unhelpful debate on why the results of the hard work of those in the supposed Cash Cow should be squandered on other subsidiaries. From this experience, I saw that turning to the conventional textbooks and their prescriptions was not at all helpful since they resolutely ignored the question of power and the political consequences of trying to follow the prescribed techniques. So I forgot about the textbooks and got on with the job. However, when it came to teaching Strategic

Management on the MBA, it was necessary to really engage with the literature and what I found rather frustrating was that it was full of techniques like the Boston Grid which simply had no connection with my experience. Of course I had to use the textbooks, but in addition I did something that I had not done very much while doing the job in industry and that was to reflect on what my experience there had actually been. What were we doing and why were we doing it?

It was not long before something rather intriguing but very puzzling became evident. I looked back over the five-year planning periods during my stay at the construction company over some thirteen years and noticed that in one of these periods the company's executives had more or less implemented the strategic plan formulated at the beginning of the period. The forecast at the beginning of this period was that following the recommended strategic actions would yield very strong growth in profits and very large inflows of cash which could be used for further investment. Unfortunately, however, despite having followed the plan, the company was incurring a loss and a very large cash outflow. The response was to put more effort into planning on the grounds that we obviously had not done enough analysis, had not made good enough forecasts, had not gathered enough information and had not dealt strongly enough with incompetent managers. Our response to this 'failure' was simply to repeat more firmly what we had been doing. It never occurred to me or to any of the others, as far as I know, that there could be something very flawed in how we were thinking. More effort was put into planning, the CEO was removed and the executive responsible for what I had called a Cash Cow became the new CEO and shortly afterwards also the chairman. In the five years that were to follow the actions taken were the exact opposite of those agreed in the strategic plan because of the skilful political activity of the new chairman and CEO, who had not agreed with the strategy in the first place but did not think it worth making a fuss about this. Instead, each time an aspect of the strategy was to be implemented, he blocked it and funnelled the cash into business areas he favoured; the results were a great success, at least for a few years. It became clear that these patterns were typical of all the five-year planning periods at this company.

At the same time as teaching on the MBA, I also did consulting work for the executive teams of some very large companies in the UK and, in addition to reflecting on my experience in the construction company, I began to think about what happened on these assignments. Whenever I went back to the companies I had worked with and asked what had happened to the strategies we had worked on, I noticed first that the top executives could rarely remember what it was that we had concluded about what the strategy should be and when I reminded them, they had usually done something different from what had been agreed and sometimes it worked and sometimes it did not. So, my experience with the construction company was not at all unique; it seemed to be a common experience, no matter what the sector or what the country. The fundamental problem was clear: over and over again we found that we were not able to forecast what the outcomes of the actions taken would be. Organizational life kept producing the unexpected, sometimes to the delight of the executives who immediately told stories about how they had turned this company around, but frequently to the disappointment of the executives. Often people working together produced not only what they had not expected but what they most definitely did not want. What disturbed me about this was that I could not explain why it was happening. In other words, I could not make sense of my experience. All of my formal education reflected the scientific conviction that with enough data and good models we would be able to forecast the consequences of our actions and so be able to rationally choose those that would yield what we wanted, which by and large was improvement of one kind or another. It was with this puzzle gnawing away at my mind that I came across, appropriately enough by chance, a book called *Chaos: The Birth of a New Science*.[1] I bought the book and read it with growing interest as I came to recognize that this 'new' science was pointing to answers to my questions and holding out the possibility that I would be able to explain why we could not forecast and so make much more sense of my own experience. So what is mathematical chaos and in what way does it demonstrate the limits of predictability?

Chaos and unpredictability

The choice of the term 'chaos' by those studying nonlinear models was unfortunate because most people immediately think that it means utter confusion. Mathematical chaos, however, is not about utter confusion but about patterns where we thought there were none. All science proceeds in terms of models, most prestigiously mathematical models of some real phenomenon. The models of traditional science are all cast in the form of linear relationships, which means that a cause is related to an effect in a proportional way. So, Newton's laws say that *if* you double the force on an object in a vacuum, *then* it will move twice as far. Of course, scientists like Newton knew that the phenomena of nature are nonlinear, but the problem with nonlinear equations is that they cannot be solved, whereas linear ones can. So although a linear model is known to be a simplification, it does make it possible to predict and it was thought that this simplifying assumption would not result in the prediction diverging very much from what actually happens. This simplifying procedure did work to very great effect in the case of many phenomena, for example in predicting the movement of the planets. What was 'new' about the models displaying chaos is that they are nonlinear so that events are not related to each other in proportional ways but are more or less than proportional. In linear models there is one cause for one effect and one effect for one cause. In nonlinear models there is more than one cause for an effect and more than one effect for one cause. These models take a particular non-linear form in which the output of the calculation in one period becomes the input of the next period, generating a never-ending history. These models cannot be solved, but the advent of powerful computers meant that they could be simulated on a computer and the patterns of movement they generated could be examined. And it turned out that for most natural phenomena the simplifying assumption of linearity has a big effect, causing the predictions of the models to diverge significantly from what actually happens.

In the early 1960s the meteorologist Lorenz was examining the weather patterns generated by a simple nonlinear model of the weather system, and he found that in certain conditions nonlinear relationships produce dynamics, that is, patterns of movement over time, which are paradoxically stable and unstable at the same time, regular and irregular at the same time.[2] This is not a matter of a balance between the opposites but the creation of a different dynamic in the ongoing tension between the opposites. We then have to talk about unstable stability, regular irregularity or predictable unpredictability.[3] Furthermore, in these conditions of paradoxical dynamics, the nonlinear relationships have the property of escalating tiny differences into very different outcomes. This has important consequences for causality and predictability.[4] It means that the long-term development of such a system cannot be predicted. This is due to the system's sensitivity to initial conditions, more popularly known as the butterfly effect, which means that the long-term trajectory of the system is highly sensitive to its starting point.

It is now accepted that the weather system is best modelled using nonlinear relationships and, as a consequence, we can now understand what has come to be called the butterfly effect. This means that when a butterfly flaps its wings in São Paulo, it alters the air pressure by a minute amount and this could be escalated into a major hurricane over Miami. Long-term predictability would then require the detection of every tiny change and the measurement of each to an infinite degree of precision. Since this is a human impossibility, the specific long-term pathway is unpredictable for all practical purposes. The long-term behaviour of such a system, therefore, is as much determined by small undetectable changes as it is by the deterministic laws governing it. Movement over the short term may be reasonably predictable because it takes time for small changes to be escalated into completely different patterns. Although unpredictable over the long term, movement of such a system is bounded; this means that there are limits to the behaviour that it is possible for the system to produce. The overall shape of weather movements can therefore be predicted, but their actual trajectory can never be predicted, apart from over the very short term. It is possible to predict the limits within which temperature will vary over a particular season in a particular geographical area, for example. Furthermore, the property of escalating small changes means that the links between cause and effect are lost. Chaos models display the unfolding of patterns already enfolded in the specification of the model so that the underlying causality is that of formative cause. Deterministic laws can therefore produce indeterminate outcomes, at least as far as any possible human experience is concerned.

The heartbeat of a healthy human also follows something like chaotic dynamics in temporal rhythms.[5] Although heartbeats are regular when averaged over a particular period of time, movements around that average display regular irregularity. A failing heart is characterized by a loss of complexity in which it moves to a regular cycle and, of course, the ultimate stability is a point attractor − the straight line.

Obviously, as I began to understand what I have just set out, I realized that this kind of thinking could help in understanding the experience of unpredictability in organizational life. If human relationships are nonlinear, and they certainly seem to be, then we will not be able to make long-term predictions of organizational futures, and this means that the failure to do so is not due to human incompetence but to the inescapable dynamics of our interactions. However, chaos models are of rather limited use for understanding organizations because they are deterministic and so cannot model learning. Nevertheless, there are developments in what we might call the sciences of uncertainty, the complexity sciences, or nonlinear dynamics, to be explored in the next section that may serve as source domains for analogies with human action, and these too display the properties of unpredictability, or more accurately the paradox of unpredictable predictability. Accepting that uncertainty is fundamental to human organizational life has important consequences.

Dominant ways of thinking and talking about management are based on the sciences of certainty, that is, on models consisting of linear relationships. In these models causality takes an *efficient* 'if … then' form: *if* action A is taken, *then* outcome B will occur. This makes it possible for a manager to make predictions of the outcomes of different actions as the basis on which they can choose in a rational manner which action to carry out. So in addition to efficient causality, an assumption of *rationalist causality* is also being made. The efficacy of the whole process of choosing aims, goals and visions and then choosing actions to realize them, so being 'in control', depends upon these forms of causality and the predictability they promise. However, if the efficient causal links are lost, as they are in mathematical chaos, then specific long-term behaviour is unpredictable. This undermines the assumption of rationalist causality. Of course, managers can still set specific goals and choose actions to achieve them, but there will be little certainty that the actions taken will actually realize the goals. If chaos theory were to indicate anything at all about human action, then currently dominant ways of thinking about management would be undermined, particularly the efficacy of long-term planning.

However, if all that the complexity sciences accomplished was to compel us to reach the conclusion that our forecasting efforts fail because they are impossible in the first place, it would be a bit depressing and anxiety provoking. Fortunately, insights coming from another branch of nonlinear dynamics, models of complex adaptive systems, offer an explanation of how phenomena develop and evolve in conditions of uncertainty. So consider now what we might learn from these models.

From the complexity sciences: local interactions and emergent global order

A complex adaptive system consists of a large population of agents, each of which interacts with some of the others in that population according to its own evolved principles of local interaction. No individual agent, or group of them, determines the local interaction principles of others, and there is no centralized direction of either the patterns of behaviour of the system as a whole or the evolution of those patterns. This local interaction is technically called self-organization, and it is this which produces emergent coherence in patterns of interaction across the whole population of agents. Local dynamics produce diversity of agent behaviour in which there emerge evolving patterns of global behaviour. Whole complex systems do not obey simple, fixed laws. Instead, individual agents respond to their own particular local contexts and even though there is no explicit coordination of their interaction, it nevertheless leads to the emergence of collective order.[6]

For example, some neuroscientists[7] think of the human brain as a complex adaptive system which consists of a very large population of neurons, perhaps ten billion of them, each of which can be thought of as an agent. The neurons are agents because they do something, namely, discharge electro-chemical energy. Each neuron agent is connected to only a small number of other agents, perhaps around 15,000, which is a tiny fraction of the total population. Through the experience of the body in which a neuron is located, connections with other neurons have evolved along with the 'rules' of its interaction with the others it is connected to, forming a pattern of the impact of one neuron agent on other neuron agents. So if we take neuron A to start with, it may be that when this neuron fires it triggers the firing of neurons X, Y and Z, while inhibiting the firing of neurons L, M and N. The firing of X, Y and Z will, of course, trigger the firing of others that they are connected to, and A only fired in the first place because it was triggered by some other neuron. What is happening is the adaptive interaction of neuron agents which is local in character because each agent is connected to only a tiny fraction of the total population, its local connections, and each is interacting with others according to its own locally evolved 'rules'. The result of all this local activity is the continuous patterning of activity across the whole population of neurons which must be coherent and orderly otherwise we would not be able to function. But these population-wide patterns emerge without any blue-print or programme for the collective pattern. They emerge only because of the local interaction of the agents.

It is easy to misunderstand the meaning of self-organization and the emergent collective order it produces. In the context of human organizations, people tend to equate self-organization with empowerment or, even worse, a free-for-all in which anyone can do anything, leading to anarchy. The example of the interaction of neurons, however, shows that self-organization is not a free-for-all; in fact it is the opposite of a free-for-all. Agent neurons are constrained to respond to others in the particular ways their evolution has brought them to – they cannot do just anything: they must respond and they must do so in particular ways so that the agents are constraining and enabling each other at the same time. This immediately resonates with the organizational reality of interdependence. Human agents can never simply do whatever they like because they will be excluded if they do. In their local interaction, human agents constrain and enable each other, which is what power means, and these patterns of power constitute social control and order. Since the term self-organization can lead to the kind of confusion just discussed, I prefer to use the term local interaction: self-organization simply means local interaction and there is nothing wonderful, emancipating or mysterious about it because both good, say democracy, and very bad, say ruthless dictatorship, patterns across a population emerge in local interaction. It follows that it is nonsense to talk about unleashing, or allowing, or stopping, self-organization simply because local interaction is what humans do whether they are allowed to or not, and since they are already always doing it there is nothing to unleash.

Furthermore, emergence is usually immediately understood as patterns which just happen, and this produces a kind of despair in managers who think that if it is going to just happen, then there is nothing for them to do. In fact, emergence means the exact opposite of 'just happening anyway'. The patterns that emerge do so only because of what every agent is doing and not doing. There is no mystery or chance in emergence; it is precisely the product of many, many local interactions. Creative–destructive, evolving and repetitively stuck, surprising and familiar, predictable and unpredictable patterns emerge across a population of agents because of what all the agents are doing and not doing in their local interactions. For me, the resonance with the organizational reality of power and the interplay of deliberate actions is very powerful. And the consequence of taking this view is profound because, instead of being determined by a prior plan, organizational change will be emerging in the local interactions of many, many people. If this is the case, it is not at all surprising that there is no scientific evidence that planned culture change produces changed culture. The change can only happen in many, many local interactions, not through some central plan or programme.

However, it is important to consider carefully how insights from the complexity sciences may be sensibly taken up in relation to human organizations. The models used in simulating the behaviour of complex adaptive systems are known as agent-based models in that they simulate the patterns formed by the local interaction of individual agents with each other. The agents, however, are digital agents occupying a space in a computer memory. Each agent is in fact a computer program, that is, a set of rules or algorithms where the rules dictate how the computer program is to interact with other computer programs. Where the agents are the same, their interaction can only produce one pattern of behaviour. Where the agents are different from each other, the rules they follow evolve and so, therefore, do the patterns emerging from their interaction. The key point revealed by these simulations is that local interactions give rise to coherent emergent patterns across a population. So, the models demonstrate a possibility, namely, a relationship between local interactions and population-wide patterns. Of course, this is an abstract relationship. Since human agents differ in major ways from digital agents, it is a highly dubious procedure to simply apply the notion of complex adaptive systems to human interaction. What is helpful, though, is to regard the complex adaptive system models as a source domain for analogies in the human sphere. When we reason by analogy, we take an abstract relationship from one domain to another and then clothe this abstract relationship with the attributes of the new domain. In the case of human beings, this must mean taking account of the fact that human agents are conscious, self-conscious, emotional, often spontaneous agents who are born into societies with long histories, including histories of traditions of thought. To take account of these attributes, therefore, it is necessary to turn to the literature in the disciplines of psychology, sociology and philosophy. It means exploring these disciplines to understand how local interaction and population-wide patterning might be thought about in relation to human beings.

This move from natural science models to the disciplines of psychology, sociology and philosophy is signalled by switching from talking about complex adaptive systems to talking about *complex responsive processes of human relating*. One particularly illuminating strand of work, process sociology, does help us understand the abstract relationship between local interaction and population-wide patterns in human terms. The key figure in process sociology is Elias,[8] and the next section presents some important points that he made.

Interdependent individuals and the interplay of human intentions

Elias did not think about the relationship between the individual and society in terms of any spatial distinction between inside and outside, as in systems thinking. He argued that while the notion of a receptacle containing something inside it might be applicable to the physical aspects of a human being, it could not be applied to the personality or the mind.[9] In rejecting the notion of the individual mind as an 'internal world', he also argued against thinking of the social as an organic unity or supra-individual with a 'group mind' developing through stages of youth, maturity and old age to death.[10] Instead, he pointed to the essential interdependence of people. Elias also usually avoided any kind of systemic formulation, arguing that such formulations abstract from experience. Instead, he understood both individual and social purely in what I am calling responsive processes terms. He did not think of the individual and society as first existing and then subsequently affecting each other.[11] He suggested that we can see the connection between individual and social more precisely if we refuse to abstract from the processes of their development, of their becoming. Elias also argued against concepts of society as some kind of 'whole', arguing that the social life of human beings was full of contradictions, tensions and explosions rather than being more or less harmonious as the concept of a 'whole' implies. Furthermore, while the concept of a 'whole' implies something complete in itself, societies are always more or less incomplete, remaining open in time as a continuous flow.[12] What Elias was doing here was moving completely away from any notion of human interaction as a system and any notion of some 'whole' existing outside of that interaction and causing it. Instead, he was focusing entirely on the processes of interaction between human bodies. Elias argued that the concept of the whole applied to human action simply created a mystery in order to solve a mystery.

In order to understand the nature of human interaction, Elias made a detailed study of changes in the way Western people have experienced themselves over hundreds of years and pointed to how social order *emerges* in interactions between people.[13] Elias argued that what we now call Western civilization is not the result of any kind of calculated long-term planning. Individual people did not form an intention to change civilization and then gradually realize this intention through rational, purposive measures. It is not conceivable that the evolution of society could have been planned because that would suppose that modern rational, calculating individuals with a degree of self-mastery already existed centuries ago, whereas Elias's research shows that such individuals did not exist then but were, rather, themselves the products of social evolution. Societal changes produced rational, planning kinds of individuals, not the other way around. In medieval times, people experienced their self-consciousness in a completely different way, in a completely different kind of society, compared with the way we experience our self-consciousness in modern society. Elias concluded that the development of a society was not caused by 'mysterious' social forces but was the consequence of the interweaving, the *interplay* of the intentions and actions of many, many people. He talked about the moves of many interdependent players intertwining in ways that none of them could control, no matter how powerful they were. However, despite the development of a society being unplanned and outside the immediate control of its members, the interplay of individual plans and intentions nevertheless produced an orderly pattern of development, tending in a particular direction.[14]

So, Elias argued that change in society occurred in an unplanned manner but nevertheless displayed a specific type of order. His research demonstrated how the constraints imposed by others were converted into self-restraints and how many human bodily activities were progressively pushed behind the scenes of communal social life and invested with feelings of shame. Elias explained how the growing interdependence of people caused by the increasing division of labour and specialization of tasks could only be sustained by the increasing self-control of those interdependent people. In other words, increasing interdependence, taken together with the increasing state monopolization of violence, came to be reflected in the very personality structures of people. The 'civilizing' process is one of increasing self-control bringing with it the benefits of social order but also the disadvantages of neurotic behaviour associated with such self-control and increasing anxiety about contravening social norms. Furthermore, this civilizing trend is easily reversed by any threat to, or breakdown in, social order. Although this transformation of societies and personality structures could not have been planned and intended, it was not simply a sequence of unstructured changes.[15] Elias looked for an explanation of how it was possible that orderly population-wide formations, which no human being had intended, arose in the human world:

> *It is simple enough: plans and actions, the emotional and rational impulses of individual people, constantly interweave in a friendly or hostile way.* This basic tissue resulting from many single plans and actions of men can give rise to changes and patterns that no individual person has planned or created. From this interdependence of people arises an order sui generis, an order more compelling and stronger than the will and reason of the individual people composing it. *It is the order of interweaving human impulses and strivings, the social order, which determines the course of historical change; it underlies the civilizing process.*[16]

Although it is highly unlikely that Elias was ever aware of the complexity sciences, what he is describing here is what complexity scientists call local interaction (technically called self-organization) and emergence. Elias is arguing that individuals and groups are interacting with each other, in their local situations, in intentional, planned ways.

However, the widespread, population-wide consequences of the interplay of these intentions and plans cannot be foreseen by any of them – long-term population-wide patterns emerge without an overall plan or blueprint. Elias explains that long-term consequences cannot be foreseen because the interplay of the actions, plans and purposes of many individuals constantly gives rise to something that has not been planned, intended or created by any of those individuals. Elias pointed to the important fact that individuals pursuing their plans are always in relationship with each other in a group or power figuration. While individuals can plan their own actions, they cannot plan the actions of others and so cannot plan the interplay of plans and actions or plan and control population-wide 'outcomes'. The fact that each person depends on others means that none can simply realize their plans. However, this does not mean that anarchy, or disorder, results. Elias talks about a trend or direction in the evolution of the consequences of the interweaving of individual plans and intentions. In other words, he is talking about local interaction (self-organization) and emergence. We can understand what he is talking about by reflecting on almost any story of developing organizational life over time. One of my favourite examples is provided by how the successful Facebook business emerged in the interplay of intentions in many local interactions.

The emergence of Facebook in the interplay of intentions

Mezrich tells the story of Mark Zuckerberg,[17] founder of Facebook in which his shareholding is currently worth billions of dollars. Mark was an 18-year-old undergraduate student at Harvard University in 2003, majoring in computer science, when he met and formed a friendship with another undergraduate student, Eduardo Severin, at a Jewish fraternity group called Alpha Epsilon Pi. Mark had a reputation as a computer hacker listed by the FBI and as a person who had turned down a $1 million job at Microsoft in order to come to Harvard. It was this reputation that had attracted Eduardo to Mark. Around this time, Mark broke into Harvard University's computer system and copied over the photographs of every girl on campus from the databases. He then created a website which he called Facemash.com and which enabled subscribers to compare the pictures of the girls and vote for the one they thought was the hottest, the votes being used to calculate who the hottest 'chick' on campus was. He emailed the website address to a few of his friends, asking what they thought of it and then went to one of his classes. On his return he found that his computer screen was frozen because it was acting as a server for Facemash.com, a development which both surprised and alarmed him. The friends to whom he had emailed the website address had in turn passed it to their friends and it had rapidly spread through the student body. However, the address also found its way to members of the Institute of Politics and of a women's issues organization called Fuerza Latina. From there it seems that someone had forwarded it to the Association of Black Women at Harvard and to *Crimson*, the college newspaper. In less than two hours the site had logged 22,000 votes, and 400 students had gone on the site in the previous 30 minutes. Mark had not meant this to go out before he found out about the legality of copying the pictures, and he feared that he was in big trouble. We can see here how Mark forms a rather frivolous intention to create a particular kind of website and a perhaps humorous intention to send it to his friends. They intentionally send it to others, some of whom intentionally send it to women's organizations whose members intentionally respond in an outraged manner. What emerges is a pattern of interaction, which we can call a scandal, which Mark and his immediate friends certainly did not intend, particularly given the punishment that might be inflicted on Mark.

Elsewhere on campus at this time, twin brothers Tyler and Cameron Winklevoss, members of the secretive Porcellian, Harvard's oldest all-male club, and sons of a very wealthy father, as well as champion rowers who would go on to compete in the 2008 Olympics, were developing a secret project with Divya Narendra – another intention. The project was to establish a website called the Harvard Connection to put Harvard's social life online, making it possible for busy men like Tyler and Cameron to meet girls without wasting time going to parties and wandering around the campus looking for girls. However, to set up such a website they needed a computer expert to write the code. Finding such a person was Divya's job. As they sat discussing the problem in the canteen, Divya drew attention to an article in the *Crimson* which reported on Facemash.com and the voting on girls. The Facemash.com website had aroused much opposition from feminist groups on the campus, and the traffic on Facemash.com had clogged the university's bandwidth so that professors could not access their emails. Mark had closed the site down but was having to face the consequences of stealing the pictures. Mark looked like the right person to develop the Harvard Connection website. So an unexpected intention emerges in response to the outcomes of Mark's and others' intentions.

After Mark's disciplinary hearing, the Winklevoss twins sought him out and told him what they were trying to do on Harvard Connection. Mark liked the idea of a website for meeting girls and felt the programming would not present a problem. The Winklevoss twins told Mark that they thought the site would make money and they wanted Mark to be at the centre of it. For the next two months the partnership seemed to be going well, but after that no real progress was forthcoming. The Winklevoss twins and Divya put pressure on Mark but still nothing happened. By January 2004 Mark had met up with his friend Eduardo again and outlined how the Facemash.com idea could be extended to enable male and female students to find out about each other in an informal, friendly online community. He saw this as a sort of exclusive social network – you could only get on the site through the recommendation of someone who was already a member. Real online social circles could be created by the people themselves putting up their own pictures and profiles and inviting their friends to join. He proposed calling it Facebook. Eduardo knew that there was a similar but not very good website called Friendster, which was not exclusive and few at Harvard used it. He also knew about the rapidly growing MySpace site, but that was not really about communicating. Mark mentioned the project proposed by the Winklevoss twins, but he regarded it as simply a dating website to enable men to find sexual partners. Mark had decided that this was not worth his time. Eduardo had money and agreed to fund the development of the social networks site, providing

$1,000 in the first instance. Mark set up a company owned 70 per cent by him and 30 per cent by Eduardo, whom Mark thought should be chief financial officer. By the end of the month Facebook was ready to go and Eduardo thought it should be introduced to members of his fraternity club, Phoenix. Within two weeks 5,000 members had signed up, representing 85 per cent of Harvard's undergraduates. So here we see the interplay of the intentions of the Winklevoss twins, Mark and Eduardo producing the emergent outcome called Facebook.com, part of a wider emerging pattern of electronic social networks. No one is following step-by-step procedures to deal with a problem situation, and no one is formulating any kind of strategic plan for a new organization or a whole new industry.

Returning to the story, the Winklevoss twins complained to Larry Summers, president of Harvard and former US treasury secretary, that Mark had stolen their idea in contravention of Harvard rules. Summers said that it was a personal issue between them and Mark and had nothing to do with the university. Meanwhile Facebook was not only changing Harvard's social scene — it was spreading to other colleges. Eduardo wanted to push it with advertisers but Mark wanted to keep it a fun site. He slept through advertising and marketing meetings arranged with sponsors by Eduardo. Then Mark and Eduardo agreed to meet Sean Parker, a 24-year-old Silicon Valley entrepreneur, only 4 years older than Mark. Sean, who had never been to college, was one of the creators of the website Napster while he was still at high school, which enabled college students to get the music they wanted. Eventually this failed, but Sean started another site called Plaxo. Sean told them that 85 per cent of Stanford students had joined Facebook within twenty-four hours of an article appearing in the *Stanford Daily*.

By the summer of 2004, only months after the setting up of Facebook, Sean had persuaded Mark to move to Palo Alto near Silicon Valley in California, where he lived in a quiet suburban house with a team of young programmers. Eduardo, still funding Facebook, had gone to New York to take up an internship at an investment bank and so was not involved in the day-to-day activities of Facebook. Sean sought to ally himself with Mark in order to build the billion-dollar business that had so far eluded him. Eduardo quit his investment bank job on his first day and then managed to get advertisers for Facebook. He was concerned about Sean's growing importance and the way he was approaching the business by taking Mark to one party after another to meet fundraisers and celebrities. Facebook surpassed 500,000 members by August 2004. There was now a need for more servers, full-time staff and permanent offices and lawyers, and all this required more funds than the $18,000 that Eduardo had so far invested. Eduardo therefore returned to New York while Mark carried on partying with Sean in San Francisco. Mark tried to persuade Eduardo to move to California but he refused. Sean introduced investors without Eduardo, who then wrote an angry letter to Mark and froze the company account. So, following Sean's advice, Mark reincorporated Facebook as a Delaware company to protect it from Eduardo, and Mark put his own money into this company. Then the Winklevoss twins took out a lawsuit against Mark which would use up $200,000 in legal defence costs. Mark and Sean went to see Peter Thiel, founder of PayPal and head of venture fund Clarium Capital. Thiel provide $500,000 seed money in exchange for 7 per cent of the reincorporated company and a seat on the board. Sean also became a shareholder. Eduardo would still get his 30 per cent, but this would be diluted if he did not contribute and accept that he could not be the head of business development. Eduardo went back to Harvard to complete his degree. By April 2005 Facebook was everywhere in America. Facebook then issued new shares to Mark, Sean and others but diluted Eduardo's holding to almost nothing. Sean was to be the new president of the company and Eduardo was edged out. By July 2009 there were 250 million users and the company was worth billions of dollars.

The book by Mezrich, from which this story has been taken, is based only on Mezrich's interviews with Eduardo and has therefore been criticized for being biased and not factual. This highlights the problem of trying to tell or find out what actually happened – all players have their story and each differs to some extent from the others, especially relating to feelings, ethics and power. So, usually, the so-called factual accounts focus on agreed-upon events and rationally reconstructed stories of the past which brush aside emotions, unethical conduct and anything which might be called irrational. However, what the stories make clear, no matter whose particular version is taken, is how population-wide patterns of interaction have emerged in many, many local interactions between a number of people, such as Mark, Eduardo, Sean, the Winklevoss twins and many others. There is no polarity of intention and emergence because patterns are emerging in the interplay of many intentions reflecting all kinds of emotions and ethical or unethical actions. This is a very different picture of creativity and innovation in organizations from that presented by the dominant discourse.

Conclusion

This chapter has pointed to some important insights to be gained from the complexity sciences, developed only over the past fifty or so years. Contrary to traditional science's linear models, which assume fundamental certainty in the universe, the nonlinear models of the complexity sciences reveal the fundamental uncertainty of the universe. It is a property of nonlinear interactions that they generate unpredictable outcomes. So in thinking about organizations, if we move from assuming underlying certainty to assuming underlying uncertainty, we begin to think in ways close to our ordinary, everyday experience. The sciences of uncertainty also demonstrate that local interaction produces coherent emergent patterns across populations. Furthermore, it is when the agents engaged in this local interaction differ from each other that the evolution of patterns of interaction locally and across populations becomes possible. All of these insights point to an alternative way of thinking about organizations compared to the dominant discourse.

This chapter has also shown how, long before the emergence of the complexity sciences, Elias produced an explanation of how population-wide patterns of civilization emerge in many local interactions and how those population-wide patterns are taken up in the personalities of the agents interacting locally. He was in fact showing how the abstract relationship between local interaction and emergent population-wide pattern can be clothed in the attributes of human agents and so help us to understand how all groups, including organizations, evolve. This way of understanding organizational life as the emergence of organization-wide patterns arising in the interplay of intentions in local interactions turns the dominant discourse on its head. It shows how it is impossible for powerful people to realize their chosen strategic outcomes, how it is impossible for them to change organizations as a whole, and how it is impossible for them to design whole organizational systems that will keep them under control.

Since local interaction is of the utmost importance, it is necessary to take up any insights psychology, sociology and philosophy have to offer us on the nature of local interaction between human agents, and this is what the next chapter will attend to.

ure of local interactions: communication

rican pragmatist sociologist G. H. Mead held that human consciousness and
iousness, that is, minds, are not possible without human societies, which
at mind and society must have evolved together.[1] An explanation of the
of mind must start with rudimentary forms of social behaviour displayed by
ammals that do not have minds in the human sense and then identify what
needed for human–like minds to emerge in social behaviour, so providing
-based account of how mind and society have evolved together. Starting
higher mammals, we can see that they relate to each other in a responsive
with a *gesture* by one animal evoking a *response* from another in the con-
of gestures. Gesture and response together constitute a social act in which
arises for both so that knowing is a property of interaction, or relationship.
nple, one dog may make the gesture of baring its teeth in a snarl, and this
forth a response of counter-snarl, or of flight, or of crouching. The meaning
animals of the social act of snarl and counter-snarl is aggression, while that
and flight is victory and defeat, and the meaning of the social act of snarl and
ng is dominance and submission. This makes it clear that meaning does not lie
gesture alone but in the social act as a whole; meaning arises in the responsive
nteraction between actors. The gesture points to how the meaning might
in the response. Here meaning is emerging in the action of the living present in
the immediate future (response) acts back on the past (gesture) to change its
ng. Meaning is not simply located in the past (gesture) or the future (response)
o in the interaction between the two in the living present. In this way, the
t is not simply a point separating the past from the future because it has a time
re. Meaning does not arise first in each individual and then in the action of
itting, as in the dominant discourse, but arises in the interaction between the
unicating individuals.

arly, there are immediately important implications for communication in organi-
s. When a CEO, for example, communicates with members of an organization,
eaning does not lie simply in the communication but at the same time in
sponses to it. No matter how clearly worded the communication is, it will be
reted in many different ways in local situations and therefore mean different things
fferent people in a way that the CEO cannot control. Effective communication,
fore, cannot be regarded as a one-off event because it is an ongoing process of
tiation. Effective communication requires staying in the conversation.

eturning to the example of the dogs, we can see gesture–response patterns of
petition and cooperation which constitute the kind of society that is widely found in
re. Mostly, such societies rest on functional specialization where, for example, ant
ties are structured by specialization into workers and breeders, while mammals
tend to specialize into hunters and breeders and into those that are dominant
those that are submissive. At this stage, meaning is implicit in the social act itself,
those acting are unaware of that implicit meaning. Humans must have evolved
n mammals with similar rudimentary social structures to those found in present

3

UNDERSTANDING ORG
ACTIVITIES AS THE GAN

Implications for leadership and
tools and techniques

The Ame
self-cons
means th
evolution
higher m
would b
an actio
with the
manner,
versation
meaning
For exa
may cal
to both
of snarl
crouchi
in the
social
emerg
which
meani
but al
preser
structu
transn
comm

Introduction

The purpose of this chapter is to explore the nature
human agents because it is in this local interaction that the
the patterns of interaction we call organizations and so
are doing as they interact with each other in their own l
whatever it is that they accomplish, is that they never-
each other. The first requirement for understanding the o
between people, therefore, is to understand the nature
communicating with each other, human beings inevitab
power relations and in the inevitable inequality and differ
generate conflict. It is the conflict arising in difference t
organizational and social evolution. But there is nothing ab
and it does not just happen; whatever happens does so preci
agent is choosing and doing as well as not choosing and not d
do always reflects ideology, the norms and values that we ta

Complex responsive processes are the activities of comm
and ideology-based intending, choosing and acting. It is in the
interact with each other, and what we produce in this intera
patterns of interaction that we call societies, institutions, ind
groups. In addition, it is necessary to take account of the
agents, human agents are capable of reflecting upon the popul
are emerging in their interaction and these articulations are ta
in ongoing local interaction. In other words, in addition to u
of ordinary local interaction, we need to understand the w
which is being reflected in this ongoing local interaction. (
might understand human communication.

Cl
zation
the
the
inter
for
ther
negc

R
com
nati
soc
ma
and
and
fro

day species of mammals. The mammal ancestors of humans must have evolved central nervous systems that enabled them to gesture to others in a manner that was capable of *evoking in themselves the same range of responses as in those to whom they were gesturing*. This would happen if, for example, the snarl of one called forth in itself the fleeting feelings associated with counter-snarl, flight or submissive posture, just as they did in the one to whom the gesture of snarl was being made. Mead described such a gesture as a significant symbol, where a significant symbol is one that calls forth the same response in the gesturer as in the one to whom it is directed. Significant symbols, therefore, make it possible for the gesturer to 'know' what he or she is doing. This simple idea is, I think, a profound insight. If, when one makes a gesture to another, one is able to experience in one's own body a similar response to that which the gesture provokes in another body, then one can 'know' what one is doing; one is conscious and can intuit something about the range of likely responses from the other. The body, with its nervous system, becomes central to understanding how animals 'know' anything. There is here no split whatsoever between mind and body, or intellect and emotion.

As individuals interact with each other in this way, the possibility arises of a pause before making a gesture. In a kind of private role play, emerging in the repeated experience of public interaction, one individual learns to take the attitude, the tendency to act, of the other, enabling a kind of trial run in advance of actually completing or even starting the gesture. Will it call forth aggression, fright, flight or submission? What will be the consequences in each case? In this way, *rudimentary forms of thinking develop, taking the form of private role playing*, that is, gestures made by a body to itself, calling forth responses in itself. Mead said that humans are fundamentally role-playing animals. The simultaneous private and public role plays so far discussed all take place without verbal language. Mead then argued that the gesture which is particularly useful in calling forth the same attitude in oneself as in the other is the vocal gesture because we can hear the sounds we make in much the same way as others hear them, while we cannot see the facial gestures we make as others see them, for example. The development of more sophisticated patterns of vocal gesturing, that is, of the language form of significant symbols, is thus of major importance in the development of consciousness and of sophisticated forms of society. Mind, that is, the private role plays and silent conversations with oneself, and society, that is, the public conversation of gestures between people, emerge together in the medium of language. However, since speaking and listening are actions of bodies, and since bodies are never without feelings, the medium of language is also always the medium of feelings. There is no question of separating mind and society as different hierarchical levels, and both mind and society are understood as responsive temporal processes of communication which are in no way systems.

Mead takes his argument further when he suggests how private role play evolves in increasingly complex ways. As more and more interactions are experienced with others, so more roles and wider ranges of possible responses enter into the role-playing activities that precede the gestures or, to be more accurate, are continuously intertwined with public gesturing and responding. In this way, the capacity to take the attitude of many others evolves and this becomes generalized. Each engaged in the conversation of gestures can now take the attitude of what Mead calls the *generalized other*. In childhood most of us are warned by our parents to take account of how 'others' will respond to what we are doing or saying. These 'others' and what 'they' think of you are not actual individuals but generalizations across a particular society. Eventually, individuals develop the capacity to take the attitude of the whole group, or what Mead calls the game. In other words, creatures have now evolved that are capable of taking the social attitude as they gesture and respond to each other. The result is much more sophisticated processes of cooperative interaction because there is now mindful, social behaviour with increasingly sophisticated forms of cooperation and competition.

The next step in this evolutionary process is the linking of the attitude of specific and generalized others, of the whole group and the nature of the games they are preoccupied in, with a 'me'. In other words, there evolves a capacity to take the attitude of others not just towards one's gestures but also towards one's self. The 'me' is a person's perception of the configuration of the gestures/responses of the others/society to him or her as a subject, or an 'I'. What has evolved here is the capacity to be an object to oneself, a 'me'. A self, as the relationship between 'me' and 'I', has therefore emerged, as well as an awareness of that self, that is, self-consciousness. In this interaction, the 'I' is the response to the perceived gesture of the group/society to oneself, that is, the 'me'. The 'me' is the attitude of others to the 'I' and they cannot be separated. Mead argues, very importantly, that this 'I' response to one's perception of the attitude of the group to oneself (the 'me') is not a given but is always potentially unpredictable in that there is no predetermined way in which the 'I' might respond to the 'me'. In other words, each of us may respond in many spontaneously different ways to our perception of the views others have of us. Here, Mead is pointing to the importance of difference, or diversity, in the emergence of the new, that is, in the potential for transformation, and to the 'I' as the creative response. Mead says:

> The 'I' ... never can exist as an object of consciousness, but the very conversa-
> tional character of our inner experience, the very process of replying to one's
> own talk, implies an 'I' behind the scenes who answers to the gestures, the
> symbols, that arise in consciousness. ... The self-consciousness, actual self in
> social intercourse is the objective 'me' or 'me's' with the process of response
> continually going on and implying a fictitious 'I' always out of sight of himself.[2]

In what I have been describing above it is evident that the conversation of gestures, the complex responsive processes of interaction between agents, creates history while that history is forming them. The history referred to here is both the history of the society any person is born into and the life history of the person in that society. It is through ongoing history that people develop some capacity to predict the potential consequences of their gestures to others, and it is through history that people learn to take the attitude of the generalized other.

Although a beginning and an end might be ascribed to a particular sequence of communicative interactions, that description is purely arbitrary, for even before a particular episode begins, even between total strangers, each has a history of experience. That history has patterned the private role playing of each individual in particular ways that enact, that is, selectively enable and constrain, what that individual responds to both privately and publicly. That history establishes what aspects of the gesturing of the other will be striking, will call forth, or evoke, a response and what kind of response it will evoke. These processes of enactment and evocation are made possible, and at the same time limited, by previous history. And when they are not strangers, the history of their own personal relating to each other, and the histories of the groups they are part of, also become relevant. However, this history is not some kind of 'true' factual account but a reproduction in the living present that always leaves room for potential transformation. Furthermore, the collective and individual histories reproduced in the living present of communicative action are extending those histories into the future. The responsive relating of people may be thought of as forming narrative at the same time as that narrative forms their relating. In other words, the experience of the living present, like the past, is structured in narrative-like ways.

I use the term narrative-like, rather than narrative, in order to make an important distinction. A narrative or story is normally thought of in its 'told' sense. A narrative is normally someone's narrative, told from the perspective of a narrator. It normally has a beginning, an end and a plot that moves the listener/reader from the beginning to the end in a more or less linear sequence. This kind of 'narrative told'[3] must be distinguished from the narrative-like process that is narrative in its making. Interaction in the manner described above evolves as narrative-like themes that normally have no single narrator's perspective. Beginnings and endings are rather arbitrary and there are many plots emerging simultaneously. The narrative told is retrospective while narrative-in-its-making is currently emerging in the living present. The former is inevitably linear while the latter is intrinsically nonlinear.

The private role play, the silent conversation, of each individual and their public interactions can be thought of as themes and variations reproducing history. It is these themes and variations that organize an individual's experience in the living present. However, what those particular themes are at particular moments will depend just as much on the cues being presented by others as upon the personal history of a particular individual. Each individual is simultaneously evoking and provoking responses from others so that the particular personal organizing themes emerging for any one of them will depend as much on the others as on the individual concerned. Put like this, it becomes clear that no one individual can be organizing his or her experience in isolation because they are all simultaneously evoking and provoking responses in each other. Together they immediately constitute complex responsive processes of a recursive, reflexive, self-referential kind. And as they do so, themes emerge that organize their experience of being together, out of which further themes continuously emerge.

The currents of communicative interaction, therefore, do not constitute some harmonious whole, and the living present is as much about conflict and competition as it is about harmony and cooperation. Indeed, without this paradox there could be no transformation. Looking backwards or forwards, no one is able to fully articulate what the themes were or how they linked into each other in reinforcing and contradictory ways. Each articulation is an act of interpretation in the living present as part of communicative interaction in the living present. Each act of interpretation in the living present reconstructs the past, potentially changing its meaning. Furthermore, no one can articulate all the themes in the process of communicative interaction in the living present of a particular local situation, each interpretation being yet another gesture in the ongoing flow of gesture–response. It is even less possible for anyone to articulate all the interacting themes across an organization, an industry or a society. Again, any attempt is simply a localized interpretation in the living present. Nevertheless, coherence emerges in the vast complexity of communicative interactions across enormous numbers of local situations because of the intrinsic capacity of local interaction to form coherent patterns in the interplay of the intentions of people. However, the pattern of this coherence is not predictable in advance, and it involves both destruction and creation, both stability and instability. Human interaction is imperfect communication between people, generating misunderstanding. Diversity arises in misunderstanding and in the cross-fertilization of concepts through interaction between different patterns of conversation. This is where the tension between conformity and deviance becomes important. It is this deviance that imparts the internal capacity to spontaneously evolve new patterns of conversation.

The nature of local interactions: power relations

I have already referred to the sociologist Elias in the last chapter. He held that power is not a thing that a person carries around and gives to others or takes away from them.[4] Such a view of power is very much tied up with the notion that we are independent autonomous individuals, 'closed' off from each other. However, for Elias there are no autonomous human beings simply because individuals are quite obviously dependent on each other in an essential and fundamental way – society is the society of interdependent individuals. We can accomplish nothing without each other, without cooperating and competing with each other. In other words, we need each other for many different reasons – we need others to love and to hate; we need others to depend upon or rebel against; we need others to victimize or be victimized by; we need enemies for wars and friends and opponents for peace. It follows that to claim that humans are essentially interdependent is to claim a fundamental 'fact' about life, not simply an ideological position that interdependence and relating are good, because our interdependence accounts for the horrific destructiveness of human action as well as its creative beauty. The ideology arises in our judgment of what is beautifully creative and what is horrifically destructive about relating to each other. Interdependence explains how both the good and the bad arise, indeed how particular judgments or ideologies arise. If human individuals are interdependent in this way, it follows that we need each other and it is this need which explains why *power* is an aspect of *every act of human relating*. Since I need others, I cannot do whatever I please, and since they need me, neither can they. We constrain each other at the same time as enabling each other and it is this paradoxical activity that constitutes power. Furthermore, since need is rarely equal, the pattern of power relations will always be skewed more to one than to another. So if I need you more than you need me, then the power distribution is tilted towards you. However, if as we relate to each other, we discover that now you need me more than I need you, then the pattern of power relations moves and is tilted towards me.

Power, then, refers to usually fluid patterns of perceived need and is expressed as figurations of relationships. These figurations are social patterns of grouping in which some are included and others excluded, and it is in being included in this group and excluded from that group that we acquire identity. I am included in a group called academics and excluded from a group called footballers, so when asked *who I am*, I say that *I am* a teacher: collective 'we' identity is inseparable from individual 'I' identity so that individual identity is fundamentally social, a matter of power relations. I am claiming as a fact of our experience that humans need each other and that relative need will rarely be equal, meaning that power is always an aspect of every act of human relating and that it is always expressed in patterns of inclusion and exclusion that give identity. I am also claiming that it is in these very acts of power relating as the ordinary politics of everyday life that ideology arises as our judgment of what is good and what is right about our acts of power relating. At the same time, these ideological judgments are shaping our acts of power relating. Figurations of power can come to have a kind of semi–permanence in which they are expressed in institutional arrangements. Figurations of power are essentially membership categories reflecting ideologies of inclusion and exclusion. For example, particular ideologies of deference and the role of women may be reflected in a particular grouping which includes senior men while excluding junior men, and all women are excluded. This pattern of inclusion and exclusion sustains the power positions of the senior men. This process of power relating, with its dynamic of inclusion and exclusion, is ubiquitous in all human interaction.

The typical dynamics of inclusion and exclusion are vividly illustrated in a study of a small town in Leicestershire, England.[5] The town was founded in the late nineteenth century by an industrialist who built a factory and also a village to house the ordinary workers who were to be employed in the factory. Life continued in the village until the Second World War broke out in Europe in 1939, and soon after this the government took the factory over to make products for the war effort. The government expanded the factory and built a number of new houses in what came to be called the 'estate' located right next to the village, in which were housed working-class people whose homes had been bombed in East London, some eighty miles away. Nearly a quarter of a century later those dwelling in the village and those dwelling in the estate still constituted two quite separate communities. Although the men from both communities worked every day together in the factory without any problems and although their children went to the same local schools, there was no social intercourse outside factory and school. There was a pub in the village in which only people from the village met for a drink and a gossip in the evening, and there was a pub in the estate which was used only by people from the estate. Women from the village never visited women from the estate and their children did not play with estate children outside school hours. It was also noticeable that the elected local government consisted entirely of village dwellers.

This situation was very odd because there was no immediately obvious difference between the two groups of people: both groups were white English people; both used the same language and after a quarter of a century there was not much difference in their accents; and both comprised working-class people. The only difference was that one group, the newcomers, had been there for only a quarter of a century, whereas the other group, the established, had been there for over a century. A study of the gossip prevailing in both communities revealed that the villagers described estate dwellers as rather dirty people who did not maintain their houses and gardens. They were not well educated and their children behaved badly. The villagers described themselves as clean people who maintained their homes and gardens in good condition, were educated and had well-behaved children. The villagers were thus articulating an ideology which polarized the two groups in terms of binary opposites with all bad ascribed to the estate dwellers and all good to the villagers. This enabled them to denigrate the estate dwellers without any difficulty and made it feel natural that they should occupy the power positions. What is being demonstrated here is how a simplistic ideology which splits good from bad, locating them in different groups, sustains the pattern of power relations between the groups. People are being included in one group and excluded from another in a dynamic which expresses a pattern of power relations reflecting an underlying ideology.

Furthermore, the prime mechanism sustaining this ideology is gossip: praise gossip is directed by villagers to their own group and blame gossip or stigma is directed to the other. On enquiry it became evident how the estate dwellers had taken into their own self-perception the assertions about them made by the villagers. Estate dwellers reluctantly agreed that their neighbours did tend to be rather dirty people who did not maintain their properties and had rather badly behaved children. The stigma articulated by the one group had been driven into the self-perception of the other group. The two groups were unconsciously caught in processes in which they served a function for each other, the function being to do with the maintenance of superiority and inferiority. Ideology can thus take the form of communication that preserves the current order by making that current order seem natural. Ideology here is mutually reproduced in ongoing communicative action rather than being some fundamental hidden cause located somewhere. Ideology is a patterning process, that is, narrative themes of inclusion and exclusion which are iterated.

This inclusion–exclusion dynamic was also intimately linked to the identities of members of both groups. Those living in the village had the identity of village dwellers with all its positive attributes – when asked 'who are you?', they could reply 'I am a villager'. If a villager questioned the simple binary distinction being drawn about village and estate, he or she would take the risk of antagonizing neighbours and this could well lead to exclusion. The sustaining of identity, therefore, required compliance with the ideology. Similarly, estate dwellers derived their identities from membership of the despised estate group and would also risk exclusion if they challenged this. Both sides had come to think of themselves as a 'we', a group with common attachments, likes, dislikes and attributes that had emerged simply because of their being together over a period of time. They had developed an identity.

However, eventually what usually happens is that some 'deviants' in one or other or both of the groups take issue with the ideology and oppose it, often in a way that can be described as 'shrill cries from the margin'. The official, legitimate ideology underlying public transcripts and strategic poses conflicts with the unofficial shadow ideologies of the deviants, at first expressed as hidden transcripts through subtle acts of resistance but then as often extreme acts of rebellion.

Directing attention to the dynamics of inclusion and exclusion, to be found in every human organization, enables us to understand the impact on organizational life of the particular groupings to be found in organizations, for example power struggles between academics and managers in universities; between managers and physicians in hospitals; between marketing and production people in some organizations. The manner in which these groups interact with each other directly affects the performance and evolution of an organization. The importance of these groupings for the maintenance of identity also helps to explain why so many mergers and acquisitions create enormous difficulties; they threaten and destroy identities, and the anxiety and resistance this creates are the cause of the problems.

The nature of local interactions: ideology and choices

Ideology has already been referred to a number of times in the previous section, which drew attention to the relationship between it and power. This section considers the nature of ideology. Ideology may be thought of as the combination of norms and values.

Norms are experienced as obligatory and constraining so that they inevitably restrict opportunities for action, being intimately connected with morals in that they provide criteria for what *ought* to be done, what is *right*. Norms, then, provide a basis for evaluating and choosing between desires and actions, and they emerge and evolve as people in a society become more and more interdependent and as the use of violence is monopolized by the state.[6] Desires are taken more and more behind the scenes of daily life as more detailed norms emerge about what can and cannot be done in public and these norms become part of individual personality structures, adherence to which is sustained by the social process of shame. Norms, therefore, are constraints arising in social evolution that act to restrain the actions and even desires of interdependent individuals, so much so that the constraints become thematic patterns of individual identities. In complex responsive process terms, norms are themes organizing experience in a constraining way. However, norms are inseparable although different from values.

Values and ideals, unlike norms, are attractive and compelling in a voluntary, committed sense; they motivate and open up opportunities for action. Values attract us, giving life meaning and purpose, and so are experienced not as restrictive but as the highest expression of our free will, presenting a paradox of compulsion and voluntary commitment at the same time. Values are intimately connected with ethics in that they provide criteria for judging what *is* the *good* in action, differentiating between good and bad desires, as well as good and bad norms. Values are essentially concerned with what it is good to desire. When we reject a perfectly realizable desire because we believe it is unacceptable, then we are distinguishing between higher and lower virtues or vices, profound and superficial feelings, noble and base desires. Such evaluations refer to feelings such as outrage, guilt and admiration and they indicate a life we hold to be of higher value, a view of the kind of person we want to be. Values, as inspiring, attractively compelling motivations to act towards the good, are continually arising in social interaction, that is, in our ongoing negotiation with each other and ourselves as we go on together, as inescapable aspects of self-formation. It follows that values are contingent upon the particular action situations in which we find ourselves and although they have general and durable qualities, their motivational impact on action must be negotiated afresh, must be particularized, in each action situation. Imagination idealizes contingent possibilities and creates an imaginary relation to a wholeness, a unity of experience, which does not exist but seems real because we have experienced it so intensely.[7] This is not a solitary but a social process and it is not necessarily good – the same process produces values that others may judge to be evil. Values may be good or bad or both, depending upon who is doing the judging. These processes point to the particular problems that arise from the tendencies to idealize imagined wholes and immerse ourselves in imagined participation in them.

Values do not arise either from conscious intentions or through justification and discussion, although such intention, justification and discussion may be applied later. Values cannot be produced rationally. A purpose in life cannot be prescribed. Instead, the subjective experience of values arises in specific action contexts and types of intense experience. Values and value commitments arise in the course of self-formation through processes of idealizing key intense experiences and through the imaginative construction of a whole self to yield general and durable motivations for action directed towards what is judged as the good. These generalized idealizations must always be particularized in specific action situations as people negotiate their going on together. Values cannot be prescribed or deliberately chosen by anyone because they emerge, and continue to be iterated, in intense interactive experiences involving self-formation and self-transcendence. To claim that someone could choose values for others would be to claim that this someone could form the identity, or self, of others and form the self-transcendence of others.

Further insight into the nature of values comes from Mead's notion of cult values.[8] He pointed to how people have a tendency to individualize and idealize a collective and treat it 'as if' *it* had overriding motives or values, amounting to a process in which the collective constitutes a 'cult'. Members of 'cults' forget the 'as if' nature of their construct and act in a manner driven by the cult's values. Cults are maintained when leaders present to people's imagination a future free from obstacles that could prevent them from being what they all want to be. The visions that leaders of organizations are nowadays supposed to have are examples of this. A cult provides a feeling of enlarged personality in which individuals participate and from which they derive their value as persons. Mead said that they were the most precious part of our heritage, and examples of cult values are democracy, treating others with respect, regarding life as sacred, and belief in being American or British. However, it is important to stress that cult values can be good or bad or both. Cult values would include 'ethnic purity' and 'loving your neighbour'. Processes of idealization are far from unproblematic and could easily lead to actions that others outside the cult will come to regard as bad, even evil. It is in such cultish behaviour that we carry out the most terrible treatment of each other. The danger arises from focusing on the cult values themselves, on the values of the personalized institution or system, and directly applying them as overriding universal norms, conformity to which constitutes the requirement of continuing membership of the institution. Normally, however, idealization is accompanied by functionalization. Idealizations, or cult values, emerge in the historical evolution of any group or institution, to which they are ascribed, and they can become functional values in the everyday interactions between members of the institution rather than being simply applied in a way that enforces the conformity of a cult. For example, the cult value of a hospital might be to 'provide each patient with the best possible care'. However, such a cult value has to be repeatedly functionalized in many unique specific situations throughout the day. As soon as cult values become functional values in real daily interaction, conflict arises and it is this conflict that must be negotiated by people in their practical interaction with each other.

Another philosopher, MacIntyre,[9] has also pointed to the relationship between conflict, ideology and control. He argues that conflict, arguments, contestability and unpredictability are all essential features of social reality in our experience but in dominant theories they feature in only a marginal way, so denying their centrality. This is because the theories themselves express a particular ideology in the following way. Social reality is characterized by rival interpretations of social reality. On the one hand, there is the claim made by the dominant discourse that there is an incontestable underlying social structure which forms order and consensus. On the other hand, there is the claim that social reality is processes of interaction involving rivalry and conflict. In this interpretive rivalry, the dominant discourse around structure causing action has prevailed and, in so prevailing, it is regarded as 'the facts' which render the contesting interpretation invisible. The theory has become an ideology in that, although partially true, it obscures alternatives and so distorts understanding. In describing the social processes in which people recognize each other, the philosopher Honneth[10] distinguishes between a form of recognition which allows full intersubjective autonomy and what he calls ideological recognition, which imposes a regulative form of subjectivity on people as a condition for recognition and so continues the domination of a particular pattern of power relations. For Honneth, as for MacIntyre, ideology distorts understanding.

To summarize, the theory of complex responsive processes describes how ideologies emerge and evolve and how they are always reflected in the choices people make and the actions they take in their local situations, and these ideologies both sustain and challenge current patterns of power relations. Here ideology is defined as the tension between the obligatory restrictions of norms, as social forms of control, and the voluntary compulsions of values, as social motivators. Ideology as norms and values is thus social processes in which what is generalized as norms and idealized as values is made particular and functional in specific situations at specific times involving specific people. These social processes of ideology, therefore, constitute particular understandings of the social and since they focus attention and action selectively, they also inevitably distort understanding and these distortions can only change in ongoing ideological conflicts.

Local interaction: the impact of the social background

The previous three sections have explored the complex responsive processes of relating that occur between people as they go about their work in their local situations: they converse, they form power figurations and they make choices on the basis of their ideologies, all normal, everyday activities in which people go on together and accomplish whatever they accomplish. In such responsive local activity there emerge across a population the much wider patterns of organization, institution and the social. There is, however, an important additional aspect and this has to do with not only how these ordinary local interactions form the broader population-wide patterns but also how the local interactions are themselves, at the same time, formed by those population-wide patterns. In other words, all local interaction expresses the wider social background, and this section is concerned with how we might think about this.

In an earlier section of this chapter, attention was drawn to Mead's argument that in every interaction we are always also taking the attitude of the generalized other, by which he meant the social milieu in which we live. In another formulation of this idea he used the term 'social object'.[11] Social objects are generalized tendencies, common to large numbers of people, to act in similar ways in similar situations. These generalized tendencies to act are iterated in each living present as rather repetitive, habitual patterns of action. However, in their continual iteration, these general tendencies to act are normally particularized in the specific situation and the specific present the actors find themselves in. Such particularization is inevitably a conflictual process of interpretation as the meaning of the generalization is established in a specific situation. The possibility of transformation, that is, further evolution, of the social object arises in this particularizing because of the potential for spontaneity to generate variety in human action and the capacity of nonlinear interaction to amplify consequent small differences in the action of particularization. While physical objects are to be found in nature, social objects can only be experienced in their particularization in complex social acts in the living present. Social objects do not have any existence outside of such particularizing social acts.

A similar notion used by some other sociologists[12] is the habitus, which is the common assumptions, attitudes, feelings, behaviours and durable dispositions of people in a group or a society which they learn from each other, and they become so deeply ingrained as personality characteristics that they constitute the 'second nature' of human beings. This 'second nature' cannot be understood as something essentially individual because it is essentially social phenomena. Social habitus refers to what people in a group inherit both as specific language and as specific forms of civilization, that is, specific forms of self-regulation, which they absorb by learning just as they do for their specific language. What we experience as habitus today has emerged in a history of our group, nation and wider civilization. The fortunes of a nation become crystallized as institutions which shape the habitus and are sedimented in the habits of its individual members.[13] Habitus is the social background understanding, a shared common sense, which enables agents to make sense of what they are encountering so making practice possible. It is somatic, it arises from concrete, physical, bodily action, and it consists of durable, transposable dispositions. Habitus and personality are inseparable from each other.

Another formulation of generalized other, social object or habitus is 'the game'. French sociologist Pierre Bourdieu contrasts the notion that agents act on the basis of reason with the notion that agents act on the basis of interests.[14] In their ordinary activities, agents are engaged in a game which they take very seriously and regard as worth the effort because they have an interest in it; they are invested in it and they participate in the game, recognizing the game and the stakes. They are preoccupied by the game rather than acting rationally to achieve goals. We acquire our interest in particular social games through our living in the society we are born into. Our minds are structured by this social experience, which is imprinted in our bodies as a feel for the game, and to talk about mapping and measuring of our minds is to immediately obscure our understanding of the thoroughly social nature of mind and self. Agents are caught up in various social games and have the dispositions to recognize the stakes at play. They are invested in the stakes and play the game with each other through enacting the habitual social customs and ways of thinking into which they are born. Much of this is unconscious as agents embody schemes of perception on the basis of which they act rather than setting objectives for what they do. Agents are absorbed in their affairs and act in ways which are inscribed in the game itself. A feel for the game develops in a history of refining the skill of anticipating the moves of others, so achieving some mastery over the unfolding game. Social agents have 'strategies' which only rarely reflect a true strategic intention. We are absorbed in the affairs of the organization in our local interactions, conducting skilful performances which give us some mastery of organizational continuity and change. While the individual with the capacity for powerful individual agency exercised in a rational, detached way is what is publicly presented, the reality of ordinary interaction, of ordinary experience, is that of participating, largely unconsciously, in games, in the habitus in which we live.

I use the term *immersing* to describe what we are doing as we interact locally, preoccupied in the game, in ways which unconsciously reflect the generalizations and idealizations, the habitus, of our society. The word *immerse* means to be absorbed in some interest or situation where one devotes oneself fully to that interest or situation, throwing oneself into it and engaging others to be so immersed. Immersing is an activity of bringing together, filling in, expanding, elaborating, complexifying and taking into account greater detail and diversity. It is our preoccupation with the game, our expression of the habitus in which we live, our direct involvement in our ordinary, everyday local interactions. Such activity, essentially ideology-based acts of choice, inevitably generates conflict. Immersing, therefore, refers to activities taking the form of: the ordinary, everyday politics of life; the patterning of the power relations between people; acts of politeness and face-saving; practising the arts of resistance; denial, scapegoating and blaming as defensive ways of living with the anxieties of ordinary, everyday life; the spontaneity and improvisation required if we are to respond appropriately in the unique contingent situations we so often face; the attachment to others, as well as the empathy with, and trust in, those others, and also aggression, competition, rivalry, mistrust and hatred; the creative imagination of alternative ways of living and doing and the inevitable destruction of others' ways of living; altruism and generosity as well as selfishness and meanness.

However, we also have the capacity to become aware of our preoccupation with the game, to reflect upon our practical action, which expresses the habitus in which we live, in an effort to make conscious sense of what we are doing. To live simply immersed in the above ways would be to live a life devoid of all thought, reflection or meaning-making. Thought, reflection and meaning-making are all activities of *abstracting*, the opposite of the activities of immersing. The most common under-standing of abstract is that it denotes theory as the opposite of something practical, but in its original sense it means 'to draw away from, to separate from'. All forms of thinking about and reflecting upon experience necessarily involve abstracting or drawing away from that experience, which becomes an object of perception and not simply the subject of experience. Abstractions are articulations of both local and global patterns of interaction. They are attempts to describe habitus and the game rather than just participate in them. However, such activities of articulation always occur in local interaction and it is in such local interaction that the meaning of these abstractions emerges. Experience is thus an inseparable interplay between the activ-ities of immersing and abstracting, of participating and reflecting, in which each is simultaneously forming and being formed by the other.

People continue to make sense of the population-wide patterns of interaction they live in through the stories they tell and the myths they spin. We still articulate the general/ideal in stories, rumours and fantasies about distant powerful figures despite the social and individual evolution of the past centuries. The point about the narrative forms of our articulations is that they stay close to our experience of local interaction in that they provide descriptions and accounts of that local interac-tion itself, even in mythical form. Articulations of these generalizations and idealizations in narrative form involve selecting and simplifying and, in that sense, abstracting from experience. However, the selection is not only simplification but also elaboration. Narrative articulations of experience require interpretation in particular contingent situations. Their aim is not simplicity, standardization and uniformity, as we shall see below is the case in later forms of abstracting, but rather their aim is the opening up of accounts of experience for greater exploration in order to develop deeper understanding.

However, the conscious simplifying generalization of narrative does amount to abstracting from, that is, simplifying and generalizing, the detail of each uniquely experienced situation. Insofar as the characters and situations in stories are stereotypes, narratives abstract from and categorize the detail of experience. We might call this articulation in narratives and philosophical arguments, *first order abstracting* from the experience of local interaction, So people do not think entirely in terms of specific objects, such as this table or that table, but instead they think in terms of a general, and so abstract, category of tables. However, over the last few centuries social evolution has produced modern agents who engage in a kind of generalizing about their experience that is articulated primarily in propositional forms. What emerged was a particularly rigorous form of simplification, a stronger form of abstracting from the experience of local interaction than before, namely, the scientific method, which we might call *second order abstracting*.

This is a form of simplification by abstraction which manipulates the categories of first order abstractions and therefore operates at yet another remove from direct experience. This abstraction from the abstraction of categories of experience makes it easier to split the second order abstraction off from the experience through reification and so lose the sense of the paradox of immersing and abstracting at the same time. Second order abstracting activity seeks to simplify, standardize and measure, so reducing elaboration, multiple interpretations and mystery. The consequent clarity and uniformity make it much easier to exert some control on the activities of others from a distance. Local interaction in the modern world, therefore, necessarily includes the formulation and interpretation of second order abstractions as one aspect of what we are doing together in organizations. Certainly, to be included in groups of managers one must be a skilled participant in the dominant discourse conducted in terms of second order abstractions. This activity of second order abstracting involves: objectifying and categorizing; measuring and standardizing; averaging out differences within categories and interactions between categories; analysing the data so produced using mathematical, statistical and other analytical techniques; selecting regularities and stabilities and forming hypotheses about relationships between entities, particularly causal connections; modelling, forecasting, specifying probabilities, articulating rules and schemas; prescribing rules, laws and norms; setting targets, planning, monitoring and envisioning.

Implications for leadership and management tools and techniques

Complex responsive processes of interaction describe what people are already doing in organizations. They accomplish their work by engaging in conversation; they engage in the power relations of inclusion and exclusion; they make choices reflecting their ideologies; they abstract from their experience to understand what is going on; they carry out procedures and take up rules and other techniques. When presented with this reflection of what they are already actually doing, many ask a rather strange question. They ask how they are to apply complex responsive processes, how they are to use it in practice. This is strange because they are already engaging in complex responsive processes as described in this chapter. So how would they apply or use, say, conversation? They are already conversing. The theory is useful not because it yields general prescriptions or general techniques. It is useful because it directs attention to what we are actually doing, matters which are rarely reflected upon. It is useful because it directs attention away from just the techniques to the processes in which the techniques are being used. The dominant discourse focuses attention on the techniques and largely ignores the processes of using them. However, even when I make this point, people mostly continue to insist that the most important issue is to find a set of tools and techniques that will produce success. They continue to believe that a way of thinking which produces a deeper understanding of what they and others are doing is not worth much if it does not produce a new set of tools and techniques. The rest of the chapters in this book will be exploring what is meant by the tools and techniques of leadership and management and just how we might understand what they are and how they are used from the perspective of complex responsive processes of interaction.

In trying to understand what managers are doing when they use tools and techniques, it seems useful, to me, to distinguish between a number of categories:

- the tools of instrumental rationality;
- the techniques of power;
- institutional techniques;
- the techniques of practical judgment.

The next chapter will deal with the first of these categories and subsequent chapters will explore the others.

Conclusion

When they go home at the end of each work day, most people have something to say to those they live with about what they have experienced at work. What they have to say is inevitably expressed in the form of stories, in the form of narrative in which they make sense of their stories. The stories will involve recalling the conversation in local interaction with others, recounting who said what to whom, what the responses were and what it all meant. The stories will often be about what more powerful people are doing and how one feels about it. They may be about how one is manoeuvring to avoid having some of one's staff made redundant or scheming about what actions to take to have one's budget increased, or trying to work out how to be included in some more powerful group or to resist the encroachment of some more powerful group. In the course of these stories the narrator will probably talk about what he or she has chosen or is choosing to do, and this will always reflect what one believes in, ideology, even though mostly we are not conscious of what this ideology is about. The narrative is likely to include items of gossip and may also be about trying to make sense of the bigger picture across the organization, industry or society. In other words, the ordinary narrative of everyday work life is about the complex responsive processes of conversation, power and ideology, reflecting choices engaged in with others in orderly and disorderly local interactions. What this chapter has been doing, therefore, is exploring in a little more detail these ordinary processes of organizational life which could be summarized as the ongoing ordinary politics of everyday lived experience in organizations.

In all of this activity, leaders and managers talk about using tools and techniques, and the rest of this book will be concerned with how we might think about the tools and techniques from the perspective of the complex responsive processes of interacting with each other in ordinary organizational life. First, the next chapter takes a look at the tools and techniques of instrumental rationality.

4

THE LEADERSHIP AND MANAGEMENT TOOLS AND TECHNIQUES OF INSTRUMENTAL RATIONALITY

Rules and step-by-step procedures

Introduction

In the dominant discourse, leaders, managers and powerful coalitions of them are supposed to objectively observe their organizations and use the tools of rational analysis to select appropriate objectives, targets and visions, and then to formulate strategies of macro change and design organizational structures and procedures to implement them, and then to use rational monitoring procedures to secure control over movement into the future. Powerful coalitions of managers are supposed to know what is happening through environmental scanning and internal resource analyses, on the basis of which they are supposed to choose the best outcomes for their organization and design the systems, including learning systems, which will enable them to be in control of the strategic direction of their organization 'going forward' so that improvement and success are secured. Recognizing that there is uncertainty, leaders and managers are supposed to conduct risk analyses of what might go wrong and to develop contingency plans to cope with the risks. Over the last hundred years business-school researchers and management consultants have developed a plethora of what are called tools and techniques to be used by leaders and managers to carry out the activities just mentioned. In essence all of these tools and techniques are prescriptions that are supposed to make it possible to choose improved organizational outcomes and results well in advance of acting. In other words, they are instruments for choosing and controlling the future of an organization, for choosing and realizing its aims, and they have been developed through rational analysis and measurement. There is an implicitly assumed theory of efficient causality which holds out the promise that *if* a manager uses the tool properly, *then* an improved outcome will be realized. It is in this sense that we can speak of them as the tools and techniques of analytical, technical, calculative or instrumental rationality. In what follows, I will refer to them as the tools and techniques of instrumental rationality. The dominant discourse focuses attention on, and is conducted primarily in terms of, these tools and techniques which are to be applied to organizations understood to be systems subject to environmental forces.

In the last two chapters I have outlined an alternative to the dominant discourse, one which focuses attention on the wider processes of leading and managing in which leaders and managers may well be using the tools and techniques of the dominant discourse but they are understood to constitute only a relatively minor aspect of what leaders and managers are actually doing. In other words, the focus of attention is on the interdependence of human agents and, therefore, on the forms of human interaction. This alternative discourse is conducted in terms of human, bodily processes of conversation, power relations and evaluative choices that reflect ideologies. It is in these processes that all of us, leaders, managers and members of organizations, accomplish together whatever it is that we accomplish. It is in these local processes of interaction, in the interplay of all our intentions, that there emerge the population-wide patterns of interaction that we call organizations and their evolution. It makes no sense to refer to these processes of interaction as tools in any way, certainly not as tools of instrumental rationality, because they are the life processes in which our very selves, our identities, emerge. In focusing attention on the interplay of human choices, as opposed to the autonomous individual's choices assumed by the tools of instrumental rationality, the theory of complex responsive processes confronts us with the fundamental uncertainty of organizational life, indeed of all human life. This, of course, greatly problematizes the tools of instrumental rationality and many managers find this rather disturbing. The frequent response I get from some managers is a dogmatic statement, unaccompanied by any rational justification, that there have to be tools of management because otherwise nothing useful or improved would get done. They claim that there must be some way of deciding in advance what a good action looks like. From yet other managers I experience an insistent demand that if I am going to problematize one set of tools, then I must put forward an alternative toolkit. I am pressed to present prescriptions for success according to the theory of complex responsive processes and asked to provide case studies of organizations that have successfully implemented such prescriptions. I am told that if I cannot do this, then the theory is of no practical use. In other words, there is an enormous pressure to present the theory of complex responsive processes in the terms of the dominant discourse. Of course, doing this would immediately neuter the theory and that certainly would make it useless.

What I am trying to explore is not about different prescriptions for what leaders and managers should do to be successful, surely there are already enough, but rather about a way of thinking about what people are already doing in organizations that produces both success and failure. Focusing attention on what we are already doing cannot produce new, universal, generalized prescriptions because, by definition, we are focusing on what we are already doing rather than on what researchers and consultants think we should be doing. However, what focusing attention on what we are already doing can produce is wider and deeper understanding of what we are already doing. In other words, the theory focuses attention on how we are thinking, or more importantly how we are not thinking, about what we are doing. This may help us to move on from endless repetition in ways that will emerge and so cannot be set out in advance. In focusing attention on what leaders and managers are already doing, it is clear that they do talk about using tools and techniques; and since they do believe that certain prescriptions lead to success, I am interested in trying to understand the nature of this talk. After all, we know that in organizational life we strike a strategic pose and talk publicly in particular ways while actually accomplishing what we accomplish in ways that differ from our public transcripts. So the interesting question becomes one of understanding what people are doing when they apply or use a management tool and what the organizational consequences of doing so are. I ended the last chapter with a categorization of the tools and techniques people in organizations use, the first category being the tools of instrumental rationality, and it is the purpose of this chapter to think about the nature of the tools and techniques of instrumental rationality. The next section of this chapter describes the tools of instrumental rationality and the section after that explores the nature of these tools and techniques. The next chapter presents a critique of the tools and techniques and some typical responses that this critique evokes.

Before moving to the next section, however, I want to clarify the distinction between a tool and a technique. Tools are artifacts used to increase and extend human capacities and as such they regulate human activity and enable the realization of goals. The tools of instrumental rationality, as understood in the dominant discourse, are applied by individuals to achieve individual and collective goals, aims and purposes. So in organizational life a tool may be a physical artifact such as a computer or, more frequently, what is meant by the term tool is a conceptual framework, such as a SWOT (strengths, weaknesses, opportunities and threats) categorization. Technique refers to how the tool is used, and in the dominant discourse on instrumental rationality this would be a systematic procedure for accomplishing a complex task using the tool. So the technique of using SWOT is to compile a careful and comprehensive list in each category of strengths, weaknesses, opportunities and threats. However, in what follows I will not differentiate between what is a tool and what is a technique because both fall into the category of instrumental rationality and it is this that I want to focus attention on.

The management tools of instrumental rationality

This section will consider what managers, consultants and academics identify as the management tools and techniques that can be described as those of instrumental rationality in that they are instruments prescribed for achieving improved organizational outcomes in rational, analytical ways. These will all be very familiar to the great majority of people likely to be reading this book. The purpose of listing them is to make what I am talking about both clear and specific. This will form the basis of the discussion on the characteristics of this group of tools and techniques in the next section. Examples will be given of tools and techniques of instrumental rationality in the following categories:

- planning and strategy tools;
- decision–making tools;
- monitoring and control tools;
- generalized motivation tools;
- tools for improving and developing organizations;
- second order systems tools and techniques.

To be included as an example in each of the above categories, a tool or technique has to take an instrumental form. In other words, it must be used as an instrument in realizing some kind of intention for the organization. Such tools and techniques inevitably reflect an 'if–then' causal structure: *if* leader-managers apply tool A, *then* they will achieve outcome B. The following examples of instrumental rationality tools and techniques were easily obtained by simple Google searches of the offerings of management consultants and by examining a few textbooks. The tools and techniques presented are analytical and usually claimed to be scientific and supported by scientific evidence. Of course, in actuality leader-managers often do not use any of the tools and even if they do, they may be using them for purposes other than those proclaimed; besides this, they are also doing many other things. These other things, as well as the less obvious purposes for using tools and techniques, will be covered in the next five chapters, particularly Chapter 9 on practical judgment. Consider first planning and strategy tools.

Planning and strategy tools

Planning and strategizing activities are usually presented by academics and consultants as a sequence of steps to be carried out, usually starting with an analysis of the environment of the organization. Managers are presented with a number of tools to be used to carry out this analysis, for example:

- The PESTEL[1] framework which categorizes environmental factors into six categories: political, economic, social, technological, environmental and legal. This framework is used to produce lists of key drivers and how they are likely to change, so enabling managers to focus on the most important drivers and secure success.
- Scenarios which set out a number of possible futures.
- Porter's five market forces framework,[2] listing key aspects of market or industry structure: threat of entry, threat of substitutes, power of buyers, power of suppliers and competitive rivalry. Analysis of these forces is used to determine the attractiveness of a market.
- Industry life-cycle models showing how industries go through phases: development, growth, shake-out, maturity, decline.

Having carried out the analysis of the environment, the next step for managers is to analyse the resource and competence base of their organization. Here, too, managers are provided with a number of tools, for example:

- VRIN capabilities,[3] which is an acronym for value, rarity, inimitability, non-substitutability. This framework is to be used to identify the competitive advantage of the resource–competence base.
- benchmarking;
- Porter's value chain analysis,[4] covering inbound logistics, operations, outbound logistics, marketing and sales, and service;
- SWOT, which is a list of strengths, weaknesses, opportunities and threats.

Tools are also provided for managers to express strategic purpose, for example:

- statements of missions, vision and values;
- setting objectives or targets for what is to be achieved;
- mapping of stakeholders and their interests.

The importance of organizational culture may be recognized and this leads to the provision of tools to analyse the culture and how it may support or block the strategy. If the culture is blocking the strategy, then either the strategy or the culture must be changed. An example of a culture analysis tool is:

- The cultural web,[5] which consists of a number of elements: paradigm, symbols, power structures, organizational structures, control systems, rituals and routines, stories.

There are, of course, many other categories of strategic analysis and a plethora of other tools, but this sample is indicative of all of them. They are usually presented in diagrammatic form, the most popular of these forms being a 2x2 matrix, and this in itself is seen as a tool. Tools to generate the required data for analysis include methods of quantification, measurement, statistics, probability analysis, questionnaires and surveys.

Decision-making tools

Plans and strategies provide general frameworks within which leader-managers are supposed to make specific decisions, for example investment decisions. Examples of the tools and techniques recommended for making decisions are as follows:

- A decision tree shows a complete picture of a potential decision and allows a manager to graph alternative decision paths. Generally, decision trees are used to evaluate decisions under conditions of risk. Decision trees force a manager to be explicit in analysing conditions associated with future decisions and in determining the outcome of different alternatives.
- Payback analysis shows how long it will take to recoup an investment.

- Discounted cash flow analysis is used to calculate the Net Present Value and Internal Rates of Return of future cash flows resulting from a particular investment over the next 25 years, and this requires using the tool of forecasting the cash flows and interest rates.
- Simulation is basically model-building, in which the simulator is trying to gain understanding by replicating something and then manipulating it by adjusting the variables used to build the model. Simulation attempts to imitate an existing system or situation in a simplified manner.
- Stages of problem identification (routines of recognition and diagnosis), development (routines of search, screen and design) and selection (routines of evaluation/choice and authorization).[6] This sequence was identified in research on decision-making processes in conditions of novelty, complexity and open-endedness. Although the steps were described as difficult, discontinuous and recursive, they still consist of the steps found in most of the tools and techniques of decision-making.
- Computerized decision-making models.

Monitoring and control tools

Once strategies have been set and decisions have been made, their results need to be monitored in budgets and reports, which rely on the following tools, for example:

- objectives and targets to achieve improvement;
- forecasts of outcomes of actions to achieve objectives and targets;
- measurement of actual outcomes and identification of the gap between forecast and actual, leading to actions to close the gap;
- project control techniques such as Gant charts and flow charts.

Generalized motivation tools

Since it is members of the organization who will have to implement the strategies and decisions, it is important that they be motivated to do so and for this purpose there are also generalized tools and techniques of motivation. For example, there are the following:

- performance appraisal following standard steps, leading to reward and punishment;
- construction of league tables and the naming and shaming of poor performers;
- team building awaydays for which there are a number of standard tools, such as exercises to be performed and games to be played;
- public recognition and praise, including the granting of awards;
- employee training and management development which focuses on the tools;
- reducing communication barriers at each stage of the communication process. At the first stage, the source of the message must be clear on why they are communicating, and what they want to communicate, which should be useful and accurate. The next stage is the message, that is, the information to be communicated.

Then there is the encoding stage, which is the process of transferring the information in a form that can be sent and correctly decoded by the receiver. Next, there is the channel, such as face-to-face meetings, telephone and videoconferencing, letters, emails, memos and reports. The next stage is decoding by the receiver. Finally, there is feedback, that is, reactions to the communicated message which make it possible to detect possible misunderstandings and re-send the message. To deliver messages effectively, managers must break down the barriers at each of these stages.

Tools for improving and developing organizations

The dominant discourse is very concerned with organizational change, and this is thought to require change at the macro level of the whole organization or major parts of it. The following are examples of the tools and techniques put forward for this purpose:

- Organizational learning. Assessment instruments are available to determine whether an organization is a learning organization or not, and if it is not, a number of steps are recommended: create a shared vision; make information accessible to all; help employees to change; empower employees to act; support risk taking; manage knowledge by keeping information current, maintaining historical knowledge and dealing with high volumes of knowledge. Also available are learning style questionnaires and the well-known Myers-Briggs test, as well as many other psychological and psychometric tests to identify different personality styles and their impact on modes of learning.
- Organizational development (OD). Since this is a process of planned change to organizational structures, cultures and values, the usual planning tools and techniques are all used. Use is also made of surveys, interviews, feedback and action planning, balanced scorecards, role and responsibility mapping, culture mapping and workflow charting. The ubiquitous diagram taking the form of a 2x2 grid is widely used to present alternative forms of culture and locate an organization's own culture, using questionnaires to identify which category it falls into. This information is used to define what the culture currently is and the gap compared to what it is desired to be. Surveys of climate, satisfaction, morale can be conducted.
- Changing behaviour, values and mental models through executive and team coaching. The dominant form of coaching calls for the coach to follow a step-by-step model of the clear tasks that are to be undertaken: defining and agreeing the specific, measurable and realistic goal or outcome to be achieved; probing the coachees to identify how they will know that they have achieved their goal of solving a problem; getting the coachees to describe their current reality as their starting point in solving a problem; exploring what possible options there are for solving the problem; specifying the benefits and costs of each option. Finally, coachees need to be asked what they will do now, when they will do it, what obstacles they might encounter, how they will overcome these, how likely the option is to succeed

and what else they will do. Throughout the process there are coaching tools that can be used, such as measuring techniques, assessment instruments, psychological tests, feedback instruments, interviews and evaluation techniques.

Second order systems tools and techniques

First order systems thinking is concerned with intervening in the organizational system to define clear goals, identify problems and propose rational solutions. This involves characterizing a situation in terms of identifiable objects with well-defined properties; finding general rules that apply to situations in terms of those objects and properties; applying the rules logically to the situation and drawing conclusions as to what is to be done. The examples of tools and techniques so far given above reflect first order systems thinking. The ideology being reflected in these tools and techniques is that of command, control and efficiency. Second order systems thinking[7] moves away from a realist belief in systems, regarding systems as hypotheses and so as ways of thinking rather than as existing things. It focuses attention on the observer of the system as also a participant in the system. There is a significant ideological shift from an ideology of control and efficiency to one of participation, inclusion, emancipation and the postmodern idea of multiple discourses or realities. Despite this significant ideological shift, however, the proposed tools and techniques continue to reflect instrumental rationality in that they are instruments to be used in rational ways to produce improvement. The difference is that the tools are presented for collective use rather than simply for leaders, and the improvement sought would pay more attention to the good of those participating.

The following are examples of the tools and techniques of second order systems thinking:

- Interactive planning;[8] using this technique, members of an organization participate in the formulating of an idealized design of the future they desire. Then they carry out a systems analysis, that is, the formulation of a detailed picture of the organization as it is today. They then seek to close the gap between their present situation and the desired future.
- Designing purposeful systems;[9] this requires a decision-maker who can produce change in performance measures, a designer whose design influences the decision-maker, a design aimed at maximizing value and a built-in guarantee that the purpose can be achieved. Critical reflection on system design and operation is regarded as essential, as is the importance of moral practice. The aim of systems design is to emancipate people from domination so that they can participate in a democratic process of system design.
- Soft Systems Methodology (SSM);[10] this technique is a process of participative inquiry in which meaning arises and intentions are developed. The aim of the methodology is to integrate multiple viewpoints of free participants in order to assist them to predict and control the changes to their systems in vague situations in which there are no agreed goals. The key phases of SSM are as follows:

building a 'rich picture' of the problem situation; drawing a number of systems (viewpoints) from the 'rich picture' which are relevant to improving the problem situation; constructing a number of conceptual systems models; taking a cultural/political systems view of the interventions and rules of clients, problems solvers and other stakeholders.

- Systemic intervention;[11] this is an approach to analysing a problem situation by making boundary judgments, which are matters of values and ethics, and through the creative design of systemic methods of intervention to enable agents to look outwards at the situation and to look back to the knowledge-generating system (biological organisms, mind, social group, society) in which the agents/stakeholders are embedded. A mix of methods is used, such as critical systems heuristics and the viable systems model. Systemic intervention always has the purpose of improvement.
- System of System Methodologies (SOSM) and Total Systems Intervention (TSI);[12] these are meta-methodological frameworks relating all systems methodologies to appropriate contexts. They bring pluralism to systems thinking by defining ideal problem contexts that differ from one another in a meaningful way. Important differences in context should be reflected in differences of methodology. The tools of TSI, consisting of lists, metaphors and models, are available to assist this process, and the outcome is coordinated change that brings about improvement.
- Some writers use notions of complex systems. In one example of this use,[13] five domains are distinguished: simple, where the nature of causality is obvious and so people sense, categorize and respond to yield best practice; complicated, in which the type of causality needs to be analysed so that people sense, analyse and respond to yield good practice; complex, in which the type of causality can only be perceived in retrospect so that people probe, sense, categorize and respond to yield the emergent; chaotic, in which there is no relationship between cause and effect so that people act, sense, categorize and respond to yield the novel; disorder, a state of not knowing what type of causality exists which prompts people to fall back into their comfort zone. This tool guides people into appropriate decision processes for the context they find themselves in.

The nature of the tools and techniques of instrumental rationality

This section explores the key characteristics of the vast array of tools and techniques of instrumental rationality, examples of which were described in the previous section. The key features of these tools and techniques are as follows:

- *Efficient causality and predictability.* Each tool or technique is either explicitly or implicitly identified as a way to improve the organization by achieving greater efficiency, effectiveness and higher quality. The purpose of the tools and techniques is to achieve results and outcomes that are 'good' or at least better than they otherwise would be. Each of them has the structure of efficient causality, namely, *if* tool A is used, *then* the better outcome Y will be produced. It is this form of causality which yields predictions and also makes it possible to claim that there is scientific evidence that the tools work.

- *Second order abstractions.* All of the instrumental tools are second order abstractions, a notion explored in the previous chapter. They are abstracted from our everyday experience of organizations as simplifications which are relevant in all places at all times. They therefore have the natural science characteristics of being general and context free. However, when they are applied or used, they have to be made particular to the specific situation the users find themselves in. The effectiveness of the tools, as well as what they mean, depend crucially on this process of particularization.

- *Rules and steps.* The tools and techniques all take the form of rules or steps that managers and leaders are to follow. Those making the prescriptions for following rules show little awareness of the complex nature of rule following. How rules are followed depends crucially on the background, game, habitus or generalized other, all concepts discussed in the last chapter.

Each of these characteristics is briefly considered below.

Efficient causality and predictability

I find it striking that the management tools and techniques listed in the previous section are all variations on a small number of themes. The main theme takes the form of stages or steps involving Planning, Doing, Studying and Acting (PDSA). Furthermore, they mainly take the form of standardized lists of categories. For example, the SWOT tool is simply a framework of categories, namely, strengths, weaknesses, opportunities and threats, and each of these categories then prompts further, often very long, lists of factors. The aim is to ensure that no relevant information is left out of consideration. However, the tool itself does not assist managers to identify the relative importance of each item in a long list, so that the tool amounts to a system of classification with little indication of how to use the lists generated. The concrete-sounding label 'tool' turns out to describe that which is far from concrete. Furthermore, the SWOT tool, like all the others, is context free – it is meant to be used in any situation, every situation. When a specific group of people use it in a specific situation or context, they end up filling each generalized, abstract category with further abstractions such as 'poor quality' or 'positive image'. The context they are immersed in is the organizational game discussed in the last chapter. To take account of context, then, is to discuss the ways in which the tools are being used and the particular game the tool users are invested in. When managers take account of context, which they must if they are to act in practically sensible ways, they rapidly discover that they are using the tool for purposes other than the one it has been designed for. For example, they may actually be using the tool as a social defence against the anxiety aroused by not knowing what to do. I will argue in Chapter 6 that the tools and techniques of instrumental rationality are all actually the techniques of disciplinary power.

In highly ambiguous situations where the outcomes of actions cannot be predicted and no one is clear about just what is going on, categories based on past generalized experience are unlikely to be the kind of comprehensive guide they are claimed to be. In these circumstances, it is highly likely that important novel factors will not be taken into account through following a list. All of the tools and techniques reflect a particular, totally taken-for-granted notion of causality, namely efficient causality with its 'if–then' structure. The assumption is that *if* managers follow the sequence of steps, *if* they use the tools listed in the previous section under the heading 'planning and strategy tools', *then* they will be more likely to achieve their objectives; *if* they make lists in the SWOT categories, *then* they are more likely to include all the relevant information. It is only if this assumption about causality holds sway in actuality that the tools can do what they are supposed to and optimize decisions, or at least yield satisfactory ones. However, it was argued in Chapter 2 that analogies from the complexity sciences lead us to conclude that the simple efficient causal structure cannot apply to human interaction and so the outcomes of human interactions are fundamentally unpredictable, or more accurately they are a paradox of predictability and unpredictability at the same time.

So, the tools of instrumental rationality immediately encounter a problem in that they depend specifically on a theory of causality which underlies the possibility of prediction but that theory of causality is not reflected in the actual world of our experience. The claim that they are scientific in the same sense as the natural sciences collapses on being subjected to scrutiny and, in addition, the claim that there is scientific evidence that the tools and techniques produce success cannot be sustained. It becomes evident that the claims are just rhetoric. In a previous publication,[14] I reported on a search of the huge literature on management and organizations and found that only a tiny fraction of it does any serious research into the evidence base for the prescriptions presented. Not only was the research on the evidence base sparse, it was also contradictory and inconclusive. There are very few studies of long-term effectiveness and sample sizes are always very small. No serious natural scientist would accept it as evidence. Others have come to this conclusion too. For example, Grimshaw and Eccles[15] recently conducted a systematic review of 235 studies of guideline dissemination and implementation strategies in the healthcare sector and found that while there was some evidence of success in particular situations, there was little evidence that the particular implementation strategies associated with the success were generalizable to other behaviours and settings. They concluded that although there are many change management methodologies in general organizational settings, their applicability to healthcare professional and organizational behaviour has yet to be established. It still requires the exercise of considerable judgment on the part of decision-makers to select interventions likely to succeed, so that any important improvements seem to be a result of 'gut feel' rather than any scientific basis. However, this does not deter some consultants from making claims that their own trade-marked tool differs significantly from traditional simplistic and theoretical approaches in using validated modelling proven in the real-world workplace. This critical difference is said to allow users to achieve genuine, lasting, measurable change and growth. The evidence, however, is not presented and there is no indication of where it is to be found. What is claimed to be evidence is often derived from working with small numbers of people in artificial settings such as a university classroom, with population samples biased towards young middle-class males. Longitudinal studies rarely go beyond a year, and organizations claiming to have evidence rarely publish it because they regard it as confidential proprietary data.

Why is there such a problem with providing evidence? The answer to this question is that what is accepted as evidence must document how a particular tool produced success across a large number of cases over reasonably long periods of time. These criteria for evidence can only be met if, first, causality takes the efficient, linear form of *if* we do A, *then* we will produce outcome X, and if, second, there are many repetitive events rather than events that are usually unique in some sense. Since these conditions are not met in organizational life, scientific evidence is not possible. Instead we are going to have to continue to rely on judgment and 'gut feel', while rhetorically claiming to have evidence as part of marketing efforts.

Second order abstractions

The last chapter presented the notion of the activity of second order abstracting. It was pointed out how this involves: simplifying and generalizing; objectifying and categorizing; measuring aspects of these categories using standardized measures; averaging out differences within categories and interactions between categories; analysing the data using mathematical, statistical and other analytical techniques; selecting regularities and stabilities, particularly causal connections; modelling, forecasting and mapping; prescribing rules; setting targets; planning; monitoring; and envisioning. Clearly, all of the tools and techniques of instrumental rationality are second order abstractions so defined. The last chapter also pointed out that in themselves tools and techniques are simply abstract gestures that can only find meaning in the responses of the specific people who are using them in the specific situations in which they are using them. As previous chapters argued, such responses will be processes of conversation, power relating and ideology-based choices. In other words, the tools and techniques cannot be simply applied in an instrumental way because their use can only ever occur in the ordinary politics of daily organizational life. This means that the use of the tools of instrumental rationality cannot be rational in an objective, instrumental sense. Their use will arouse emotion, threaten or sustain existing power relations, provoke resistance and conflict between different ideologies. Instrumental rationality turns out to be a fiction in ordinary everyday life in organizations.

Rules and steps

The tools and techniques of instrumental rationality take the form of rules or steps and these require interpretation. Taylor,[16] a philosopher, argues that we need some notion of a rule because so much social behaviour is regular. However, following a rule is not a straightforward matter. Taylor argues that understanding anything always relies upon a background that is taken for granted. To be able to follow a rule, one has to understand what it means and to do that one has to rely on the taken-for-granted background. Those who lack a particular background are extremely likely to misunderstand the rule and therefore not know what to do, or they will do the wrong thing. Taylor points to Wittgenstein's argument that 'obeying a rule' is a social practice in which people are expressing the unarticulated – people are acting without reasons but on the basis of experience. Practice requires continual interpretation and re-interpretation of what a rule means in specific situations. Taylor gives a simple example of a stranger asking for directions to a place. He is told to follow the arrow on the road signs. However, if he has just come from a place in which there are no arrows, or knowledge of arrows, the stranger will not know that following an arrow means taking the direction which the tip of the arrow is pointing to. He might just as easily think that following the arrow means going in the direction of the feathers. Taylor argues that when we say that our understanding is situated in practice, this means that it is implicit in our activity, even that activity we cannot represent in explicit formulations. Intelligent action is sensitive to situations and goals which we have not necessarily formulated as representations. So, following a given rule will produce variations of activity depending on particular situations and individual goals. Understanding relies on the background and it is embodied:

> That is, our bodily know-how, and the way we act and move, can encode components of our understanding of self and the world. I know my way around a familiar environment in being able to get from any place to any place with ease and assurance.[17]

As explained in the previous chapter, for Mead the background required to understand and so follow a rule is a social object or generalized other, while for Bourdieu and Elias it is habitus and for all three it is the game.

Conclusion

In my experience, many people in organizations talk about management tools and techniques in a rather loose and taken-for-granted way as if we all know exactly what is meant by such a tool or technique. However, if we are to think at all seriously about the matter of tools and techniques, then we need to be clear on what they are and just what is being assumed when it is recommended that they be used. This chapter has, therefore, set out a long but by no means exhaustive list of what people normally mean when they talk about the tools and techniques of leadership and management. The tools and techniques are prescribed in the belief that they will enable leaders and managers to choose an improved future for their organizations and to control movement towards that future. This chapter has explored how this belief is based on a taken-for-granted underlying assumption of efficient causality. The prescriptions all take the form: *if* you apply tool M, *then* you will get result X. It is only if organizational life takes the form of taking an action which produces a predictable outcome that we can apply the tools as recommended. This chapter has argued that the inevitably uncertain and ambiguous processes of interaction between people which produce organizations do not take a linear form and efficient causality does not apply. The claim that the use of particular tools and techniques will enable leaders and managers to choose and control future direction simply cannot be sustained in any rational argument. This conclusion is reinforced when it is understood that the tools and techniques of instrumental rationality are actually second order abstractions from lived experience in organizations. Such abstractions have to be made particular in particular contingent situations characterized by some degree of uniqueness. What the tools or techniques actually mean will depend upon how they are taken up in contingent local interaction. The effect of attempting to apply the tool or technique will therefore be characterized by considerable uncertainty. Finally, the tools and techniques take the form of rules and procedures, and it is clear that following a rule is a complex matter depending on the nature of the society that those attempting to follow the rule live in. This chapter, then, seriously problematizes the whole notion of leadership and management tools and techniques. The next chapter takes this conclusion further by arguing that expert action does not take the form of following rules. Experts leave the rules, and so the tools and techniques, behind and exercise practical judgment derived from their experience, a matter to be addressed in Chapter 9.

5

THE LIMITATIONS OF THE TOOLS AND TECHNIQUES OF INSTRUMENTAL RATIONALITY

Incompatibility with expert performance

Introduction

This chapter concerns the analysis of the instrumentally rational tools and techniques of leadership and management. There is a well-known argument that those who are proficient in and expert at performing an activity do not use rules or tools at all. Following rules seems relevant when moving from novice to competent actor, but to go further than competence requires going beyond the rules. Insistence on following rules traps people at the level of competent performer and blocks the development of expertise. The expert and the merely competent actually display different forms of knowing. This chapter looks at the work underlying this conclusion. It then provides a general critique of the tools and techniques of instrumental rationality and concludes with a consideration of tools and techniques in relation to leadership.

Competence, perhaps, but not proficiency or expertise

Hubert Dreyfus, a philosopher, and his brother Stuart Dreyfus,[1] an industrial engineer, developed a critique of the claims of computer scientists who were developing artificial intelligence (AI). The AI scientists sought to program computers to think like experts, and in the 1980s they claimed that they were on the verge of doing so. In order to develop intelligent computers they interviewed experts, such as physicians, and questioned them to extract the rules lying behind their effortless judgments. They assumed that experts acted on the basis of rules, just as all humans were claimed to do by cognitivist psychology, but that these rules had slipped out of awareness. However, the AI community encountered a serious difficulty because the experts were unable to articulate rules which determined what they did. Dreyfus and Dreyfus argued that this was because experts do not follow rules at all, and they predicted, therefore, that the AI scientists would never be able to produce expert computers.

Their prediction was realized and the AI project is now a backwater of information technology development. Dreyfus and Dreyfus argued that human understanding is more than knowing facts and rules; it is, more importantly, the skill of knowing how to find a way of acting in the world. Heuristic and algorithmic rules, instrumentally rational tools and techniques, cannot cope with the unpredictable, unique situations which require intuition, the ability to cope with accidents and to tolerate ambiguity, all characteristics of expertise.

Dreyfus and Dreyfus presented a model of the stages of development of expertise in which the acquirer of expertise moves from the stage of being a novice, to the stage of being an advanced beginner, to the stage of competent practitioner, then to being proficient and finally to being expert. So, for example, according to this model, a leader-manager[2] would acquire the practice of managing by starting as a novice and learning the rules and context-free facts pertinent to the practice of leading-managing. The novice adheres rigidly to rules and plans, shows no sensitivity to context and does not exercise discretionary judgment. The next step, now as advanced beginner, is to begin to apply these rules and facts in the practice of management, and this inevitably means encountering the context of specific time and place. As managers develop more practical experience, they find that they are able to undertake more and more complex actions in specific contexts but experience some difficulty when facing competing priorities. Further training provides conscious decision-making techniques. The manager is now a competent practitioner, and Dreyfus and Dreyfus observe that some people may never get beyond this level of competence. The first three phases of development, therefore, describe the acquisition of what has been referred to in the previous chapter as the tools and techniques of instrumental rationality, which the Dreyfus brothers refer to as calculative rationality.

Although some people get stuck at the level of competent practitioner, some do move to the next stage, that of the proficient practitioner. They recognize similar patterns between the current situation they face and previous ones they have experienced; they have the intuitive ability to respond to patterns without having to follow rules. Such practitioners act on experience-based intuition, responding to situational cues when faced with difficulties in identifying what is going on. In the final stage, the expert practitioner is all that the proficient one is, only more so, in that the skills of experts have become so much a part of them that they are unaware of the skills they are acting upon.

> What should stand out is the progression from the analytic behavior of the detached subject, consciously decomposing his environment into recognizable elements, and following abstract rules, to involved skilled behavior based on an accumulation of concrete experiences and the unconscious recognition of new situations as similar to whole remembered ones.[3]

Dreyfus and Dreyfus describe the acquisition of expertise as a movement from practice based on instrumental rationality to one that reflects what they call deliberative rationality, by which they mean deliberating on what they are doing as experts.

Another writer, Flyvbjerg,[4] draws on the work of the Dreyfus brothers and brings it together with Aristotle's concept of phronesis in order to understand the nature of expertise. Aristotle distinguished between three different modes of knowing anything.

First, *episteme* is the scientific way of knowing in which knowledge is universal, invariable and context-free. It takes the form of statements of timeless laws and is metaphysics in the sense that it posits forces and causal factors behind phenomena, which govern them. For example, in the dominant mode of thinking organizations are systems consisting of parts that interact to form them. Markets are driven by forces of competition. In epistemic thinking about organizations there are forces, systems and drivers of action lying behind that action and causing it. We can observe the action but not the systems, forces and drivers themselves, and this is why the epistemic approach can be described as metaphysical. In the dominant discourse, theories of organization and management clearly reflect the epistemic way of knowing.

The second form of knowing is *techne*. Techne is about how to do something as craft or art and so is pragmatic, based on practical instrumental rationality governed by a conscious goal. In this way of knowing, knowledge takes the form of comprehensive, precise rules, principles and propositions. This knowledge is analytical and consists of small, explicit, logical steps. Such knowledge is universal, context-free, impersonal and often quantitative. It is logically derived from initial assumptions and seeks to produce certainty while avoiding uncertainty. All the tools and techniques of instrumental rationality clearly express the techne way of knowing.

The third way of knowing is *phronesis*. Phronesis is often translated as practical wisdom or practical judgment. It is pragmatic, context-dependent and oriented towards action. It is forms of knowledge embedded in local experience and thus comprises a wide range of practical skills in adapting to changing circumstances. Phronetic knowledge is acquired through experience, and it can only be understood by taking a reflective stance in relation to that experience. Since that experience is always social, phronesis is essentially a social way of knowing very much concerned with our being in the world and therefore with ordinary everyday politics and ethics. Phronesis arises in experience but, being concerned with differing contexts, it is contingent and produces new practical insights. It is essentially self-knowledge rather than theoretical speculation. It is based on concrete action, and it cannot be taught in the usual formal ways. Phronetic knowledge is very difficult to articulate and cannot be reduced to rules, principles or propositions, which means that the tools and techniques of technical rationality cannot produce the kind of practical judgment required of an expert manager. This does not mean that experts never use rules for one purpose or another; it simply means that their exercise of practical judgment itself cannot be reduced to any rules and so while practical judgment and the use of rules may proceed in parallel, the one necessarily precludes the other. Phronesis, then, is the same as proficiency and expertise. The dominant discourse on organizations and their management reflects episteme, and its tools represent the techne way of knowing. It takes little account of phronesis; in fact, the insistence on the tools and techniques precludes phronesis, that is, practical judgment. Practical judgment is of great importance but care needs to be taken not to idealize it and simply dismiss episteme and techne. The practical judgments of experts are essential for operating in the world of uncertainty we live in, but such judgments also frequently turn out to be wrong, unproductive, destructive and sometimes catastrophic. This cannot be used to claim that the tools of instrumental rationality must be used to avoid such catastrophes – since the tools do not work as they are proclaimed to, there is no use relying on them because they cannot guarantee against catastrophes. This means accepting that leaders, managers and others have no option but to rely on practical judgment and keep on dealing with the successes and failures produced. It is essential, therefore, not to lose sight of the social nature of practical judgment – it is not the possession of the autonomous individual but the activity of interdependent individuals in relation to each other in which they negotiate what they can accept as ethical. Practical judgment also clearly involves power and ideology.

Dreyfus and Dreyfus focus on individuals and they present the acquisition of expertise in sequential stages. However, in the above paragraph, I have interpreted what they say as social and, furthermore, I would argue that phronesis does not simply preclude episteme and techne. It seems to me that expert managers may well take up the tools of the dominant discourse in the processes of exercising practical judgment. It follows that phronesis and techne often occur at the same time rather than in clear steps and practical judgment is about taking account of the wider processes of power and ideology in which the tools and techniques are used, frequently for purposes other than those they are publicly proclaimed to serve. Conceptual distinctions between the competent employing techne, on the one hand, and proficient experts using phronesis, on the other, are useful in thinking about what we are doing, but in actuality they cannot exist in pure form. Practical judgment and reflexivity will be the topics of Chapter 9, which will explore the question of whether we can talk about leadership and management techniques of practical judgment.

The notion of expert can be expressed in different ways. In what is, perhaps, its most common expression, it describes an individual who knows what he or she is doing in advance of doing it: an expert knows it all and tells others what they should do. Obviously the notion of expert in the above discussion is completely different. First, the term describes a particular kind of social interaction in which those with the greater experience-based capacities for practical judgment interact with those displaying less of this capacity in order to be able to go on doing something together. Second, an expert in this sense does not know it all because this is impossible in ambiguous and uncertain situations. Instead, such an expert risks making practical judgments and then responds in an ongoing manner to the consequences.

Critique of the tools and techniques of instrumental rationality and responses to the critique

The tools and techniques of instrumental rationality are based on the possibility of prediction. Since the world is characterized by important degrees of unpredictability, the tools and techniques cannot fulfil their proclaimed purpose of enabling managers to choose favourable outcomes. The 'outcomes' continually emerge in the interplay of human choices and no one can control this interplay. Next, the tools and techniques of instrumental rationality are second order abstractions. While these are necessary in a society in which some control from a distance is important, they always have to be particularized in specific situations which are never exactly the same as other situations, and this means ambiguity, uncertainty and unpredictability in how the tools and techniques are used. The tools and techniques in practice do not, therefore, take the clear-cut simplicity of their presentation. Furthermore, the tools and techniques of instrumental rationality take the form of rules and, in prescribing their use, account is not taken of the fact that rules need to be interpreted in particular situations, and this means that how the rules are followed is a reflection of the wider society, of habitus. It follows that straightforward, simple application of rules to conduct is not possible. Finally, those who reach capacities of proficiency and expertise do not rely on rules at all, and insisting that rules be followed amounts to the destruction of proficiency and expertise. We therefore need to focus attention on how expert managers move beyond rules, tools and techniques in their actions as experts. They carry on responding to the uncertainty of organizational life and the ongoing consequences of their actions by exercising practical judgment developed in their experience. In acting according to practical judgment when choosing their next actions, accepting that they cannot control the consequences, they frequently use the tools of technical rationality for purposes other than those that are publicly proclaimed. While they cannot control 'outcomes', they can and do control the bodies and the actions of the bodies of members of an organization using the techniques of disciplinary power to be explored in the next chapter. This is a pretty devastating critique, so how have managers and other organizational members been responding to it?

Many recognize the validity of the critique in their experience and find it liberating, while others find it depressing because they interpret it to mean that they cannot improve the world as they had hoped and relying on expert judgment does not seem to them to be enough. Yet others say that they agree with the critique, but the belief in tools and techniques of instrumental rationality is so strong that they immediately start talking about dynamic tools instead of static ones and claiming that there is scientific evidence for certain propositions about the development of the human mind, allowing standard patterns to be mapped and measured. Of course, what I have written in this chapter is contesting all of this and is certainly denying the assertion of a scientific base that allows us to know anything about human interaction and human minds as a fact. While agreeing with the need to change ways of thinking and focus on local interaction, some people seem unable to recognize the fundamental characteristics outlined in the previous chapter which logically and necessarily apply to all instrumentally rational tools and techniques, whether they are claimed to be dynamic or not, and there seems to be a strong resistance to seeing that the fundamental characteristics of tools and techniques undermine the claims of all of them to be able to produce success. Instead they claim, but present no logical argument to back the claim up, that there is not a fundamental problem with the tools of instrumental rationality; it is just that the tools being employed are inadequate conceptually and analytically. The belief is that the problem with tools and techniques can be overcome through using the 'right' ones in a more flexible manner, continually reassessing assumptions and goals so as to maintain alignment and increase the speed of response. For example, some claim that the human mind can be trained to deal with complexity by following a scientifically validated development path which can be measured. Some people even argue that everything we do and are, including our minds, is a tool or technique and that it is necessary to use the language of tools and techniques because it is familiar.

Another interpretation of the points I have been making about tools and techniques is that they amount to a dismissal of any kind of prescription, a distancing from the command and control model of management and the promotion of the view that organizations should be self-organizing and fluid and therefore require no managerial intervention at all. This, of course, is a total misunderstanding of the viewpoint of complex responsive processes. First, there is no dismissal of hierarchy or command and control forms of management. Instead, there is an exploration of how they emerge and are dynamically sustained, like any other pattern of relating, hierarchical or not, command and control or not. All emerge in local interactional processes of communication, power relating and ideology reflecting choices. Furthermore, self-organization means, quite simply, local interaction and this is not necessarily fluid. So there is absolutely no implication that managerial 'intervention' is not required; rather, there is an exploration of just how managers participate in ongoing interaction in influential ways and why they are only influential if they display expertise and practical judgment.

People repeatedly claim that 'we' cannot wait for evolution to provide us with effective organizations. There is the insistence that 'you' need intelligent design using the tool of knowledge. It is quite common in discussions around a complex responsive processes view of organizations to hear people referring repeatedly to what 'we' must have and what 'you' need if organizations are to run effectively. However, there seems to be no sensing that this way of talking implies an ability to take a viewpoint outside the interactions of others, to observe matters such as their thinking and their values, as well as the tasks they are to perform and the functions they are to take up. The complex responsive processes perspective denies the possibility of the external observer, arguing that no one can get outside their experience of interacting with others. There is no external, presumably powerful and intelligent 'we' or 'you', only us who are trying to accomplish something together. In other words, the theory of complex responsive processes takes a view in which interdependent people are interacting with each other locally and the interplay of their plans and intentions gives rise to emergent patterns across a population. How these ordinary individuals come to think emerges in an ongoing social process, as do the tasks they develop and perform. We, here meaning all of us and encompassing the more powerful and the less powerful, are forming and being formed at the same time by our interactions with each other. We are discovering together, in conflict and difference, what to do. When the external observer position is taken, people sense nothing problematic in claiming the 'we'/'you' can align the thinking/values of others with their tasks; fit them and their values to functions; support them with resources; position them in relation to each other; allow them to own parts of the responsiveness. For a long time, managers have been talking about 'aligning' or 'fitting' people and tasks, values and functions. For decades, managers have been talking about designing and constructing learning, dynamic, intelligent organizations which allow people to actualize themselves. But there is no evidence that we actually know how to do any of this or that anything like it actually happens.

From a complex responsive processes perspective, it is impossible for anyone to do any of this aligning and fitting, designing and constructing whole organizations. The argument is against reifying and anthropomorphizing an organization – organizations are not things or persons so they cannot learn, be intelligent or anything else. Organizations are simply imaginative constructs around the patterns in interaction between human persons who can learn and be intelligent, or not, as social selves emerging in social interaction. What is being drawn to attention, then, is the inevitably immersing and at the same time abstracting activities that we have no choice but to engage in together. Attention is also being drawn to the conversational nature of organization in which patterns of power relations emerge, which are sustained by our ideologies and reflected in the choices we make. All of this emerges in the interplay of all our choices and no one can control this interplay, and nor can they align it or fit it to anything.

Another response to my argument about the problematic nature of the tools and techniques of instrumental rationality is to claim that thinking and doing are separate and that knowledge is the tool for thinking. For me, it is a false dichotomy to split thinking and doing since thinking is action and doing reflects past patterns of thought modified a little or a lot by current thinking. Instead, it is necessary to hold the paradox of thought and action, theory and practice. In actual experience it is not possible to split 'feelings and thoughts' from 'actions' because feelings and thoughts are the actions of a body just like any other 'actions' the body takes. Thoughts do not simply lead to actions because at the same time thoughts as actions provoke and evoke other actions, and these other actions provoke the actions of further thought as actions in a never ending process with no beginning and no end. It is quite artificial to cut this ongoing process into 'thought' leading to 'action', or indeed 'action' leading to 'thought'. It is also not helpful to think in terms of individual minds having lenses which determine 'thoughts and feelings' which then determine 'actions'. We are all born into families and groups which are part of larger groups called communities, organizations and societies. All of these groupings have long histories in which ways of acting-thinking have evolved. All of us are born into such groupings and acquire our patterns of action-thought in our ongoing interactions with those around us. My mind as the action of my body directed to itself is thoroughly social. There is no mind without the group and no group without human minds – individuals and groups are inseparable, being simply aspects of the same phenomenon of fundamental interdependence. From this perspective it is not sensible to talk about my mind in terms of lenses – I can only talk about my mind as historical, socially constructed and ongoing narrative. It also follows from the view I am taking that human interactions, or the knowledge emerging from them, cannot sensibly be thought about as a tool in any sense because these are the processes of social and individual life itself – our very identities are arising in such processes so it would be meaningless and demeaning to call them tools or instruments of any kind. We are talking about ourselves not some instrumental rationality we use.

If our ways of thinking, our systems of thought, our 'mental models' are all tools, then who is using the tools? Who are the agents, who must be separate from the tools if we are to talk about using them? The unquestioned assumption in stating that we use our minds as tools is the Cartesian split between mind and body, making it possible to say that a body is using the thinking thing called a mind to do something. But what is this thinking thing? Surely I am the way I think and I think the way I think because we think the way we think. It makes no sense to talk about myself as the tool of myself. My mind is not a thing, but conversational processes that I silently engage in all day and night. These silent processes are social and are always taking up my habitual perception of the attitude of society towards 'me' as the object to which the subject 'I' responds, constituting phases in an inseparable dialectic of 'I–me'. The subject and the object cannot be split in the process of self-consciousness. How can 'I', the agent, be using a tool which is 'me'? A hammer is a meaningless object until a body uses it or at least recognizes it. Can thought ever be a meaningless object until a body uses it? If so, where is the thought when the body is not using it?

There are ideologies of control lying behind the insistence on the need for instrumentally rational tools and techniques. In reflecting these ideologies, some believe that without the tools and techniques organizations would not be able to produce success; indeed, they would be ungovernable. Others believe that without the tools and techniques it would be impossible to improve the human condition or take action to sustain the planet. There is a very powerful belief that 'we' must be able to improve whole organizations intentionally. For some, these beliefs are impervious to reason, perhaps because it is too disappointing to accept the humbler realization that success and failure, sustainability and destruction, all emerge across populations through myriad local interactions and all anyone can do is participate as meaningfully and as influentially as possible, acting on practical judgment, in these local interactions.

Having discussed the instrumentally rational tools and techniques of management, this chapter will conclude with a consideration of leadership tools and techniques, which are also tools of instrumental rationality. Chapter 1 described the way in which leadership and management have come to be understood as different activities. I argued against such a split and claimed that leadership and management are so intertwined that it is meaningless to split them. However, those arguing for the split claim that leadership is about choosing a vision for an organization's future and choosing its culture and values, while management is about implementation. It is relevant, therefore, to consider separately what are proposed as the tools and techniques of leadership. This will make it clear that they are little different from the tools of management and so also take the form of instrumental rationality, subject to the same problems as those outlined earlier in this chapter and in the previous chapter. These tools and techniques are presented at leadership development programmes, and I will use modern leadership development programmes to highlight the tools and techniques proposed for leaders.

The tools and techniques of leadership: development programmes and models of leadership

Since the 1990s there has been a rapid growth in the provision of leadership development programmes, provided not just by the elite business schools and consultancies but even more by the education and development departments of most organizations. Leadership academies and programmes have been established by governments and others to provide for leadership development, for example: the International Leadership Association, the Institute of Leadership and Management in the UK, and programmes for the military, defence, health and higher education. Even academic researchers at universities are invited to go on leadership programmes. This trend is not confined to the UK but is as much in evidence throughout Europe and North America. Such programmes are now common in developing countries too. Participants on these programmes are introduced to one or more of the leadership theories, usually presented in a 'model' claimed to be specific to the sector mounting the programmes. It is quite common for participants to be presented with: exercises using various games; experience of the theatre, for example actors and directors may interpret the leadership qualities of, say, Shakespeare's Henry V; conducting an orchestra; engaging in various outdoor activities such as trekking through the wilds and dealing with hazards such as mountains and river crossings. The aim is for participants to have the experience of leading teams in addition to understanding the theories of leadership so that they will be more likely to apply them in practice. Also participants are often asked to identify the leadership qualities of great leaders, such as Mahatma Gandhi, Nelson Mandela and Mother Teresa, so that they might imitate them in order to improve their own leadership skills.

In terms of the time devoted to them, these programmes range from one-off events lasting only a few hours to a series of sessions extending over a few hours or a few days. The programmes are usually commissioned by managers in the Human Resources (HR) functions of organizations, and these commissioners usually play a significant role in designing the programme together with training the providers, usually consultancies. The HR commissioners and, indeed, the consultants actually providing the training are often people with no significant leadership experience of their own but who can present the models and supervise the exercises. For example, I was recently contacted by an HR manager in a major international bank. I was informed that the whole middle layer of management in this company across the world, amounting to many thousands of people, were to be put through a leadership development programme. They would each attend one session lasting five hours. I was asked to attend a meeting of the HR managers charged with delivering this programme. I met with five of them from the UK, the USA, India and Hong Kong and was struck by the fact that they were all young women around thirty years old who all had the same very clear idea of what a leadership programme was. I was asked to explain how my contribution would assist the participants on the programme to realize their visions and what I would do to make sure that they were 'all on the same page'.

Consider the nature of the leadership models that are being provided as the basis for leadership development.

Leadership models

One example of such a model is that used by the UK's Royal Navy on its action-centred leadership and command training. Here leadership is defined as the influencing of others so that they willingly do what the leader wants them to do. Leadership is defined as the cognitive skill, personal qualities, behaviour and ethos required to inspire others to commit. The model consists of two 'forces', the command of authority and the influence of leadership, manifested in a cycle of plan, organize, execute and control. Management is at the centre of this circular activity, the implementers of it.

Another example is provided by the model of leadership used in the UK's National Health Service (NHS) leadership programmes. The NHS commissioned consultants, the Hay Group, to develop a robust model of leadership specific to the NHS. The consultants gathered information through interviewing NHS stakeholders, running expert panels and other groups, and gathering user and other data. They did all this to obtain information on what people in the NHS thought were the leadership traits of good leaders. They then analysed this data as well as data from existing competency models, benchmarks and relevant strategic materials. This led them to produce the NHS Leadership Qualities Framework, which they depicted as a circle. The top of the circle lists the activities required for leaders to set the direction, which are: broad scanning, intellectual flexibility, seizing the future, driving for results and displaying political astuteness. The bottom half of the circle lists the leadership activities required to deliver the service and these are: leading change through people, holding to account, empowering others, effective and strategic influencing and collaborative working. The middle of the circle represents the personal qualities required of leaders: self-belief, self-awareness, self-management, drive for improvement and personal integrity.

The first point to note is that, although developed specifically for the NHS, it is fundamentally not all that different from the Royal Navy programme, and both are immediately recognizable as reflections of the dominant discourse on leadership and strategy – they are exactly the same as the tools and techniques of instrumental rationality described in the last chapter. Another example along much the same lines is the Senior Strategic Leadership Programme of the Leadership Foundation for Higher Education in the UK, which is aimed at senior people who need to secure the commitment of others through inspirational motivation. There is also a programme for those lower down in the hierarchy, called Preparing for Senior Leadership, and this aims to assist those facing the challenge of corporate leadership: planning, innovation, creativity and implementing effective and sustainable change. There is another programme for professional information services staff, called the Future Leaders

Programme, which aims to assist participants to take a more visionary and strategic approach to building world-class leadership capabilities.

It is immediately apparent how abstract, idealized and edifying these models all are. It is also interesting that these lists of activities and traits are presented in a simple, rational-sounding manner as if each item on the list is well understood. However, I would argue that there is not one item on these lists that is well understood – all continue to be the subjects of debate.

Furthermore, it is taken for granted that the activities identified in the models actually are what 'leaders' normally do in their daily work lives. Alvesson and Sveningsson argue that the leadership literature pays little attention to the more mundane tasks that leaders and managers carry out.[5] In their interviews with leaders and managers, they found that those interviewed themselves drew attention to the more mundane aspects of their work. These mundane tasks include 'administration, solving practical and technical problems, giving and asking for information, chatting, gossiping, listening and creating a good working atmosphere'.[6] They argue that what leaders actually do does not differ all that much from what non-leaders do – they problematize the notion of leadership being something extraordinary, constituting a distinct and special kind of work. In another study,[7] the same authors reported how managers as leaders describe their work in terms of visions, values and strategies, claiming to refrain from directing the details of the work those reporting to them carry out. However, when asked to be specific, these same manager-leaders talk about administrative tasks and how it is necessary for them to be directive with regard to the work of those who report to them. When they talk about leadership, they dismiss micro-management as bad leadership; but when they describe what they do, the description indicates that in actuality leaders and managers do engage significantly in micro-management. The authors conclude that the rhetoric employed therefore does not describe what managers and leaders actually do. I would draw attention to this finding that managers make the statement that micro-management is bad but then later, in another context, claim that it is something they have to do and so something good. This is a neat example of George Orwell's *Nineteen Eighty-Four* Doublethink,[8] where people hold two contradictory statements at the same time but do not notice the contradiction. The mundane nature of leadership work is also brought out by the accounts that Tobin[9] and Taylor[10] give of their own experience of doing leadership in hospitals in the United States.

Finally, there are no leaders anywhere who are unconstrained – every leader has to deal in some way with a higher leader or some group to which they are accountable. The tight constraints on leaders are ignored in the edifying, idealized models of leadership in the dominant discourse.

So are managers and leaders being put through all these leadership programmes because they are not doing what the models define as the 'best' way to lead? Are they to leave behind the more mundane activities they find themselves spending time on and shake off the constraints? It seems clear that the programmes aim to produce some kind of personal change in participants so that they willingly carry out what is required to be an effective, good leader. In other words, leadership development programmes, simply a new name for what used to be called management training programmes, are really about training people to act in disciplined ways, preparing them for the roles that they are required to take up in organizations. They certainly cannot be actually training people to choose the future because this is impossible. The next chapter will explore how the tools and techniques of instrumental rationality are actually the techniques of disciplinary power through which people are persuaded to willingly carry out what is expected of them as good leaders.

Conclusion

For the reasons given in the previous chapter, the tools and techniques of instrumental rationality cannot be the cause of change or improvement; on the contrary, they can sometimes, as we have seen in this chapter, be harmful by restricting spontaneity and blocking the development of practical judgment. However, many of them are essential in modern organizations and societies where some degree of control has to be exercised from a distance, and this use has to depend on practical judgment if it is to be beneficial rather than harmful. So, if the tools and techniques are used, but not actually for their proclaimed purpose, what are they actually used for? In Chapter 9 there will be an exploration of how these tools are used to provide a veneer of rationality, as the rhetoric of ordinary politics and as social defences against the anxiety provoked by not knowing and not being in control. Before that, however, the next chapter will consider how the tools and techniques of instrumental rationality are, in reality, the techniques of disciplinary power.

6

THE LEADERSHIP AND MANAGEMENT TECHNIQUES OF DISCIPLINARY POWER

Surveillance and normalization

Introduction

The French philosopher Michel Foucault described in careful detail how modern hospitals, prisons, schools and workplaces evolved as institutions in which the techniques of disciplinary power constitute the major form of their governance.[1] He argues that discipline is a specific form of power which operates through the use of simple instruments of hierarchical observation, normalizing judgments and examination. This chapter will explore how modern leadership and management practices employ these specific instruments of disciplinary power, and it will make the point that the tools and techniques of instrumental rationality discussed in the last two chapters are indeed the same as the instruments of disciplinary power. The aim of disciplinary power is that of controlling the bodies of people in a group, organization or society and the actions of those bodies. So, while the tools and techniques of technical rationality cannot achieve their stated purpose, namely, setting and controlling future outcomes, they do succeed in providing the means leaders and managers can use to control the bodies and their activities even though this is not what they are claimed to be used for. However, modern organizations and societies could not exist without the techniques of disciplinary power, although it is, of course, as we will see in the next chapter, possible to practise them in ways which become highly dictatorial and ultimately, at the extreme, fascist.

In the theory of complex responsive processes, global organizational change emerges in local interaction and any overall global design can only find meaning in local interaction between individuals and groups of them. This chapter will consider how the techniques of disciplinary power are taken up and responded to in local interactions between members of an organization. It will be argued that modern leaders are not autonomous leaders who can design cultures because they are themselves subjected to the techniques of disciplinary power. They are, however, prime agents administering the techniques of discipline. As they use these techniques to supervise others, they are themselves perpetually supervised in globally co-created interactive processes which powerful individuals can only design and control if they employ the techniques of terror.

It should be borne in mind that disciplinary power and its techniques are not simply negative aspects of organizational life. Foucault argues that power creates knowledge – it creates the reality we live in. Sophisticated modern organizations and societies need the techniques of discipline to sustain sufficient order for the carrying out of complex tasks. However, covering over the nature of disciplinary power with a mystifying discourse in terms of some fantasy of leadership, and covering over the use of the tools and techniques of instrumental rationality as techniques of discipline by claiming that their function is to improve outcomes, mean that we lose awareness of the ethical dimension of what we are doing and do not notice when disciplinary techniques are taken to the extremes of domination to be discussed in the next chapter. We lose sight of the significant constraints on every leader's freedom to choose the future of their organizations. We also cover over the practice of the arts of resistance to forms of domination and so have only a partial understanding of our own experience of organizational life. It is easy then to slip into thinking that it is acceptable to practise coercive persuasion, to be discussed in the next chapter, arguing that it is necessary for the greater good of improvement.

First, consider what Foucault has to say about the nature of disciplinary power.

Disciplinary power

For Michel Foucault:

> power is not something that can be possessed, and is not a form of fight; power is never anything more than a relationship that can, and must, be studied only by looking at the interplay between the terms of that relationship.[2]

This view leads him to differentiate between sovereign power and its exact opposite, the disciplinary form of power, which complemented and to some extent supplanted sovereign power. Sovereign power is exercised over the land and its produce, while disciplinary power is exercised over bodies and what they do. Sovereign power is concerned with goods and wealth, and its instruments and techniques are juridical in the form of obligations which grant absolute power to a physical sovereign. Disciplinary power employs techniques of surveillance and normalization to be discussed below. Although the new form of disciplinary power became more and more prominent, as the basis of industrial capitalism, sovereign power did continue to exist as an ideology of rights and organizer of juridical codes. Foucault argues that sovereign power survives as public rights which conceal the domination of bodies by disciplinary power. Disciplinary power also complemented and to some extent supplanted the other prominent form of power in the years up to the seventeenth century, namely, pastoral power largely exercised by the Church. Here, God and, through God, the sovereign are conceived of as the shepherds of the people. The clergy of the Church are the shepherds charged with saving the souls of people. This is a beneficent form of power, exercised over a population of people rather than a territory as in sovereign power, aimed at doing good for people in return for complete obedience. A key technique of this form of power is the confessional.

Foucault describes how, in the late seventeenth and early eighteenth centuries in Western Europe, there emerged techniques of disciplinary power which operated on the human body as the object and target of power.[3] Sets of regulations and calculated methods of controlling or correcting the operations of the body were developed in the army, the school, the hospital and the workplace. So, for example, the army developed as a profession through the specification in meticulous detail of the posture, movement and appearance of the body. Similar developments occurred in hospitals, schools and workplaces. These techniques operate in a way that constantly supervises the processes of bodily activity rather than the results of that activity. Instead of focusing on behaviour or language, the focus is on the internal organization, economy and efficiency of bodily movements. Disciplinary power operates in such a way that the operations of the body are meticulously controlled and imposes upon it docility and utility. The body becomes more obedient and more useful. The disciplinary techniques are applied not to masses but to all individuals, controlling the movement, gestures and attitudes of all. Foucault talks about a mechanics of power, a political anatomy and a micro-physics of power which explores, breaks down and rearranges the body. The mechanics of power made it possible for one body to exercise a hold on other bodies and get them to do what it wanted with the speed and efficiency desired. Foucault stresses how this is accomplished in the meticulous supervision and inspection of the detail of bodily activity.

The key distinguishing features of processes of discipline are as follows. First, they distribute individuals in space. Each individual has his or her own place in partitioned space, for example at work stations in a factory or in an office, and this space enables supervisors to know where people are and to control their coming and going, as well as what they are doing. It also prevents confused groupings of people from forming. Architecture plays an important role in creating spaces which enable the control of bodies. The techniques of discipline rank bodies in relation to each other and so individualize them.

> In organizing 'cells', 'places' and ranks, the disciplines create complex spaces that are at once architectural, functional and hierarchical. It is spaces that provide fixed positions and permit circulation; they carve out individual segments and establish operational links, they mark places and indicate values; they guarantee the obedience of individuals, but also a better economy of time and gesture.[4]

Second, the disciplinary processes establish rhythms of activity through timetables and the regulation of repetitive cycles of activity. They specify the time individuals must arrive for work and when they can depart and punish contraventions of these time boundaries.

Foucault also identifies the emergence of a new form of power in the second half of the eighteenth century, one which did not supplant but complemented and overlapped with disciplinary power. He calls this bio power, by which he means the state control of the biological. While disciplinary power controls individual bodies so that they can be kept under surveillance, trained and used, bio power is directed at the population in general and the patterns of birth, sexuality, death, production and illness. Disciplinary power individualizes while bio power massifies. Bio power and bio politics are concerned with birth rates, the mortality rate, rates of particular illnesses and amounts of products produced. These all came to be measured so that they could be operated on by policies. Bio power, then, depends very much on statistics, which originally meant information on and for the state. The state began to intervene in phenomena relating to birth, such as contraception and health. These concerns led to the development of forms of medicine concerned with public hygiene, involving campaigns to teach people about healthy living. Bio politics was also concerned with matters such as old age, and it established charitable institutions and institutions of insurance, savings and safety measures. Furthermore, bio politics developed a concern about the environment.

> Bio politics deals with the population, with the population as political problem, as a problem that is at once scientific and political, as a biological problem and as power's problem.[5]

The techniques introduced by bio politics are forecasts, statistical estimates and measurements to enable intervention at a general rather than an individual level. Regulatory mechanisms are established to maintain an equilibrium, an average, and compensate for variations. The mechanisms seek to compensate for the random variations within a population and so optimize state life.

Disciplinary and bio power largely replaced the power of sovereignty and pastoral power. Disciplinary and bio power differ from each other in the following way:

> Both technologies are obviously technologies of the body, but one is a technology in which the body is individualized as an organism endowed with capacities, while the other is a technology in which bodies are replaced by general biological processes.[6]

Returning now to disciplinary power, the following paragraphs will describe the techniques of this form of power. As mentioned above, for Foucault disciplinary power amounted to the uninterrupted, constant supervision of the physical activities of people across the institutions of society. It had the effect of imposing bodily docility and utility on people that Foucault calls 'disciplines'. This emergent global pattern arose in many, often minor, processes in response to, for example, military and industrial needs or outbreaks of epidemic diseases, and constituted a new form of power, exercised particularly at the micro level. Foucault argues that discipline employs a number of techniques: the physical enclosure of people in prisons, poor houses, hospitals, schools and factories; the partitioning of individuals so that each has his or her own place, making it possible to control presences and absences, communicate, supervise, conduct, judge, assess and calculate qualities and merits, and avoid disruptive groupings of people. The techniques of discipline allocate individuals to functionally useful spaces. Discipline 'constructs a machine whose effect will be maximized by the elementary parts of which it is composed'.[7]

Foucault shows how the modern institutions of mental hospitals, hospitals in general, prisons, schools and workplaces have evolved as institutions which take up the disciplinary form of power. The aim of disciplinary power is to establish strict discipline in society, and this is primarily done by corrective training. Discipline is the training of individuals so that they become more economically and socially useful in a more stable society. This training produces individual identities which conform to societal norms. Discipline, then, is specific techniques of power which treat individuals as both objects and instruments. Disciplinary power operates through the use of simple instruments of hierarchical observation, normalizing judgments and examination.[8]

First, consider what Foucault means by *hierarchical observation*. This is a technique that coerces people through employing ways of observing what they do. Foucault sees the school building as a mechanism for training which relies heavily on observation. He describes how the designers of the nineteenth-century Ecole Militaire in Paris paid enormous attention to details that allowed continuing observation. For example, accommodation for the students consisted of bedrooms distributed along a corridor, with an officer's room between every ten student rooms, thus enabling the students' behaviour to be observed. Hospital buildings in nineteenth-century France were also developed to enable observation of patients. Industrial buildings were designed to enable observation of the workforce. A key technique of disciplinary power is, therefore, one of surveillance, involving control and checking to encourage obedience and work. The task of surveillance across large numbers of people is, of course, enormous, and it therefore needs to be split up into smaller units. This is the function of hierarchy – a pyramid of units with one level applying surveillance to the level below it, which in turn observes the next level down and so on. Foucault describes how the difficulties of carrying out surveillance were particularly acute in workshops and factories as they increased in size and employed more and more specialized workers. These problems could only be dealt with by the development of the functions of supervision throughout the workplace.

> Surveillance thus becomes a decisive economic operator both as an internal part of the production machinery and as a specific mechanism in the disciplinary power.[9]

Foucault argues that although surveillance has to be carried out by individuals, such activities of individual surveillance have to be understood in the context of a whole network of relations from the top of the hierarchy to the bottom, from the bottom to the top, and from side to side. All supervisors are themselves also perpetually supervised. It is through this network of relations that surveillance anonymously and automatically makes its contribution to disciplinary power.

> Discipline makes possible the operation of a relational power that sustains itself by its own mechanisms and which, for the spectacle of public events, substitutes the uninterrupted play of calculated gazes.[10]

In the disciplinary society, leaders can be understood as those who supervise, who oversee the carrying out of surveillance, but they are not themselves autonomous or unconstrained because they too are under surveillance. Over the last few decades, organizations have evolved highly sophisticated forms of surveillance made possible by technology. Many offices now have closed circuit televisions, ostensibly for security purposes, but they nevertheless make continuous surveillance of staff possible and managers do make use of them. Members of staff who forget the television cameras do so at their peril. One needs to remain aware of the possibility of being constantly observed by some hidden observer. I was told of what happened to two people who thought that the secure room in their offices, used to store personal details, was not on the television circuit. They were wrong and so when they engaged in sexual activity that was observed by a manager, they were dismissed from their positions. Everyone uses computers in offices, but many probably do not realize that every key stroke can be, and often is, recorded. All office emails are usually retained over very long periods. Telephone calls are recorded and managers of call centres frequently listen in. Swipe cards are used to enter and leave a building so that timekeeping can be checked. The scope of disciplinary power is steadily increasing as the technology provides more comprehensive techniques of discipline. Hacking into computer databases and the leaking of information, as well as increasingly intrusive media investigations, all increase the surveillance we are subjected to.

Leaders and managers are key agents in instigating and sustaining the techniques of disciplinary power. However, it is important to remember that even the agents of disciplinary power are themselves subjected to the very same disciplinary techniques. The leader is not an unconstrained autonomous individual at all but an actor in a whole network of surveillance in which no one escapes the surveillance. All are perpetually supervised, even the supervisors themselves. It is also important to remember that such techniques are required to sustain the patterns of order in complex modern societies. However, they are also 'dark' techniques and, when taken to the extreme, they create a totalizing domination, which Orwell's *Nineteen Eighty-Four* describes in depressing detail.

Next, consider what Foucault means by *normalizing judgment*. Discipline can be thought of as conformity to norms and this, at least in part, is sustained through some kind of penal mechanism. During the nineteenth century, workshops and schools were increasingly characterized by penalties imposed on members for contravening micro-norms to do with lateness, absences, interruptions of tasks, lack of attention, lack of zeal, impoliteness, disobedience, insolence, idle chatter, incorrect attitudes and indecency. The penalties took the form of subtle procedures of minor deprivation and petty humiliation. Since disciplinary punishment has the purpose of reducing gaps between actual behaviour and conformity to the norms, it has to operate in a way that is corrective. Punishment, then, ideally takes the form of corrective training which must be more than simply punishment; it must also include a system of rewards for compliant behaviour. This requires that behaviour be judged along a continuum from a 'good' to a 'bad' pole. This continuum can even be quantified, making it possible to distinguish between individuals on the basis of where they are on the continuum according to ranks or grades. In this way gaps are marked and individuals are punished and rewarded. Through comparing, differentiating, ranking, homogenizing and excluding, the punishment–reward system normalizes individuals. The 'normal' is a principle of coercion. The judgments on gaps in realizing norms, measuring and ranking individuals and the imposition of penalties and rewards are techniques of disciplinary power which are carried out by hierarchical layers of supervisors. Each is supervised in this way by those higher in the hierarchy, and even the highest role in the hierarchy is also subjected to normalizing judgment.

> In a sense the power of normalization imposes homogeneity; but it individualizes by making it possible to measure the gaps, to determine levels, to fix specialities and to render the differences useful by fitting them one to another.[11]

In today's organizations, all of the normalizing techniques of disciplinary power have been significantly developed to cover more and more detailed activities of the members of an organization, and no one escapes the mutually imposed normalizing processes. It is now quite common for role-holders at all hierarchical levels to be judged on performance as frequently as every six months. More and more detailed targets are set for more and more micro-activities, providing the benchmarks for judgments on gaps. Salaries and bonuses are awarded on the basis of judgments about the meeting of targets, and persistent failure to meet targets may also be punished by removing the judged failure from the role and even from the organization. Foucault also identified corrective training as a form of punishment. Programmes of corrective training have proliferated through all categories of organizations across the world. For example, supervisors of postgraduate research at universities now go on supervisor training programmes and examiners of research degrees go on exam training programmes. Leadership programmes are also a form of corrective training in which the focus is on 'good' leadership and the extent to which programme participants fall short of the characteristics of 'good' leaders. Leadership programmes seek to promote compliance, as do all corrective training programmes. Leaders at all levels of the supervisory hierarchy are those who employ the normalizing techniques of disciplinary power. Even CEOs cannot escape performance judgments.

For Foucault, the third technique of disciplinary power is *the examination*. The technique of the examination combines the techniques of hierarchical observation and normalizing judgment. It is a form of ritualized surveillance that qualifies, classifies and so punishes individuals, and objectifies them. The procedures of examination and review came to be accompanied by systems of registration and documentation, which became essential techniques of disciplinary power. This made it possible to classify, form categories, determine averages and fix norms. Foucault traces these developments through the army, hospitals, schools and workplaces. The examination makes it possible to describe, judge and compare individuals with each other and thus fixes individual differences.

The effects of disciplinary power in organizations

As already mentioned, it is not necessary or even helpful to focus only on the negative effects of power in organizations. Foucault is quite emphatic on this point:

> We must cease once and for all to describe the effects of power in negative terms: it 'excludes', it 'represses', it 'censors', it 'abstracts', it 'masks', it 'conceals'. In fact, power produces; it produces reality; it produces domains of objects and rituals of truth. The individual and the knowledge that may be gained of him belong to this production.[12]

Foucault is basically arguing that as they evolve, institutions take over the techniques of power and in so doing create institutional reality and knowledge. An institution may be defined as customs, practices, relationships or behavioural patterns of importance in the life of a society, such as those dedicated to health, education and public service. Foucault traces the evolution of disciplinary power and how it was taken over by specialized institutions:

> 'Discipline' may be identified neither with an institution nor with an apparatus; it is a type of power, a modality for its exercise, comprising a whole set of instruments, techniques, procedures, levels of application, targets; it is a 'physics' or 'anatomy' of power, a technology and it may be taken over by 'specialized' institutions (the penitentiaries or 'houses of correction' of the nineteenth century), or by institutions that use it as an essential instrument for a particular end (schools, hospitals), or by pre-existing authorities that find in it a means of reinforcing or reorganizing their internal mechanisms of power ... [13]

Foucault argues that the techniques of disciplinary power actually create knowledge. Thus it was the development of mental institutions that created knowledge of the mind, psychology, and the development of hospitals created knowledge of the body, modern medicine. The workplaces of the industrial revolution created knowledge about the control of workers. Modern organizational forms of workplaces have taken over the techniques of disciplinary power and, in turn, these techniques have made the development of modern organizations possible.

> First the hospital, then the school, then, later, the workshop were not simply 'reordered' by the disciplines; they became, thanks to them, apparatuses such that any mechanism of objectification could be used in them as an instrument

of subjection, and any growth of power could give rise in them to possible branches of knowledge; it was this link, proper to the technological systems, that made possible within the disciplinary element the formation of clinical medicine, psychiatry, child psychology, educational psychology, the rationalization of labor.[14]

The techniques of disciplinary power, such as 'time-tables, corrective training, exercises, total and detailed surveillance',[15] are used 'to extract from bodies the maximum time and force'.[16]

I want to develop these points further by exploring the role of leadership programmes in modern organizations. Following Foucault, they may be thought of as corrective training.

Thinking about leadership programmes

The currently dominant ideology of leadership may make it feel natural to train people to apply the techniques of disciplinary power in an unreflexive way. From a complex responsive processes perspective, the techniques of disciplinary power are themselves complex responsive processes of relating between people. They constitute themes emerging in communicative interaction; they constitute patterns of power relations and, in current times, they reflect ideologies of autonomous leadership and managerialism. The techniques are generalizations which are taken up and made particular in local interactions. They are social objects and key aspects of habitus. The techniques of discipline are clearly responsive processes having the aim of sustaining conformity and social order and so the status quo. The techniques are often presented as techniques of change but when one remembers that they are applied with the authority of the most powerful, one can see that, in effect, they are only about change which is thought to sustain existing power relations and so, in effect, are not about change at all but about staying the same. For example, leadership programmes frequently do not seek to provoke reflective and reflexive thinking but they can create a form of propaganda,[17] for example through playing games, which blocks conversation and so sustains the status quo. Propaganda and spin cover over what is actually happening and amount to a subtle form of prohibition in which people are persuaded not to talk about what they feel. The actual patterns of behaviour emerging in the application of the techniques depend upon the local interactions in which they are particularized. In effect both stability and change are emerging in local responses to generalized patterns of discipline and coercive persuasion. If one understands change in this way, the particular need for techniques of disciplinary power is open for critical appraisal – in themselves they produce no change or even stability; it is only the responses to them that produce stability and change. Thinking in this way would lead one to question many of the approaches adopted on many, but not all, leadership programmes.

The first rather curious feature of leadership development programmes is that they are so often supervised and even delivered by rather young people without much leadership experience and certainly not leadership experience in a senior role. But it gets even more curious when one reflects upon the number of people going through these programmes. Leadership is, on most programmes, unquestioningly taken to be the activities of individual leaders choosing and realizing their own visions for their organizations. It is held that they need to do this so that they can provide direction to their followers and ensure that all are on 'the same page'. Leaders are supposed to set the values and the culture and to inspire and persuade their followers to adhere to them. However, it is the very highly paid executives at the top of any organization who are the ones really charged with the vision for the organization and the ones really supposed to change the culture. Given this, it is curious that top executives rarely go on leadership programmes. Instead it is usually very large numbers of middle managers who go on them. When one thinks of the numbers of managers going through these programmes each year, one has to conclude that around the world there must be at least many hundreds of thousands of middle manager participants each year. Is it possible for so many people, running into the millions over a number of years, to display the leadership qualities of the great individual leaders and actually perform the activities called for in the leadership models they are exposed to? Are all these people actually realizing their visions and changing the values and cultures of those around them? Are they all unconstrained?

Even stranger, if leadership is required at all levels of an organization, a requirement indicated by the training of all levels of managers as leaders, then all managers are being turned into leaders. If all middle managers are now leaders, what has happened to the managers, the technicians who are supposed to implement the visions? Has the much vaunted distinction between leaders and managers now in reality disappeared without many noticing it? For me, the mere raising of these questions indicates a need to explore just what is going on in these leadership programmes and what their purpose actually is. Chapter 1 drew attention to the distinction that has been made between leaders and managers and pointed to Khurana's contention that the emphasis on leadership arose as a means by which organizational executives could retain their status as professionals. Clearly this claim to status is not being made simply for top executives; middle managers are now also being accorded professional status by being trained as leaders. It seems that the underlying purpose of the proliferation of leadership programmes may be primarily that of re-branding and re-presenting, in a more favourable, rather idealized form, the roles of executives in organizations. Curiously, in so doing they destroy the notion that leaders are distinct from managers because they are all now leaders. However, I want to argue that there is far more to it than simply re-branding organizational executives. I think that there is an even more fundamental purpose of leadership programmes.

Ostensibly the leadership programmes are about developing the competences or skills that the autonomous leader requires in order to bring about change. Actually, however, leadership programmes are themselves institutionalized techniques of discipline. Behind the idealized, romanticized, simplistic view of leadership, the programmes train agents, called leaders, to instigate and sustain disciplinary power. It seems to me that all leadership development programmes will inevitably reflect the disciplinary society and the need for agents who sustain disciplinary power. Foucault is clear that the techniques of disciplinary power are not necessarily negative. Complex modern organizations cannot function without the techniques of surveillance, hierarchical normalization and corrective training. However, when leadership theories and leadership development programmes focus attention on idealized and, thus, unrealistic theories, the effect is to obscure the actual experience of leadership. The idealizations and the unrealistic views on what it is possible for leaders to achieve cover over the fact that leaders are actually influential agents who instigate and sustain disciplinary power. The danger then is that the techniques of disciplinary power are utilized in completely taken-for-granted ways which are not open to question or critical reflection. This makes it possible for the techniques to be taken up in increasingly extreme ways which produce counterproductive domination and block creativity and innovation. Also, focusing attention purely on simplistic idealizations and myths about what it is possible for leaders to do renders people blind to the hidden transcripts and arts of resistance which are local responses to the techniques and will have important effects on what happens.

I would argue that today's leaders are the agents of discipline in society and the process of training large numbers of managers as leaders is a key activity sustaining the disciplinary society. Leadership and leadership development programmes are far more about order and discipline than they are about change and creativity.

The theory of complex responsive processes, however, specifically focuses attention on both the generalized global techniques of disciplinary power and the responses they call forth in local interactions. Furthermore, the theory produces an understanding of leadership as social processes between interdependent people, not simply the choices of the 'autonomous' individual, and this move to the central importance of interdependence invites critical reflection on what we are doing together. If one understands leadership as roles arising in complex responsive processes of mutual recognition, the work of effective leaders is not just to use techniques of disciplinary power but also to foster reflection on what they as leaders/managers and others are doing together in the belief that stability, change and the sustaining of disciplinary power all emerge in such reflection. This is not dialogue but ordinary processes of conversation reflecting the difficulties arising from difference and conflict, in which people are paying attention to their own complex responsive process of relating to each other. In focusing on power, difference and conflict, thinking in terms of complex responsive processes immediately problematizes processes seeking to produce conformity, coherence and harmony. Attention is drawn to how processes of conformity and harmony, while sustaining necessary stability, also cover over conflict and difference and so make the ongoing evolution of work patterns more difficult. In this reflection people will be forming judgments as to whether the techniques of discipline and coercion are ethical or not and what ideologies they reflect. They may, for example, judge that in present times we are taking the techniques of power required for our kind of society to extremes which undermine what we think is our kind of society. We might then conclude that we need to find ways to reverse the ever increasing surveillance, for example.

From the perspective of complex responsive processes, it is in the many local interactions between people that continuity and stability are dynamically sustained as habitual interactions are continuously iterated. However, habitual interactions are not exactly the same at all times because people can also be spontaneous, adjusting their responses in the light of changes in their situations, and these small adjustments can escalate into significant changes to habitual patterns of interactions. Local interaction is thus dynamically sustaining continuity and giving rise to emergent change at the same time. If these local interactions involve the techniques of discipline, and they are highly likely to be involved given the disciplinary nature of modern society, then the effects of these techniques depend on just how people are taking them up. This means that the techniques of disciplinary power will produce effects that are uncertain. This is all the more evident once we understand that learning and changes in patterns of thinking emerge in ordinary conversation and the conflictual conduct of the ordinary politics of organizational life. The part that leaders can usefully play in these ordinary processes lies in the manner in which they themselves participate in these ordinary processes through questioning attitudes so as to open up further conversation. Leadership emerges in social processes of mutual recognition, and the actions of leaders are not totally confined to using the techniques of disciplinary power, although in modern organizations and societies these remain actions of enormous importance.

Conclusion

The previous two chapters concluded that it is impossible for the tools and techniques of instrumental rationality to accomplish what is proclaimed to be their use, namely, the control of future outcomes. There are four reasons for this. First, the tools and techniques reflect a theory of efficient causality which is too simplistic to explain human interaction and the consequence of this is that the ability to forecast outcomes of actions, which is the basis for the tools and techniques of instrumental rationality, is compromised. Second, the tools and techniques of instrumental rationality are second order abstractions which must be particularized if they are to be used in practical situations, and this particularization inevitably involves ideology, power and the politics of ordinary organizational life, from which it follows that in practice they actually cannot take instrumentally rational forms. Third, the tools and techniques are expressed as rules, and for human beings following a rule is highly complex in that the meaning of a rule can only arise in the habitus of the community in which the rule is to be followed, so that rules cannot be the context-free universals claimed – following rules will produce variations of activity in different situations. Finally, experts do not follow rules but, rather, exercise practical judgment based on experience so that the tools and techniques of instrumental rationality fall away as far as expertise is concerned.

Despite this compelling critique, leaders and managers still claim to be using the tools and techniques of technical rationality. This chapter has argued that they do this not to control the outcomes of actions, which is impossible, but to control the bodies of organizational members and the actions of those bodies. As the tools and techniques of instrumental rationality are in practice the techniques of the exercise of disciplinary power in which embodied human persons are supervised by managers in a hierarchy, by those reporting to them in this hierarchy and by colleagues. These are social processes from which no one escapes – the supervisors are themselves perpetually supervised. The techniques of disciplinary power actually create knowledge and provide enabling constraints on people, making generative learning possible. They provide the stability and continuity without which organizations and societies could not function. These techniques are, however, not simply applied as universals for they too have to be particularized in specific situations and specific people. It is in this particularization that people practise the arts of resistance and 'game the rules' to make the techniques functional and to contest the potential for domination. When the techniques of disciplinary power are simply applied in unreflexive ways, they create the potential for bullying and domination, in the extreme taking the form of fascist and totalitarian organizations and societies, points which will be explored in the next chapter.

Forms of power give rise to forms of institutions – they are reflected and actualized in specific institutional forms. Chapter 8 will inquire into the institutional forms produced by sovereign power, pastoral power, disciplinary power and bio power. It will be concerned with how institutions function and affect the activities of leaders and managers. The next chapter, however, describes how we can easily be caught up in mindless patterns of interaction, which can be described as 'institutionalized bullying', reflecting the taken-for-granted, unreflexive exercise of the techniques of discipline. It also considers the techniques of coercive persuasion.

7

TAKING THE TECHNIQUES OF DISCIPLINARY POWER TO THE EXTREME

Domination and coercive persuasion

Introduction

The discussion on the techniques of disciplinary power in the last chapter is followed in this chapter by a consideration of another technique defined by American management academic Edgar Schein as coercive persuasion.[1] Schein, well known for his view of the leader's role as essentially one of defining and changing an organization's culture,[2] also claims that all such culture change must involve coercive persuasion, or brainwashing, since people will naturally resist suggestions that they change fundamental aspects of how they think. Leaders then become instigators and organizers of coercive persuasion. A theory of leaders as those who have the skills required to choose outcomes for the whole organization, and to choose the values organizational members should follow to implement their chosen outcomes, reflects an ideology of leadership which, perhaps, makes it feel natural to use techniques of coercive persuasion to change how people think in order to act for the general good – it is the general good which justifies the coercion. Schein's underlying, taken-for-granted assumption is that it is possible for powerful individuals to design culture change for the organization as a whole and to change the values and beliefs of people using coercive persuasion. In the views of Schein and others in the dominant discourse, leaders are assumed to be unconstrained in making their choices for the future of a whole organization, and it is assumed that coercive persuasion can overcome the resistances people practise to thwart domination.

I will argue that there is a fundamental distinction between the techniques of disciplinary power, discussed in the last chapter, and those of coercive persuasion. The former are aimed at controlling the bodies of people in a group, organization or society and the actions of those bodies. Modern organizations and societies could not exist without the techniques of disciplinary power, although it is, of course, possible to practise them in ways which become highly dictatorial and ultimately, at the extreme, fascist. Whether such techniques are ethical or not will, therefore, depend on the particular circumstances in which they are used and on what the consequences for people and their work are. Coercive persuasion has a completely different aim – it is aimed not at bodies and their activities in general but at the specific activity of mind. It seeks to foster dependency and, by definition, block questioning and reflexive thinking. It is, therefore, inimical to learning. The techniques of discipline, however, could create conditions in which learning is possible, just as Foucault argues, although they could also be used in unreflective ways to produce fascist environments that block learning. The aim of coercive persuasion is to break down the personalities of people and reconstruct them in ways that are chosen by the most powerful. For me, this can never be ethical and I cannot see how it can have any legitimate place in organizational life. It is, I think, important to pay serious attention to what is being proposed in applying the techniques of coercive persuasion.

Coercive persuasion

Schein locates leadership in the rational autonomous individual who develops the skills required to choose the direction of an organization and then chooses the values, or culture, required to realize such a direction. The issue then becomes one of changing the mindsets of members of the organization so that they subscribe to the new culture, believe in the new values and willingly act upon them. But just how are these others to be brought to this willing state? Not surprisingly, there are rather different views on what is involved in these change processes.

One answer to this question is typified by the learning organization theory of Senge.[3] Leaders inspire people by inviting them into dialogue where they suspend assumptions and so learn and change. Well-intentioned rational people, engaged in dialogue under inspiring leaders with vision, will willingly change. The contention here is that double loop,[4] or generative, learning takes place if leaders develop the right capacities for such learning. These capacities produce voluntary learning which people find pleasurable and inspiring. The belief is that a skilful leader can bring about change through building teams whose members participate in dialogue in which they will willingly, even joyfully, change their mental models. The problem, however, is that this view of learning is a highly idealistic and simplistic view of human nature that takes no account of threats to identity, power relations, conflicting ideologies, conflictual politics and anxiety. However, when the idealized process is actually taken up by people in their local interactions, the process is not nearly as benign as it seems. It easily becomes a cult-like experience in which people are pressured to participate in what is quite a prescriptive mode of conversation – failure to submit to peer pressure and conform to the usually oppressive conversational rules, which allow only for 'constructive conflict', immediately creates the threat of exclusion. Schein takes a very different view and thinks that leaders can only bring about generative learning and change cultures through processes of coercive persuasion. At first glance, dialogue looks like the civilized alternative to Schein's prescription of coercive persuasion, but it is, in practice, not all that different. In both cases powerful individuals take it to be their role to set the rules and situations for others to learn; in both cases ordinary differences and conflicts are avoided, even though they are pre-requisites for any kind of creative learning; in both cases powerful individuals are seeking to get others to willingly act on the new values of leadership. The rest of this chapter explores what Schein means by coercive persuasion.

The techniques of coercive persuasion

In 1961 Schein published a book on his research into the interrogation and indoc-trination of military and civilian prisoners in China during the Korean War in the 1950s. These prisoners included significant numbers of foreigners and he noticed that when they were repatriated, there was one group who had submitted to the interrogation and indoctrination and, amongst other things, signed confessions of crimes they had not committed. In order to avoid being subjected to unbearable pressure, they collaborated and allowed themselves to be used for propaganda purposes. However, they never really accepted their guilt and, as soon as they were free, they abandoned the compliant, collaborative ways of thinking they had feigned. They were coerced but had not been persuaded; they had simply engaged in superficial, adaptive learning. However, there was also a significant group of freed prisoners who continued to believe that they had been guilty of betraying the people and were grateful for the way the Chinese captors had treated them. Schein claims that these people had undergone a significant learning process, although an undesirable one from our point of view. They had not engaged simply in adaptive learning but in double loop, generative learning in that they had been persuaded to change their beliefs through coercion. Schein describes the process this group went through as coercive persuasion, popularly known as brainwashing, which he likened to a conversion process. He then goes on to argue that all culture change requires generative learning, which people resist and so will only come about in a process of coercive persuasion. It is the leader, the one whose role it is to bring about generative learning and change cultures, who must instigate and organize this process. The effort to empower people and make them generative learners so that they become more productive and creative requires a major move in the thinking of organizational members who are used to bureaucratic norms and top-down control systems. They have to be coercively persuaded to change the way they think – this is what generative learning is according to Schein.

> In the typical organizational context the new ways of working that are touted as culture change are usually seen as necessary for organizational survival and growth. So, paradoxically, the required generative learning process is coercively imposed on most of the managers and employees which puts them into a situation comparable to the prisoners in a political prison. It is not a spontaneous joyful process to give up one's beliefs, values and concepts and anchors for judgment. It is not a particularly comfortable situation to be subjected to re-engineering or culture change programs with the clear threat that unless one participates wholeheartedly one might lose one's job.[5]

Schein argues that coercive persuasion is conducted by taking the following steps:

1. Those who are to be coercively persuaded are *prevented in some way from leaving the learning experience*, for example through a feeling that they will lose their livelihood if they leave. It is very difficult for anyone in an organization to decline an invitation to a change or leadership programme and nearly impossible to leave once one is there.
2. The learners must be subjected to *intense interpersonal and psychological pressure to destabilize their individual senses of self and disconfirm current beliefs and values*. The level of survival anxiety must be high so that people surrender psychologically and put themselves into the hands of those providing the learning experience. Many people find the prospect of attending some compulsory training programme highly anxiety provoking. They fear exposing themselves and often feel that their performance on the programme will be judged and their managers informed. Also, many of the games and exercises people on programmes find they must engage in are infantilizing and create intense dynamics of dependency.
3. The learners are *put into teams so that those at more advanced stages of moving to the new culture can mentor those at less advanced stages*. Peer pressure plays a part in shifting doubt and also in creating feelings of safety. The emphasis on teams and team work is apparent on most development programmes, and this applies particularly to leadership development programmes where participants must learn how to be team members and how to run effective teams as team leader. The pressures team members place on each other clearly produce compliance, but the feeling of belonging that goes along with this also produces feelings of safety in anxiety-provoking situations.
4. *The team is rewarded if all its members demonstrate that they have learned the new collective values*. For example, it is widespread practice on leadership programmes for some admired senior executive to attend the end of the programme to listen to team presentations. Teams demonstrating that they have learned what they were supposed to learn and so have supposedly become more creative are rewarded with the praise of the admired senior executive.
5. *The new values or points of view are presented in many different forms*, such as lectures and informal discussions among team members, or games and exercises.

I have used examples of how each point made by Schein on coercive persuasion might be found in the conduct of leadership programmes. However, it is easy to point to each of them in any process of significant learning. People engaged in, say, a doctoral programme at a university are, of course, not physically prevented from leaving the programme, but they may still find it very difficult to leave, even though they might be having difficulties continuing, because of feelings of failure and loss of face. They are also highly likely to experience the kind of inquiry and reflection required for doctoral research as anxiety provoking, destabilizing of their taken-for-granted ways of thinking and therefore of their identities. They may well be learning in groups or teams, feeling rewarded by the praise of supervisors and punished by their criticism. So, does this mean that all significant learning processes amount to coercive persuasion, that is, brainwashing? For me the answer is that this is not the case because, as Schein describes it, coercive persuasion is consciously intended by powerful individuals whose aim is to change the way people are currently thinking to the way that those powerful individuals have decided that they should be thinking. In other words, powerful individuals are consciously working at changing the very identities of people so that they will conform. The powerful quite intentionally block any attempt by anyone to reflect on what they are being coercively persuaded to do. This total prevention of reflexivity is vital to the success of coercive persuasion – any reflexive activity is bound to disrupt any destabilizing arising from intense interpersonal and psychological pressure. Clearly, significant learning processes cannot amount to coercive persuasion where those conducting the processes are intending not to promote conformity but rather its opposite by seeking to improve the capacity of participants to think for themselves – when people are continually invited to take a reflexive stance, there can be no coercive persuasion.

The key aspects of coercive persuasion are, firstly, the intention of powerful individuals to change the very way people think to the way that they have decided by intentionally destabilizing their sense of self and, secondly, the blocking of any questioning, reflective, reflexive attitudes. Processes of disciplinary power differ from coercive persuasion for three reasons. First, the function fulfilled by the techniques of discipline is the location and control of human bodies and their activities in order to render them docile and so more productive. These techniques are not single-mindedly targeted at the particular bodily activity which we call 'mind', as is the case with coercive persuasion. Of course, rendering people 'docile' does also amount to some change in the bodily activity of mind but not in a way that blocks thought and reflexivity. Second, the techniques of disciplinary power are not applied to others by powerful individuals who are themselves not subjected to discipline – they are not the choices of individuals. Instead, they are social processes in which everyone is supervising and being supervised, even the most powerful. Third, working with the techniques of disciplinary power does not inherently and necessarily mean blocking all questioning, reflection and reflexivity except when those techniques are taken to the extreme and applied in fascist power structures, in which case they amount to coercive persuasion. It is essential, therefore, that, in using the techniques of disciplinary power, people do so in a reflexive manner. It is this that prevents the techniques of disciplinary power from being used in abusive and unproductive ways.

However, to return to Schein, he holds that as the techniques of coercive persuasion are applied, people experience cognitive redefinition as concepts and values are semantically redefined and standards, or anchors, of judgment are altered. The question, however, is whether they do produce changes in what people believe.

Richard Ofshe[6] argues that reform programmes operating according to the techniques of coercive persuasion have a very poor record of actually changing the beliefs of individuals, so that on this criterion they are abject failures and a waste of money. But on the basis of other criteria, he says that they are impressive. They are impressive in their ability to re-socialize people (whom he calls targets) so preparing them to conduct themselves in an appropriate way for the roles they are to take up in their organizations. For him, reform programmes are role-training regimes.

> If identified as training programs, it is clear that the goals of such programs are to reshape behavior and that they are organized around issues of social control important to the organizations that operate the programs. Their objective then appears to be behavioral training of the target, which results in an ability to present self, values, aspirations, and past history in a style appropriate to the ideology of the controlling organization; to train an ability to reason in terms of the ideology; and to train a willingness to accept direction from those in authority with minimum apparent resistance. Belief changes that follow from successfully coercing or inducing the person to behave in the prescribed manner can be thought of as by-products of the training experience.[7]

So, what programmes of coercive persuasion accomplish is not what Schein seems to claim. He argues that generative learning requires coercive persuasion. However, what he discovered in his study of prisoners subjected to coercive persuasion was that only some people succumbed to it. Most adapted on the surface and waited for freedom. I would argue that the same pattern occurs in leadership and other change programmes. The participants show all the appearance of making the change in public, but in private they display well-developed skills of resistance.[8] I think Ofshe's observation is insightful. The programmes do not really change the beliefs of many people, but they do train them in the public display of willing acceptance. Ofshe is correct, I think, in regarding them as role-training exercises.

If one is to accept the view that it is the role of leaders to change the values of their followers in ways the leaders have decided in order for them all to share the same values and so improve the organization, then one also has to accept that full-blown coercive persuasion is the only way to do this, and even then success is not guaranteed. Perhaps this is why there has been such a singular lack of success in changing people's values. More importantly, however, as Schein recognized, the use of coercive persuasion has ethical implications. I would go further and claim that giving advice to leaders to change people's values, as well as practising coercive per-suasion, is always unethical and therefore unacceptable. Such a strong claim about ethics cannot be made about the techniques of disciplinary power. It is only when they are carried to extremes that they become unethical and it is for this reason that they need to be used in reflexive ways, a matter to be taken up in Chapter 9.

Taking account of these points leads one to a very different conceptualization of what roles leadership and leadership training actually play in our society. Some leadership programmes do encourage a reflective stance and do invite participants to question taken-for-granted views on leadership, and so they may well encourage change. In my view, many more, especially in-house programmes in organizations, do not. Instead they provide what Foucault would call 'corrective training'. They train people to take up ways of talking and acting so that they conduct themselves in an appropriate manner. In this process of role training, conformity is encouraged. So, despite leaders being presented as bringers of change and leadership development programmes as the process of acquiring the skills necessary to bring about change, in fact what is actually happening is that leaders are bringers of order and continuity and leadership development programmes are training them in the kind of conformity required to sustain order and continuity. The programmes are a training in the techniques of disciplinary power, whether they encourage reflexivity or not, but those that do encourage reflexivity are more likely to avoid dangerous and unproductive extremes.

Foucault takes a very different approach from that typified by Schein and Senge. Foucault takes a social perspective in which the individual is not taken to be autonomous but to be an agent in a society in which all are subject to the domination of disciplinary power. Foucault carefully traces the evolution of institutions over long time periods in order to understand how the techniques of discipline are taken up in our modern organizations. The power of any individual to change disciplinary societies is highly limited. What Schein, Senge and others in these traditions propose is severely problematized by Foucault's analysis.

In Foucault's terms, techniques of disciplinary power enable some more powerful agents to act upon the conduct, even the will, of others to sustain them in patterns of sufficient docility so that their activities are more productive. However, interdependence means that even those more powerful individuals do not escape the techniques also being applied to them. For Schein, however, these powerful agents are autonomous individuals acting on others, without themselves being acted upon, in order to change the values and thought patterns of others. For Foucault, the powerful agents are not autonomous individuals because they too are being supervised by yet other groups of powerful agents. All, powerful and weak, are completely caught up in sustaining the disciplinary society over which none have absolute control because the controllers are themselves being controlled as they all live out the power of discipline. The habitual patterns of behaviour in modern organizations, that is, the habitus, social object or generalized other, consist of institutionalized techniques of discipline.

Complex responsive processes of discipline

The theory of complex responsive processes is based on the view, derived by analogy from the natural complexity sciences, and the sociology of Elias and Mead, that patterns of behaviour across the populations of organizations and societies emerge in many, many local interactions. Local interaction between interdependent human agents takes the form of communication, understood as the conversation of gestures, which forms and is formed by patterns of power relations, sustained by ideologies which also form the basis of the choice human agents make. It is in the interplay between all these choices that population-wide patterns emerge, often in unexpected and undesired ways which no one, no matter how powerful, can control. Leaders, like everyone else, also engage in local interaction. It is in the conversations and negotiations with colleagues and constraining groups both inside and outside a particular organization that leaders produce statements of visions, directions and new values and cultures. These are necessarily generalized, simplified, abstract statements which constitute powerful gestures to large numbers of people. However, what then happens depends on how these abstractions are taken up in the responses of people in many, many local interactions. Organizations and societies change not simply through the statements of the powerful, but also through the responses of those to whom the statements are addressed. This perspective is, of course, the diametric opposite of the dominant discourse on change typified by Schein and Senge. It is, however, a view which is quite consistent with Foucault's analysis.

It seems to me that Schein ignores the way in which every technique of discipline, including coercive persuasion, is only ever manifested in many, many local interactions. Articulations of techniques such as coercive persuasion are always generalizations which must be perpetually made particular in particular situations. However, in these local disciplinary interactions, which may include attempts at coercive persuasion, many people are only superficially subservient and talk the dominant discourse in order to be able to go on with the minimum discomfort; their conformity is a strategic pose which they will drop as soon as they can. Indeed, in his original work on the subject Schein identified this phenomenon but then never explored it. Only a few will ever be persuaded by the techniques of coercion. Foucault focuses our attention on the micro-detail of the use of techniques of disciplinary power. His detailed analysis of the emergence of different institutions which take up the techniques of discipline makes it clear how it takes myriad local interactions in which we are all disciplining each other to constitute the disciplinary society. Foucault is also well aware of the resistance aroused by particular forms of power. In his analysis of the pastoral form of power that was so widespread throughout Europe until the seventeenth century and, in a less demanding form, even long after that, he has this to say:

> I would like to try to identify some of the points of resistance, some of the forms of attack and counter-attack that appeared *within* the field of the pastorate. If it is true that the pastorate is a highly specific form of power ... if the objective of the pastorate is men's conduct, I think equally specific movements of resistance and insubordination appeared in correlation with this that we could call specific revolts of conduct.[9]

He mentions specifically the revolts of Luther, Wycliffe, Jan Huss and the Methodist movement. After noting that medical knowledge exercises the pastoral form of power today, he goes on to point out how it arouses dissent in the refusal to take particular medications, such as vaccination, or undergo certain medical procedures, such as abortion.

As with pastoral power, so with disciplinary power, many, many people will respond to the dominations of disciplinary power by striking a strategic pose and practising the arts of resistance. Scott explores how subordinate groups of people often have to adopt a strategic pose or public transcript when dealing with the more powerful, but how they also find other ways amongst themselves of expressing what they think and feel.[10] He refers to the latter as hidden transcripts and argues that contradictions and tensions expressed in the hidden transcripts and between them and the strategic pose/public transcript have a major impact on what happens. In other words, it is vital to understand the nature of ordinary, local political interactions if one is to understand wider social evolution. The problem with studying the hidden transcripts is that they are usually clandestine and so closed to outsiders. However, they are frequently expressed more publicly in disguised form as rumours, gossip, folk tales and jokes. Scott argues that these apparently innocuous and anonymous forms of discourse are disguised ideological insubordination which provides a reasonably safe critique of power. Civility requires us to smile and exchange routine pleasantries, especially when others have the power to harm or reward us, even if we privately despise those others. In particular in the face of domination, people will express themselves in their public transcripts in ways which are ritualized and stereotypical. The public transcript will be a performance masking the hidden transcripts, which will often erupt in ways that catch the more powerful off guard. Eventually the hidden transcripts may be expressed publicly, and Scott argues that when this happens it is often experienced as a breach of etiquette, even a symbolic declaration of war. The frontier between public and hidden transcripts is a constant struggle between the dominant and the subordinate. So, confronted by leaders and their agents' use of the techniques of discipline, people are adept at striking the strategic pose and speaking in terms of public transcripts, so creating the appearance of that compliance which is called 'change'. However, privately, in the hidden transcripts, we find ways of avoiding surveillance and undermining corrective training. The use of the techniques of disciplinary power is vital for the kind of social order required to sustain long chains of interdependence, but so are the arts of resistance expressed in the hidden transcripts in preserving some flexibility and freedom.

Taking the application of the techniques of disciplinary power to extremes: institutionalized bullying

If executives are trained in the techniques of disciplinary power in ways that invite inquiring into the nature and effects of using these techniques, then the extreme effects which these techniques may lead to can be avoided. It is essential, then, not only that managers and leaders are trained in reflexive ways, but also that they continue with such reflexivity as they apply the techniques in their organizations and find the same techniques being applied to them. A possible consequence of avoiding the reflexive stance is what we might call institutionalized bullying.

I want here to explore how unconscious general patterns of institutionalized bullying emerge and are sustained in many, perhaps even most, organizations nowadays. I am using the term 'institutionalized bullying' to make it clear that it does not refer to particular individuals who are bullies and other individuals who are victims. Instead, I am talking about the largely unconscious processes we are all colluding in that produce a culture of enforced conformity for all of us as we practise the techniques of disciplinary power in unreflective ways. We are all caught up in this culture of enforced conformity and together we repeatedly co-create it as we strive in very well-intentioned ways to do our work. We are all acting with the very best of intentions, not out of malice. But as our best intentions play into each other, there emerges a pattern none of us really want. The pattern I am referring to can only be described as 'institutionalized bullying'.

Typically, someone, whom I will refer to as an objector, attempts to draw attention to some difficulties that they are encountering in carrying out their work. This difficulty arises in trying to apply standardized procedures, requirements, targets, monitoring activities and so on, to the particular situations they have to deal with. In making the attempt, the objector is trying to get recognition for some variation of the generalized, standardized, abstract procedures so that they make sense in contingent local situations. These attempts are instantly blocked, which tends to provoke feelings of frustration, anger, rage and in the end cynicism and surface compliance. The feelings involved are then expressed in gossip, ridicule and subtle acts of resistance. The result is to weaken central control in reasonably safe ways which are unlikely to be ascribable to particular individuals. The result is also to block centralized attempts to bring about 'change'. Managers can try as much as they like to change things from the centre, but things really carry on much the same as before. Eventually this kind of pattern drives out innovative behaviour.

When someone tries to modify some procedure, the typical response is one of blocking by rejecting the objector on the grounds that he or she must comply with organizational policy, organizational strategy and the wishes of top management. If the objector resists these first attempts to block and refuses to comply, then the guardians of the procedures simply restate the general, standardized procedures (mistakenly calling them the 'System') in the apparent belief that anyone raising objections must be suffering from defective understanding which can be cured by further explanations, after which, as rational people, they will simply comply. Any objectors who still persist face the prospect of damaging their careers and possibly public ridicule. Most commonly, people simply give up and comply publicly. Then they join others, sometimes from other institutions, in ridiculing their organization, and those other institutions. In fact, it goes further than this because people stop objecting in the first place to silly procedures because they know the pattern and they know that they will get nowhere. So, they strike a strategic pose, repeat the language expected of them and apparently comply as part of a public transcript. Then they find ways to do the sensible thing by subversively working around the rules and engaging together in the hidden transcripts in which they practise the arts of resistance.

However, the objector who nevertheless continues will face a further common blocking pattern which takes the following form. When the objector does not give up at the first and second blockages and breaks an unwritten code by publicly refusing to comply, even drawing the attention of the most senior managers to what is going on, some representative of authority issues thinly veiled threats couched in the form of accusations that the objector is being 'negative', 'unhelpful' and 'unacceptable'. These responses put pressure on the objector to submit to the 'System'. In my experience, most people abandon any attempt to change anything at this stage. Only someone who, perhaps mistakenly, feels that they no longer have much to lose persists beyond this point and so the patterns go on and change becomes virtually impossible since all objections have been killed off. Running through the patterns of blocking described above, there is another common blocking process which takes the form of advice. The objector is advised to look at their own behaviour. The claim is that there is in fact not much of a problem at all, certainly not one that cannot be handled by a mature and sensible person. The problem is really the objector's own feelings and lack of confidence, and the prescription is that they should 'get a grip', 'grow up' and stop causing so much trouble. This is, of course, a far from subtle process of shaming which is a highly effective form of social control that will rapidly 'see off' the objectors.

It is this pattern in which we all create the dynamics of forcing each other to comply, no matter how silly complying might be. It is this pattern that I call institutionalized bullying, and while we all continue to collude in it we hold it firmly in place so that it cannot be dislodged by any amount of expensive centralized change programmes (for which there is anyway no scientific evidence of success). The change programmes accomplish little of a positive kind and instead provoke cynicism, which in turn reinforces the pattern of bullying in an ongoing vicious circle. This kind of pattern works against creative (or even destructive) change because creativity and innovation can only arise if there is difference and deviance in interactions – a statement amply supported by the natural complexity sciences. The compliance produced by institutionalized bullying is inimical to change. Change will then only come when deviants utter 'shrill cries of protest from the margin' which those at the centre will probably classify as hysterical.

Changing this kind of institutionalized bullying pattern is of course far, far harder than changing the 'System'. Changing patterns of interaction such as the one I have described is impossible, I believe, while thinking is regarded as a luxury which no one has time for, other than occasionally, and even then perhaps briefly, at the end of a busy day. Thinking together about what we are doing and why we are doing it seems to me to be the only way to produce reasonable and lasting changes in what we do. I believe that we can only address complex processes such as this if we think together about what we are doing and why we are doing it, an activity which occurs very little indeed in most organizations. Practising the techniques of discipline is essential to sustain modern organizations, but we may be able together to ameliorate the undesirable consequences of this practice by reflecting upon what we are doing.

Further thoughts on taking the application of discipline to extremes: 'Doublethink' and 'Newspeak'

In his novel *Nineteen Eighty-Four*, George Orwell describes a disciplinary society taken to the absolute extreme of fascist totalitarianism. It is easy to interpret the processes of disciplinary power as thoroughly bad, as in Orwell's narrative. Faced with this interpretation, it is easy to make a polarized response. At one pole there would be those who would demand the eradication of the techniques of disciplinary power. At the other pole there would be those who deny that activities of appraisal and control are techniques of discipline – they are simply the tools of efficient management and to paint them in emotive language as surveillance and correction is a distortion.

Foucault argued against such polarization by pointing to how the techniques of discipline are required to sustain order in modern, highly complex societies, and I would argue that, at the same time, one has to be mindful of the strong possibility that unreflexive applications of these techniques can lead to forms of totalitarianism. While, of course, not claiming that we live in the kind of totalizing society Orwell depicts, nevertheless some of the ideas he presents do provoke thought about the nature of the discourse on leadership and organizations.

Orwell describes in *Nineteen Eighty-Four* the ubiquitous presence of Newspeak. Newspeak is an impoverished form of language in which certain words are banned and the common vocabulary is reduced. For example, the word 'bad' is banned and replaced by 'ungood'. It provides a medium of expression of a world-view and at the same makes all other modes of thought impossible – thoughts not aligned with the dominant world-view become literally unthinkable. Newspeak diminishes the range of thought by encouraging the unreflective use of jargon which expresses official views, which people simply take for granted. I think there are many examples of this kind of taken-for-granted jargon in modern organizations. People say things like: there is no appetite for this meeting; raising the bar; going step by step; run leaner; agile strategy; fast strategy; how will you help managers realize their visions?; how will you get them all on the same page? what will your offering help me do on Monday morning?; what are the tools? alignment and direction; we need to be more agile and nimble in our planning and stand ready to amend the plan; we need to implement our skills; my skill set; mindset; ball park; game plan; leverage; touch base; results–driven; thinking outside the box; out of the loop; bandwidth; best practice. Conversations between managers and leaders tend to be peppered with this kind of jargon, which has become so familiar that few contest it and so it has the effect of blocking thinking and closing down any further inquiry.

In Newspeak, Doublethink means simultaneously holding two contradictory beliefs in one's mind while accepting that both are true. In Doublethink, people know that they are falsifying reality but Doublethink allows them to think that reality is not being violated. For example, people will accept that there are severe limits to our ability to predict the outcomes of our actions. Having agreed to this, they immediately claim that we must plan for the long term – we simply need to be more flexible and agile. Doublethink is both conscious, to enable precision, and unconscious so as to prevent feelings of guilt. It is conscious deception while retaining firmness of purpose with complete honesty. In Doublethink people happily tell deliberate lies but genuinely believe in them as they forget any inconvenient facts. There are many examples of Doublethink in today's dominant ways of thinking about organizations. For example, the distinction between leaders and managers gives rise to doublethink. On the one hand, people say that leadership is distinct from management and that leaders should be sent on leadership development programmes to acquire the distinctive skills of leadership, which are at a higher level than those of management. On the other hand, they send huge numbers of middle managers on leadership programmes so that they can exercise leadership in their current roles, and this has the effect of obliterating the distinction between leaders and managers. This contradiction goes unnoticed. Managers and policy-makers call for a scientific approach based on evidence of successful application of management tools; they claim to be following evidence-based techniques. Then, if pressed, they produce the evidence, which is anecdotal and rhetorical and so not evidence at all in scientific terms. The contradiction is not noticed. If change emerges in local responses to generalizations, not in the engineering of the acceptance of choices made by leaders, then most leadership programmes provide examples of doublethink. They claim to be about how the leader should bring about change, but they really amount to the corrective training required to sustain the status quo. The contradiction is not noticed.

Doublethink differs from a paradox. In paradox, we hold together in the mind two opposites at the same time in a dialectical process in which the opposition is transformed into new patterns of thought. In paradox there is the negation of negation, but in Doublethink there is only simple negation accompanied by dualistic thinking in which we apply first one statement and then its opposite without regard to the tension between them.

Conclusion

The literature on the role of leaders in changing the values of organizations presents a technique which it is important to distinguish from the techniques of disciplinary power. This technique is coercive persuasion, or brainwashing, which is practised in training situations. It is the intentional activity of changing the values people hold to those the leader has decided they should hold. The technique is one of confining people to a situation and breaking down their sense of self. In the ensuing dependency they come to believe what they are required to believe, although many, perhaps most, simply give the appearance of believing until they can escape. It is essential to this process that all questioning be blocked and all opportunities for reflexivity be denied. The techniques of discipline operate on bodies and their activities but not in a way that necessarily blocks a reflexive stance. When leaders try to use coercive persuasion on others, such coercion will not be the direct, simple cause of change, unless it is applied in a fascist power regime in which the techniques of terror are used. In normal organizational life, intentionally destabilizing people's sense of self and identity in order to 'soften' them up for change cannot, as presented by Schein, have any straightforward consequence. It may lead to anxiety, anger and sullen resistance, which means that it is ineffective in doing the 'softening' up job. It is, then, highly ineffective, in addition to being unethical, for leaders to apply the technique of coercive persuasion in order to fulfil their roles as change agents. Coercive persuasion is always unethical and if this is the only way the values of people can be changed, then attempts to carry out this change are always unethical too. The techniques of discipline are not inherently unethical, although they can become so in the absence of reflexivity. Reflexivity is central to the ethical conduct of disciplinary power and so is a key aspect of the practice of practical judgment to be explored in Chapter 9.

8

INSTITUTIONS AND THE TECHNIQUES OF LEADERSHIP AND MANAGEMENT

Habits, rules and routines

Introduction

Organizations reflect the wider institutions of society; indeed, they are expressions of various institutions such as the law, property rights and professional bodies. Wider institutional settings, therefore, impact on what leaders and managers can and cannot do in organizations. The purpose of this chapter is to explore the nature of institutions and how they enable and constrain the activities of leaders and managers. In particular, this chapter is an inquiry into the link between institutions and the organizational techniques of management and leadership. The inquiry starts by considering what the economics and organizational literature has to say about institutions and how they change, pointing to how the central concern is with habits, rules and routines, as well as laws, rights, obligations, norms, customs, traditions and codes of conduct. Next, the literature on power and the social nature of institutions is briefly explored, before looking at the differences between the literature on institutions and the theory of complex responsive processes. Then there is a consideration of how the theory of complex responsive processes understands institutions as patterns of interaction between people, making power and ideology central to institutions. The chapter ends with a brief indication of what institutions mean for our understanding of the techniques of leadership and management.

The nature of institutions

During the first half of the twentieth century, institutional economists focused attention on economic institutions as prime shapers of economic activity.[1] They argued that institutions are the patterns and regularities of human behaviour, understood as habits, which constitute macroeconomic systems. Writing in the last quarter of the twentieth century, the New Institutional Economists argued that institutions are the rules of the game,[2] provided by constitutions and laws, which shape institutional environments consisting of, for example, property rights and norms. Institutions consist of formal rules such as constitutions and property rights and also informal rules taking the form of customs, traditions and codes of conduct. Some hold that institutions are defined as systems of established, structured algorithms and rule-like dispositions which interact with each other at the micro level to create often unpredictable macro outcomes. The algorithms and rules structure and constitute the social interactions through which people communicate. Individuals and social structures are taken to be different levels of entities which co-evolve. For some writers, institutions are both 'objective structures' and 'subjective springs' of human agency and so are located in the human mind. Examples of such institutions are language, money, laws, systems of weights and measures, and table manners. Institutions create stable expectations of the behaviour of others and so enable ordered thought and action by imposing consistency, but they are also a special kind of social structure with the potential to change agents. For some,[3] organizations are special forms of institutions having principles of sovereignty (who is in charge), chains of command and principles of membership. For others,[4] institutions are the rules of the game and organizations are the players. Institutional economists[5] argue that institutions can arise spontaneously in undesigned ways through interactions between agents or they can be designed by powerful people, but even the latter will combine designed and undesigned elements. This point has obvious implications for leaders and managers; they cannot simply design institutions, although they may discover limited possibilities to influence the further evolution of institutions and the manner in which they are expressed in their own organizations. Furthermore, leaders and managers are not outside of institutional patterns of activity but always actors in the sustaining and developing of institutions.

Institutional economists, therefore, understand the essence of an institution to be habits and rules constituting an objective system which structures social interaction, and institutions also constitute the subjective nature of human agency. They provide the consistency and stability required for an orderly society. So, how are rules and habits understood? Rules are understood to be socially transmitted norms or normative dispositions which are transmitted in language, making them potentially codifiable.[6] The rules work because they are embedded in shared habits of thought and behaviour. A habit is a largely unconscious disposition to engage in previously adopted behaviour, but habits are held to be not the same as behaviour since habit is a cause of behaviour. Habits and institutions are mutually entwined and actors and institutional structures are connected in a circle of mutual interaction. Habits are different from repetition or ritual in that they are social mechanisms which involve imitation and the repeated experience of being constrained by others, and, as such, habits are central to institutions.

Evolutionary economists have also explored the nature of institutions,[7] and for them institutions are essentially about routines, which are taken to be the equivalent of the biological gene in the social realm, and it is the routine, therefore, which is the foundation of social evolution. What they seek to explain, from a Darwinian perspective, is how variations in routines come about, how routines are selected and how the selected routines are transmitted from one period to another. They argue that routines have gene-like stability (inheritance); they also have the capacity to 'mutate' (variation); and they compete for survival (selection or choice). Routines are repetitive and persistent patterns of collective behaviour, while habits are recurrent activity patterns on the individual level; routines refer to the organizational level, while skills refer to individuals. Both routines and habits are followed in an automatic manner not requiring reflection or conscious intention. Routines coordinate and control; they economize on cognitive resources; they reduce uncertainty; they lead to inertia; they provide predictability and stability through enabling and constraining social interaction, and they embody knowledge.

Organizational routines are understood to emerge out of the interplay of individual rules[8] in local learning processes.[9] They are path-dependent and shaped by history; they adapt to experience incrementally in response to feedback about outcomes. Both routines and habits are followed in a specific context so that successful application depends on the specificities of the context. When general rules are transferred across contexts, they can only ever be incompletely specified, because one context will differ from another, and this means that routines are transferable to other contexts to a limited extent only and this in turn problematizes the notion of general best practice. This process of transferring will always require interpretation and judgment and can only result in local best practices. Rule-enforcement mechanisms play a crucial role in making routine operation possible.[10] However, this role is limited so that there is a zone of discretion within which conformity cannot be enforced but only secured through motivating governance routines. Routines can be understood as providing a 'truce' between management and workers. It follows that political or motivational arrangements underlie the working and stability of routines.

Leaders and managers do not feature all that much in the above literature on institutions. They are understood to be caught up in the same institutional processes as everyone else which they cannot control. However, they can engage influentially in the political processes of institutions, and they have some constrained ability to articulate particular rules, routines and habits and in doing so seek to affect how people interact with each other.

Institutional change

Institutions are understood to change in endogenous processes of social evolution which take the same form as Darwinian biological evolution.[11] Some writers in this tradition[12] describe the processes of social evolution in terms of changes in the relative bargaining power of rulers, and they change in the interaction between institutions and organizations as the latter compete over scarce resources. This interaction is characterized by rules that govern political actors and shape the structure of property rights, which in turn define and specify the rules for competition and cooperation in markets. The importance of formal rules is amplified in modern market economies where the growth of long-distance trade, specialization and the division of labour contribute to problems of agency, contract negotiation and enforcement. Interpersonal ties, social norms and sanctions, such as ostracism, are important in securing the commitment of agents as the basis of institutional stability, but there is also always the possibility of defection from these norms.[13] On this view, institutions reflect vested interests which reinforce path dependence, and this makes it very difficult for individuals and organizational agents to change institutions. It requires state intervention to make large-scale changes to institutions. Organizations are the players in the institutional game and if they seek institutional change, they can only do so by lobbying the government.

For other writers, managers in organizations generate, select and enforce what they judge to be superior organizational routines. Some change occurs in institutions because individuals are in different institutions at the same time.[14] As individuals adjust to the conflicting claims and divergent development of these different institutions, they develop different habits of thought and behaviour. If a significant group of individuals change habits of mind, then this can lead to changes in some institutions. So there must be overlapping institutions and heterogeneous individuals in a two-way process where individuals adapt to institutions (downward causation) and the institutions adapt in response to changes in individuals. This two-way process of adaptation could occur in wars or invasions leading to conflicts of rules. In both normal and violent adaptation what is happening is the clashing of competing rules and in this conflict some institutions will become extinct. This is the process of selection in Darwinian evolution.

Power and institutions

Institutional and evolutionary economics, then, focuses attention on the rules, habits and routines which are understood to constitute institutions and on a Darwinian form of social evolution through which they change. It is the rules, routines and habits that are evolving – there are variations of them, some form of competitive selection between them and then they are passed on to others. In the previous section I have provided a brief summary of what I think are the main positions taken by institutional and evolutionary economists. Of course this ignores some important differences between these economists.

For example, one institutional and evolutionary economist, Lawson,[15] questions the usefulness of transferring notions of Darwinian evolution to social processes. He argues that all social processes are evolutionary in an actual rather than a metaphorical way but that natural selection is a metaphor taken from biology and it is open to question how useful the metaphor is in understanding social systems. He thinks that the metaphor may be useful for certain types of change and since it is an account of dynamic processes of continuous change, it may relate to social systems which are open to the future. He points out that the interaction in biology is between species and the physical environment and variety arises by chance. Is this so for social interaction? If it is, then the notion that leaders and managers are choosing what to do and are in control of the outcomes is problematized. This is reflected, perhaps, in the ambivalence among institutional and evolutionary economists over the extent to which they think that managers can decide on what the rules, habits and routines should be. Some writers in this tradition think that managers have some ability to change rules, habits and routines but most, it seems to me, emphasize the constraints on such ability in what is primarily an evolutionary process.

Another example of differing views among institutional and evolutionary economists relates to a reliance on formal rules and state power as the source of institutional change. Critics[16] argue that this covers over ideology, cultural beliefs, norms and conventions, making it difficult to understand why actors obey some rules and not others and also follow rules not enforced by the state. Institutions are thus better understood as reflecting both formal and informal rules.

Those[17] working in what has come to be called the new institutional economic sociology seek to understand how the incentives for the actions taken by agents arise from the institutional framework within which they operate. They are interested in the micro-foundations of context, social relations and norms which shape institutional frameworks. They stress the social context in which the intentional actions of individuals are embedded and are critical of the emphasis placed by institutional economists on atomistic individuals who slavishly follow scripts written for them by the particular intersection of social categories that they happen to occupy rather than respond to the social context they find themselves in. The result is that the history of relationships and network structures is ignored and the importance of personal relations and the obligations inherent in them are overlooked. It is also argued that institutional economists place too much importance on hierarchical authority and ignore the manner in which social networks in organizations structure power relations. The writers in this group pay attention to the actual patterns of personal relationships, arguing that it is the structures of these relationships, the interpersonal ties, that display both order and disorder and both honesty and malpractice. For one writer in this group, Nee:

> An institution … is defined as *a system of interrelated informal and formal elements— customs, shared beliefs, conventions, norms, and rules—governing social relationships within which actors pursue and fix the limits of legitimate interests.* In this view, institutions are social structures which provide a conduit for collective action by facilitating and organizing the interests of actors and enforcing principal agent relationships. It follows from this interest-related definition that institutional change involves not simply remaking the formal rules, but fundamentally it requires the realignment of interests, norms and power.[18]

Similar views are expressed by writers in other disciplines. The accountant Burns points to how power and organizational conflict play important roles in both the stability and the change of routines.[19] Routines are both constraining and enabling and they also lead to inertia, often persisting even when they produce negative performance. Feldman, whose area is policy research, holds that routines can change in an internal dynamic as participants respond to the outcomes of previous iterations of a routine.[20] The political scientist McKeown argues that leaders can intervene to override the constraining effect of routines.[21]

The American philosopher Searle also stresses the role of power in relation to institutions.[22] The purpose of institutions is to create new sorts of power relationships which are denoted by terms such as rights, duties, obligations, authorizations, permissions, requirements and clarifications. Searle calls these structures of power relationships deontic powers. Institutions create reasons for action that are independent of people's desires in that the reasons are duty and obligation which we carry out even if we do not want to. However, despite his emphasis on power and collective action, he insists that the reality of institutions, like all observer-dependent reality, is in the minds of individuals and their minds are in their heads.

Pentland, whose research area is accounting and information systems, and Feldman, policy researcher, argue against the notion that routines create inertia and offer a theory of routines which encompasses change as well.[23] For them, routines have two aspects, the ostensive and the performative. The ostensive aspect is an abstract rule or narrative description of the routine (structure), which is the traditional focus of attention by researchers on routines, and the performative is the actual performance of the routine by specific people in specific situations (agency), which attracts little attention in the literature. It is the relationship between these two aspects that generates outcomes that could be stable but also display change. Routines are not simply re-enactments of past regularities because they have to be taken up by people in specific contexts in ways that are sensitive to changing contexts, thus producing variations in routines. It follows that people in organizations are not simply following rules; they are interpreting them. Since many different people are engaged in preforming routines, they will have different interpretations of how to adapt them and this will generate conflict, so that which interpretation takes hold will depend on the power and subjectivity of the agents involved. In taking this perspective, therefore, Feldman and Pentland focus attention on agency, subjectivity and power. In the end, performance is inherently improvisational. But the ostensive aspect of routines does have its uses in that they act as a guide to actions to be taken; as a way of accounting for actions that have been taken; and as a way of referring to patterns of activities that render them more comprehensible. Feldman and Pentland do not, however, move away from a Darwinian evolutionary theory but seek to understand the evolution of routines as processes of variation, selection and retention: performance generates the variety which is selected and retained in the ostensive aspects as some kind of framework, artifact or narrative. They argue that some variations are intentional and others are unintentional.

So the writers reviewed in this section move away from the focus on habits, rules and routines and explore the wider social features relevant to institutions. First, the use of the metaphor of natural selection, and with it Darwinian evolution, is questioned. Second, emphasizing formal rules and state power in relation to institutions covers over issues of power and ideology in institutions. Third, the assumption of atomistic individuals is contested and attention is focused instead on personal and social relations as constitutive of institutions, and this brings to the fore issues of power, ideology and conflict. Fourth, the notion that routines are essentially static and produce stability and inertia is questioned and instead an understanding of the ongoing interaction between the ostensive and performative aspects of routines is presented, and this brings in agency, subjectivity and power.

The differences between the theory of complex responsive processes and the theories of institutions

In this section I want to set out what I see as the principal differences between the theory of complex responsive processes presented in Chapters 2 and 3 and the theories of institutions presented in institutional economics, evolutionary economics and institutional economic sociology, which are the main disciplines concerned with institutions that are relevant to the literature on organizations. Some of the differences I will point to are also taken up by some of the writers on institutions and routines reviewed above, but I do not think that any of them combine all of the eight differences outlined below in their theories.

The first difference has to do with Darwinian evolution. As with some writers on institutions and routines,[24] the theory of complex responsive processes questions the appropriateness of applying biological metaphors of the variation, selection and retention of routines to social evolution. The theory of complex responsive processes is a theory of evolution but one that draws on aspects of Hegel's philosophy of the movement of thought in the historical evolution of society. This is a dialectical understanding of historical processes, which emphasizes how the paradoxes of domination and subjugation, that is, the dynamic tensions of conflicting power positions, are transformed into new social dynamics. Since these new dynamic patterns have been produced through the transformation rather than the obliteration of the former patterns, the original tensions remain, although in a different form, as the generators of yet further transformation. This evolutionary process is understood directly in terms of dynamically changing patterns of power relations and with them the movement of thought. These two different theories of evolution reflect two different forms of causality. The Darwinian processes of evolution imply what might be called adaptionist causality; variations are generated by some mechanism and then selected for retention by some competitive means because they represent fitter adaptations to changed conditions than others. The change in routines is caused by selective adaptation so that causality takes an adaptionist form. The Hegelian theory of evolution, however, implies what might be called transformative causality. In the theory of complex responsive processes this is reflected in the understanding that individuals form society while *at the same time* society forms them. In their communicative interaction, power relations and ideology reflecting intentions, choices and actions, people are producing emergent patterns of both continuity and change at the same time. So instead of thinking in terms of variation, selection and retention, which some certainly do understand in terms of agency, subjectivity and power,[25] the theory of complex responsive processes understands routines and habits as patterns of routinized and habitual interaction between interdependent individuals which emerge in their interaction while at the same time sustaining and transforming that interaction. In trying to make sense of what is going on in a particular organization at a particular time, therefore, attention is primarily directed to processes of conversation, power, ideology and choice, and in the course of trying to understand these we need to take account of habitual and routine interaction. This is a departure in the mode of understanding from one which immediately focuses attention on habits and routines and how they are varied, selected and retained. I think that the complex responsive processes method mainly seeks to stay close to a wider understanding of actual experience rather than just the abstractions of routine and habit.

Second, the theory of complex responsive processes moves away from the notion of system found in the theories of institutions reviewed in the previous two sections of this chapter. This is because the notion of a human system with its parts, its rules, its boundaries and its inside and outside is a spatial metaphor. It amounts to a second order abstraction and so covers over the ordinary experience of human beings as they engage in the interactions with each other that are the reality of organizational life. Instead of thinking in terms of systems, the theory of complex responsive processes is couched in terms of responsive processes of interaction taking the form of the actual conversation of gestures between people, actual power relations and actual ideologies and the choices they are reflected in, without any intervening concept. This interaction does not produce anything outside of itself – patterns of interaction simply lead to further patterns of interaction. There is, therefore, no outside cause, no outside force, no mechanism or driver. There are simply people in interaction with each other, endlessly evoking responses in each other in motivating and unmotivating ways. The practical implication of taking this view is that, in trying to understand what we are doing and what is going on around us, attention is directed to wider social processes which can be described as habitus, social object, generalized other, the background or culture. Habitual and routinized interactions are important aspects of these wider processes and always reflect them. This kind of understanding is also present in the work of some of those researching routines.[26]

Third, as with some writers on institutions,[27] the theory of complex responsive processes contests the possibility of individuals ever being autonomous and bases its reasoning on the irremovable interdependence of individuals. This interdependence means that people need each other so that they are both enabled and constrained by each other, and it is this enabling and constraining that is power. Power is thus an aspect of every human relationship and it is never equal. Power relations between groups of people are experienced as the dynamics of inclusion and exclusion, and it is this process that constitutes the 'we' identities of individuals which are inseparable from their 'I' identities. Individual selves are thus essentially social selves; the individual is the singular and the group or society is the plural of interdependent people. The personality structures of individuals are formed in social processes of interaction with others, and indeed the consciousness and self-consciousness of individuals are essentially the same processes as social interaction between those individuals. The interaction of interdependent individuals forms the social while, at the same time, the social forms them in terms of selves and identities. Habitual and routinized behaviour emerges, is dynamically sustained and changed, as aspects of wider social processes of conversation, power, ideology and choice. The advantage of thinking in terms of interdependent rather than autonomous individuals is that one abandons the myth of autonomy which sustains totally unrealistic expectations of what individuals are capable of doing. Instead, in trying to understand what is going on, one remains firmly focused on the reality of the manner in which human agents enable and constrain each other and so always socially produce what one is experiencing and capable of choosing to do. Both habits and routines are then always understood as social phenomena.

The fourth difference that characterizes the theory of complex responsive processes follows from the move in thought away from the notion of human system to understanding individuals as thoroughly social, which means that there are no levels. Thinking in terms of human systems and autonomous individuals is almost always expressed through a spatial metaphor of levels. Individuals are thought of as being at one level, while the groups they form are at a higher level, organizations at yet a higher level, and societies at an even higher level. Each level is held to display regularities peculiar to it which cannot be reduced to the level below. However, from the perspective of complex responsive processes, individuals and groups, organizations and societies, are all constituted in the same responsive processes and this means that there can be no levels – there is only movement over time. To talk in terms of levels is to talk in terms of second order abstractions. The practical relevance of moving away from the abstract notion of levels is that, instead of imagining that we are creating something outside of ourselves, we can focus our attention on how we are together co-creating what is happening to us over time.

The fifth difference between the theory of complex responsive processes and much of the literature on institutions is that the latter presents rules, habits and routines in a disembodied way that abstracts from people, while the former focuses on the experience of bodily interaction between people. This bodily interaction is understood as conversation which, following Mead, consists of the gestures human beings make to each other and the responses these gestures evoke. It is in this communicative interaction between human bodies, that is, conversation, that the thematic patterns of human experience emerge as narrative histories. The appropriate method of inquiring into this experience is that of reflexively seeking to understand what is going on in the narrative.[28] The narrative of experience is complex, meaning that it is stable and unstable at the same time, predictable and unpredictable at the same time, constant and changing at the same time, and habitual and spontaneous at the same time. If one understands human experience in its complexity, it becomes somewhat artificial to split the opposites of that experience to focus on habits and routines as stable, repetitive and predictable. For conceptual purposes, the theory of complex responsive processes identifies habits and routines as the rather repetitive themes being iterated in conversation while recognizing that in experience the repetitive iterations are never exactly the same, as people respond to the uniqueness of the ordinary situations they find themselves in. Since tiny variations in interaction can escalate into significant changes in narrative themes across a population, repetition and potential change cannot be separated in actual experience.

The sixth difference is that there is a relationship between the local (individuals) and the population of institutions (society), which of course is recognized in the literature on institutional routines, but there this relationship is mostly treated as a duality, whereas in the theory of complex responsive processes it is taken to be a paradox. A key claim made by the theory of complex responsive processes is that all human interaction is essentially local interaction. It is local in that individuals can only interact in a direct bodily way with a small number of others, and they do so in ways that reflect their own personal histories and the histories of the communities in which they live. It is from many, many local interactions that coherent patterns of activity emerge across populations. These population-wide patterns are referred to using terms with very similar meanings: habitus, social object, generalized other, game and culture. In their local interactions, interdependent individuals are interacting not just with each other but at the same time with the generalized other so that the patterning of their local interactions reflects the wider patterning of habitus, social object, game or culture. It is the paradox of local interactions forming population-wide patterns while at the same time being formed by them. The claim that individuals can only interact locally is not rebutted by the fact that individuals can use communication tools such as email, the internet, radio and television to communicate with large numbers of other individuals across a whole population. This is because the messages sent via these media are not the whole social act of communication but only a gesture. What the gesture means, and this is true of the gestures of very powerful people too, can only emerge in the response, in the interpretations of what the gesture means, and responses and interpretations are local activities. The practical import of this point is that it directs attention to the effects that habits and routines have in specific situations, at specific times, in specific places, with specific people.[29]

The seventh difference between the theory of complex responsive processes and some of the literatures on institutions is that institutions, like all other social phenomena, are understood to be patterns of interaction across populations of people which emerge and are dynamically sustained in many, many local interactions between people. Institutions are then seen as expressions of habitus, power and ideology. These matters of habitus, power and ideology are recognized in the work of some researchers into institutional life,[30] while others[31] in this tradition claim that it is misleading to define institutions as patterns of behaviour because that would mean that an institution ceases to exist when the behaviour is interrupted. The institutional economist Hodgson gives as an example the UK monarchy, arguing that if institutions are regarded as patterns of behaviour, then the monarchy would disappear when the monarch went to sleep. Instead of understanding institutions and their routines as actual behaviour, he claims that they have to be understood in terms of potential, that is, as stored behavioural capacities and capabilities which cause the actual behaviour. He argues that institutions and routines cannot be regarded as both potential and actual. It seems to me that he is reflecting a highly individualized way of thinking. Taking his example, the monarchy does not disappear when the monarch is asleep because the monarchy is institutional patterns of tendencies to act, that is, social objects, that involve many, many other people too. However, if they are all asleep, then the institution is nowhere to be found because the potential can only appear in actual behaviour, otherwise it is irrelevant. We can only know the generalized potential, the disposition, in specific local behaviour. For the theory of complex responsive processes this goes back to the point made in the last paragraph that the population-wide patterns called institutions are generalities that only have meaning in local responses. If there are no local responses, then there is no institution.

The eighth difference is that most writers on institutions and routines adopt the basics of the natural sciences method which seeks to adopt the position of the objective observer, while, according to the theory of complex responsive processes, there is no objective observer, only participants in social interaction, and no one can escape from this participation to stand outside it and observe it. The position of the participant is understood to be a paradox of immersion and abstraction or, in Elias' terms,[32] involvement and detachment. People are normally not simply immersed, or involved, in their participation; in order to understand what they are doing, they have to abstract, or detach, at the same time.[33]

Having identified eight conceptual differences between much of the literature on institutions and the theory of complex responsive processes, the next section goes on to explore what is meant by patterns of interaction, and the final section will look at whether routines can be thought of as tools and techniques of leadership and management.

Institutions and complex responsive processes: patterns of human interaction

The central assertion of the theory of complex responses is that patterns of social interaction emerge across a population, be it a society or an organization, in myriad local interactions. It is these local interactions that are described as complex responsive processes of relating encompassing communicative interaction, relations of power, and the desires, ambitions, intentions and choices of interdependent individuals which reflect values and norms, that is, ideologies. Patterns of communication, forms of power, norms and values all emerge through the interplay of individual and group choices in local interaction. Since the patterns that emerge across a whole population are arising in these many, many local interactions, they cannot be designed or intended, as a whole. Whole patterns are dynamically reproduced from moment to moment in local habitual interactions, and it is in these local interactions that they also, at the same time, change. From a complex responsive processes point of view, therefore, institutions are population-wide patterns dynamically sustained while at the same time changed in local interactions. Three key points can be made about institutions from this perspective. First, institutions as patterns of interaction across a population reflect, indeed are, the habitus, social object, the game or culture, all concepts presented in Chapter 3. Second, values and norms are constitutive of institutions. Third, forms of power are expressed in specific ways as institutions. Each of these three points will be briefly reviewed in the rest of this section.

Habitus, generalized other, social object, game and culture

Chapter 3 briefly reviewed concepts of the generalized other, social object, habitus and game. All of these notions express the point that everyone in an organization or society is acting in ways that reflect the society they live in. These notions are all ways of conceptualizing the tendency on the part of large numbers of people to act in similar ways in similar situations. They are the dispositions and tendencies of individuals in a community to act in ways acceptable in that community. Generalized other, social object, habitus and game are all generalities that have to be made particular in particular situations involving particular people in particular places, at particular times.

Another concept which has much the same meaning as notions of habitus, social object and game is that of culture. The anthropologist Geertz[34] argues that although culture involves ideas, it cannot be equated with a set of ideas in people's heads, and although it is not a physical thing, it is not some kind of super-organic entity with forces and purposes of its own. He argues that to try to conceive of culture as either subjective or objective is a mistake, as is defining culture as the beliefs people have about how they need to operate to be acceptable. Culture cannot be reduced to systematic rules or algorithms. Instead, he sees culture as symbolic action which signifies meaning. Culture consists of socially constructed structures of meaning according to which people act. Culture is not a cause of events, behaviour, institutions or processes but a context within which human action becomes intelligible. Geertz also argues that it is through social action that culture is articulated.

The concepts of habitus, game, generalized other, social object and culture are central to the theory of complex responsive processes of relating between human bodies. They all can be thought of as a paradox of habitual, routine action and improvised, spontaneous change at the same time. Since institutions are dispositions realized in action and since, in some formulations anyway, they are constituted in social relations, they are much the same as notions of habitus, generalized other, social object, game and culture. Conceiving of institutions in this wider way results in the downplaying of rules and codifications while in no way denying their roles. As a consequence of downplaying the role of rules, institutions can clearly be seen to involve expert behaviour that goes beyond any rules or codifications. It is this expertise, or practical judgment, which is essential to the functioning of institutions and to the use to which experts put rules and codifications. Conceiving of institutions in terms of habitus and social object also makes it impossible to ignore the role of ideology, of norms and values.

Norms and values

Chapter 3 presented a discussion of the nature of norms and values, key aspects of habitus and social object. Norms are understood to be obligatory restrictions on what people can do – they are essentially customs and laws. Norms arise and evolve in a history of interaction between people and they come to structure the personalities of individuals. Values are voluntary compulsions, feelings of choosing to do something that nevertheless feels compulsory in the sense of not being able to do anything else and continue to live with yourself. The experience of value arises in intense interaction in which some imaginative whole is idealized in a way that demands self-transcendence. Values are the basis of our motivation to rise above narrow self-interest in the cause of some greater good. Together norms and values constitute ideology, which is the basis on which people make evaluative choices and which also makes particular patterns of power feel natural. All institutions reflect some kind of ideology, only some of which can be expressed as rules, and all institutions, therefore, have an ethical dimension. Taking account of the ideological nature of institutions again presents a more complex conceptualization than one which focuses too heavily on rules and routines.

Forms of power

Finally, consider how institutions emerge from particular forms of power. Chapter 6 briefly discussed the four forms of power identified by Foucault, namely, sovereign, pastoral, disciplinary and bio power. Foucault moved away from what he called an 'institutional-centric'[35] approach which starts with a particular institution, say the psychiatric hospital, and focuses on its structure and procedures, its rules and routines, and the type of power and knowledge found in it. He argued, instead, that an institution could only be understood on the basis of something external, general and global, which in the case of the psychiatric hospital would be the psychiatric order, in turn part of the project of public hygiene. The institution gives concrete form to this wider order and to understand this form of order we need to go behind it to take the perspective of the technology of power which it expresses. He does not start with the functions that a particular institution performs and whether or not it is properly exercising these functions. Instead he wants to start with the strategies and tactics of the techniques of power. He also does not want to start with the norms and criteria of an already given institutional object and focuses instead on how these objects have come to be constituted. He attempts to free relations of power from institutions in order to analyse them in terms of the technologies of power. So, for example, he identifies how the pastoral form of power was institutionalized in the form of the Church.

I think this approach of relating institutions to the forms of power they express brings deeper insight into the nature of institutions. Sovereign power is that form of power exercised as centralized rule, originally the form of power employed by monarchs. Although this form of power was greatly diminished by the move away from monarchies, it has survived as the law, which in a way is the successor to monarchy. The sovereign power of the law takes institutional form in, for example, legislatures, courts and the professional bodies of lawyers. The pastoral form of power exercised by the Church has also been significantly diminished in Europe by the emergence of secular societies, but it does still survive in the institution of the reduced church. Pastoral power is also expressed in modern times by, for example, the institutions of psychotherapy and counselling and in organizations such as coaching. As argued in Chapter 6, it is the disciplinary form of power which has largely, but not completely, replaced both sovereign and pastoral power. Disciplinary power is expressed in the institutions of the military, the police, mental institutions, hospitals, schools and workplaces. Bio power is a form of power concerned with the well-being of the population and is expressed in institutions such as population censuses, surveys of health, health think-tanks, lobbying bodies pressing for smoking bans, control of alcohol consumption and weight control, and many others. Many activities of the institution of government are expressions of bio power, for example health departments. In modern private, public and not-for-profit organizations the primary form of power is clearly disciplinary power, but traces of the other forms are to be found in, say, human resource departments and health and safety departments.

Institutional techniques

Taking a more complex view of what institutions are makes it clear how heavily constrained leaders and managers are by the ideological and power nature of the institutions reflected in organizations. It is not possible for even the most powerful to change the institutions of which organizations are reflections. Nor can they change the ideologies of people in their organizations or design the forms of power employed. These all reflect wider institutional and social patterns outside their control. However, although it is extremely difficult to change habits and routines by fiat, leaders and managers do articulate routines and procedures and they do seek to enforce them using the techniques of discipline. Also, leaders do intervene to override some of the effects of routines which have emerged and are now thought to be no longer playing a productive role.[36] Leaders and managers do choose their next actions based on their desires and ideologies, but in doing so they reflect the habitus of their community and what happens depends upon the responses to their next actions in the interplay with the actions of others. So while they are significantly constrained, in participating in the ongoing complex responsive processes of organizational life leaders and managers can exert considerable influence over the activities of others. They do this by designing disciplinary and also pastoral rules and routines such as planning procedures, budgeting procedures, health and safety policies, recruitment policies and procedures, procedures required by equality laws and many more. Rules and routines can be understood, then, as institutional tools and techniques of leaders and managers. Leaders and managers have some ability to design routines that may have considerable impact on how others, and also they themselves, work together.

Conclusion

From the perspective of complex responsive processes, institutions are generalized, population-wide patterns of interaction between embodied persons which are made particular in many, many local situations. The population-wide patterns of interaction emerge and are dynamically sustained in these ongoing local interactions. In a fundamental, constitutive sense, institutions are expressions of forms of power: sovereign power, pastoral power, disciplinary power and bio power, and therefore they are also expressions of ideology. In turn, organizations are expressions of the wider institutions of society. The patterns of interaction that are institutions are local particularizations of general habits, rules and routines, most of which are unconscious. However, the theory of complex responsive processes points beyond habits, rules and routines themselves to the improvisational, spontaneous ways in which they are tailored to unique local situations. It points to the expert behaviour that is beyond rules but is essential to effective institutional activity.

Although they are largely emergent and unconscious, the habits, rules and routines of institutional life can be articulated, both formally and informally, by powerful individuals and groups. We might say that it is this possibility of designing rules and routines that enables a degree of organizational control by leaders and managers. They can and do set out routines to be followed, for example to prepare plans, work to targets, obtain approval for resource uses, hire staff, appraise staff and many more. In doing this, they are importantly using the techniques of disciplinary power discussed in Chapter 6 and also the techniques of sovereign, pastoral and bio power. It is through these means that they are able to exert considerable control over the activities of members of an organization. However, there are constraints. Articulations of designed rules and routines can only be generalizations and idealizations which only have any meaning in the particularization of local interaction, where many different interpretations of the generalized rules and routines will inevitably be made and application of the rules and routines will often raise resistance. It follows that the designed rules and routines are highly likely to be taken up in ways not expected or desired by the designers. Furthermore, rules and routines can guide competent performance, but expert performance cannot be expressed in this form which means that expert performance is to a degree outside the possibility of leadership and man-agement control. Finally, the interplay of intentions, choices and actions will yield unexpected and undesired 'outcomes', and this means that leaders and managers cannot control 'outcomes' or 'future direction'. They can, however, exercise the expertise of leadership and management to carry on responding to what emerges. In the end, the really important aspect of leadership and management is experience-based expertise and expert knowledge, which are beyond the scope of rules and routines. The next chapter turns to this crucial matter of expert performance and asks whether we can talk about 'techniques' of leadership and management expertise.

9

THE LEADERSHIP AND MANAGEMENT 'TECHNIQUES' OF PRACTICAL JUDGMENT

Reflexive inquiry, improvisation and political adroitness

Introduction

In considering the nature and possible uses of the leadership and management tools and techniques of instrumental rationality, Chapter 5 drew attention to how all of these tools and techniques take the form of rules, procedures and models. It also drew attention to the difference between competent performance, on the one hand, and proficient, expert performance, on the other. The difference is that following rules, procedures and models may produce competent performance, but proficient, expert performance requires moving beyond the rules, procedures and models. Experts are unable to articulate the rules governing their performance because they simply do not follow rules; instead, as a consequence of long experience, they exercise practical judgment in the unique situations they find themselves in.

Through experience they are able to recognize patterns, distinguishing between similarities with other situations and unique differences. The patterns they recognize are the emerging patterns of interaction that they and other people are creating. In other words, they are recognizing the emerging themes in conversation, power relations and ideology reflecting choices. The key resource any organization must rely on is surely this expert interactive capacity in the exercise of practical judgment by leaders and managers. If we cannot identify rules, procedures and models as 'drivers' of expert practical judgment, does it follow that we can say nothing about practical judgment and have to leave it as a mystery? I do not think there is anything mysterious about the exercise of practical judgment and it is the purpose of this chapter to inquire into the exercise of practical judgment and explore whether it is possible to identify any 'techniques' of practical judgment.

However, the first point to note is that if we are to continue using the term 'techniques', then we have to accept that it cannot mean what it means in the mode of instrumental rationality. In instrumental rationality, the tools and techniques take the form of simplifications and generalizations or, in other words, second order abstractions that are context free. These tools and techniques are algorithmic in nature and take the form of models, frameworks, rules and step-by-step procedures. However, none of them can address uncertainty, unpredictability, ambiguity and complexity. The exercise of practical judgment is highly context-related; it is exercised in highly uncertain and unpredictable, unique situations. It cannot, therefore, be generalized or dealt with in the manner of second order abstractions. The exercise of practical judgment calls for a wider awareness of the group, organizational and societal patterns within which some issue of importance is being dealt with. This requires a sensitive awareness of more than the focal points in a situation, namely, awareness of what is going on at the margins of what is being taken as the focus. Practical judgment is the experience-based ability to notice more of what is going on and intuit what is most important about a situation. It is the ability to cope with ambiguity and uncertainty, as well as the anxiety this generates. The second point to notice is that expertise is largely unconscious and difficult to articulate, as became clear when those trying to develop artificial intelligence found that experts could not formulate what they did in terms general enough to be simulated by a computer. Clearly, practical judgment has to be acquired and exercised in ways that cannot easily be generalized.

This does not mean, however, that there is nothing further to be said about practical judgment. The capacity for practical judgment in relation to some activity is gradually developed through actually performing the activity in question. So the technique is to do the work, ideally under the supervision of another who is already an expert. The technique, then, is one of doing the work alongside others who are more experienced, so learning by doing. For thousands of years, in most cultures, pupils or apprentices lived and worked with masters or craftsmen to acquire, for example, the expertise of cloth maker, weaver, butcher, scribe and teacher. Schön gave an analysis of this kind of relationship,[1] when he described how, for example, artists, medical practitioners, teachers and others learn their craft in a studio or other workplace where they work with, and are supervised by, those who already display expertise. In fact, it is part of the role of a manager in every organization to supervise the work of those reporting to him or her. In many organizations today, relatively inexperienced managers are formally allocated a mentor and even if this does not happen, inexperienced managers may informally find a mentor. Schön described the expert as a reflective practitioner, that is, one who thinks in the action of practising. Reflection-in-action, or, more importantly, reflexivity-in-action, can be thought of as 'techniques' of practical judgment, as can supervision and mentoring. However, it is important to note two points about these 'techniques'. First, supervisors and mentors must themselves be experts if they are to guide others on the route to expertise, and supervising/mentoring is also the exercise of practical judgment. It follows that supervising and mentoring cannot be reduced to rules, procedures and models. Second, supervision and mentoring are at their most effective in sustaining and enhancing capacities for practical judgment when they take the form of reflexive inquiry into what they and those they are supervising and mentoring are doing together and why they are doing it in the way that they are.

Furthermore, the previous paragraph makes it clear that practical judgment is not an individual possession, competence or skill set. Practical judgment is, rather, social processes. Interdependent individuals can only develop and sustain the skills of practical judgment through participation with each other. When senior leaders and managers withdraw from the hurly-burly of organizational life to live in an isolated world of privilege, they simply lose the capacity for practical judgment. This has been made clear again and again, for example by the failure of the CEO of Lehman Brothers to make practical judgments about exotic financial products – he had very little awareness of what they were and no interest in them.[2] More recently, a UK House of Commons select committee examining the phone hacking perpetrated by the *News of the World* questioned Rupert Murdoch, CEO of News Corporation, and his son, James Murdoch. It became very clear that they were completely out of touch with what is actually going on in their company, or they were not telling the truth.

Since leaders and managers can only become experts through experience, it follows that some form of mentoring is a very important way in which to foster the development of leadership and management expertise. It also follows that some form of ongoing or periodic supervision is highly important in sustaining and further developing this expertise. Management and leadership coaching might be a 'technique' of fostering practical judgment. However, a distinction should be drawn between the kind of instrumentally rational, step-following forms of coaching which focus on goals and tasks in a narrow way and the kind of more discursive and exploratory forms that coaching, understood as a kind of work therapy, might take. A coach who follows rules and step-by-step procedures when working with leaders and managers is in fact using the tools and techniques of instrumental rationality, and while these may foster competence, they cannot develop proficiency and expertise. The problem with coaching is that the coach will probably not have the kind of expertise which the client needs to develop, while a mentor who is an expert leader and manager in the client's organization will have that kind of expertise. However, a coach who is an expert in discursive forms of work therapy may assist the client to greater awareness of his or her roles in the organization. In other words, the contribution of a coach could be to encourage the development of exploratory reflexivity. Coaches who work in a discursive way with groups of leaders and managers may help to widen and deepen communication in a group and so produce greater meaning, and again this activity cannot be reduced to rules and procedures. The coach's work in the development of more fluid and complex conversation involves curbing the widespread pattern in organizations where leaders and managers focus on the future and move immediately to planning and solving problems. This can be done by exploring narratives of what those in the group have done in the past in order to develop some insight into what they have been doing and why they have been doing it in a particular way. Such conversation grounds group members in the present as they make sense of the past in the present and opens up more varied and grounded ways of taking account of the future in the present. Another 'technique' which can be used in discursive, narrative forms of coaching is that of writing. It is very helpful for leaders and managers to write short narratives of troubling events they are currently experiencing and then inquiring into these narratives in the group.

It is important, however, not to idealize mentors and coaches. Mentors and coaches may well relate to those they mentor and coach in ways that are self-satisfying, domineering and manipulative.

The rest of this chapter looks at how we might think about 'techniques' that foster and sustain the capacity for practical judgment. First, practical judgment requires ongoing reflection on the judgments made and the consequences they produce. Mindless action does not yield practical judgment; instead mindful action is required in which the actors reflexively think together about how they are thinking about what they are doing. I think, then, that we can understand the first requirement of ongoing practical judgment to be an ongoing inquiry, one that takes narrative, reflexive forms. Second, practical judgment relies on ongoing participation in the conversational life of an organization in ways that widen and deepen communication. Third, practical judgment involves some degree of spontaneity and improvisation, and there are 'techniques' which can make people more aware of this. Fourth, practical judgment is essentially the ordinary politics of everyday life where the techniques of rhetoric play a part and the matter of ethics becomes of major importance. Each of these aspects will be considered in the sections that follow.

'Technique' as a mode of inquiry: narrative and reflexivity

Chapter 4 noted that the management tools and techniques of instrumental rationality take the form of rules, procedures and models which set out the steps to be followed in carrying out any leadership and management activity. It also drew attention to the fact that experts do not follow rules but, instead, make practical judgments based on experience, where those practical judgments take account of the features of a situation that are similar to those of situations previously encountered but also features that are unique to the new situation now being faced. Practical judgment is not a rule-following activity but, rather, the activity of pattern recognition. Practical judgments exercised by leaders and managers take the form of interactions with others in the course of performing some work together and so the patterns that are being recognized are the themes emerging in conversation, power relations and ideologically based choices. These are the themes that people in a situation are forming in their interaction while at the same time those themes, in organizing the experience of being together, form them. Practical judgment, therefore, is based on the ability to recognize and understand the themes emerging in group interaction – the expert manager is one who has developed the ability to notice more aspects of group dynamics than others do and a greater ability to make sense of those aspects. Expert managers form intuitions based on experience about what is going on and why. It is in this sense that it is possible to say that the major 'technique' of practical judgment in organizations is that of inquiring into what is going on and what part one is playing in this. The 'technique' is that of inquiring into why all are doing what they are doing together.

The question then becomes how such inquiry into ambiguous and uncertain themes emerging in group interaction might be carried out and how the nature of such inquiry might be expressed, given that it cannot be expressed as rules, algorithms or step-by-step procedures and can only be expressed to a very limited extent as propositions. Since in our interaction we form living narrative themes, the form of expression that is relevant to practical judgment in highly ambiguous and uncertain situations is that of narrative. What is called for then is the practice of narrative forms of inquiry because it is in the detail of the narrative that we find ourselves participating in that we can express the themes emerging in our experience, as well as the details of context, that enable us to form judgments on what is going on and what we might do as the next step. The 'technique' of narrative inquiry involves leaders, managers and members of an organization exploring together the history of the situation they find themselves in, trying to identify how they have together created this situation. Here the 'technique' requires self-discipline on the part of all in engaging in a mode of inquiry that cannot be 'controlled'. The 'technique' involves scrapping the bullet points and turning instead to narratives that provoke further reflection. So what do we mean by reflection?

In its meaning relevant to this chapter, *to reflect* means to think deeply about a subject; some synonyms are to ponder, ruminate, contemplate or speculate. Reflection is the intellectual and emotional exercise of the mind to reason, give careful consideration to something, make inferences and decisions, and find solutions. Reflection can be directed at one's own experience in order to gain a new understanding, and there are some well-known models of the individual activity of reflecting in the literature on organizations and their management. For example, there is the well-known reflective cycle suggested by Kolb.[3] This cycle involves having an experience and then reflectively observing this experience, which leads to abstract conceptualization, which leads to some kind of conclusion as to what happened. The next step is for the individual to consider what action might be taken in future situations, followed by active experimentation to test learning conclusions as the next concrete experience is embarked upon. Another influential writer, Schön,[4] drew a distinction between 'reflection-on-action' and 'reflection-in-action'. The latter is the activity of meeting professional challenges with a kind of improvised learning in practice. Reflective practice is lifelong learning in which professionals engage in reflecting on the situations they encounter in their professional work. It involves looking to our experiences, connecting with our feelings and attending to our theories in use. Practitioners are said to have a repertoire of metaphors and images that assist in finding different ways of framing a situation, so coming to see the ways in which a new situation is similar to and different from other, past situations. *Introspection* is the activity of reflecting on one's own thoughts and feelings and forming beliefs about one's own mental states.

Reflection generally, including its introspective form, is easily understood, as in the previous paragraph, as an individual activity in which the reflector as subject is outside of that which is being reflected upon as object. The subject and the object are thought of as separate even in the introspective form where 'I' as subject reflect on 'my mental states' as objects. However, what we are trying to do in reflecting and introspecting actually requires us to practise *reflexivity*. A reflexive pronoun is the object in a sentence indicating that the object is the same as the subject in that sentence. The subject and the object are then not separate but are simultaneously present. For example, I might say that 'I was washing myself' so that the reflexive pronoun 'myself' bends back to the 'I'. So, if I say that I am reflecting on, or examining, myself, then I am couching the activity in reflexive terms. However, this reflexivity should not be understood as introspection since reflexivity involves much more than introspection, and the form of reflexivity that I want to point to in this chapter needs to be distinguished from both reflection and from introspection. Reflexivity points to the impossibility of standing outside of our experience and observing it, simply because it is we who are participating in and creating the experience, always with others. Reflexivity is the activity of noticing and thinking about the nature of our involvement in our participation with each other as we do something together. So, I am using a notion of reflexivity which can only be social. Since we are interdependent individuals, reflexivity must involve thinking about how we and others involved with us are interacting, and this will involve noticing and thinking about our history together and more widely about the history of the wider communities we are part of. Furthermore, this social activity of reflexivity is the activity of noticing and thinking about how we are thinking about our participation together. When we take a reflexive stance we are asking how we have come to think as we do, and this will involve becoming more aware of the history of the traditions of thought in our communities which we are reflecting in our interactions.

In an important sense, all humans are inevitably reflexive in that mind is the activity of a body directed back to itself. It follows that all knowing and all kinds of knowledge are self-knowing and self-knowledge. We are selves who form knowledge of ourselves and selves who know others in relation to ourselves. We might call this consciousness and self-consciousness first order reflexivity to distinguish it from an intentional inquiry into these essentially social processes of self-knowing, which we might call second order reflexivity. Second order reflexivity, therefore, is essentially social processes of narrative inquiry.

While all humans are inevitably reflexive in a first order sense, not all have developed the capacity of second order reflexivity and many find it difficult to engage in this activity. In the rest of this chapter I will use the word reflexivity in its second order sense, and it is this that constitutes a 'technique' of practical judgment.

This way of reasoning amounts to a move from simply the 'reflective practitioner' to the much more complex 'reflexive practitioner'. What does this involve? Reflexive practice involves noticing and thinking about participation with others in the accomplishment of joint tasks. What is being noticed and thought about is how actors are thinking about their engagement in social processes of communication, power relations and ideology reflecting choices which together produce emergent patterns of action. Reflexive practice is more than reflective practice because it involves people in more than reflection together on what they are doing, and that more is inquiring into how they are thinking about what they are doing. It involves asking ourselves who we are, what we are doing together, why are doing it and how we are thinking about all of these questions. Reflexivity is thinking about how we are thinking.

What this section is proposing, therefore, is that the capacity for practical judgment in organizations can be sustained and developed by the 'technique' of reflexive inquiry into the narrative of what we are doing together in ambiguous and uncertain situations.

For leaders and managers, in practical terms, this means consciously creating opportunities for groups of colleagues and others to engage in the kind of inquiry that I
have been describing. In my experience this kind of more fluid, more searching
inquiry is rarely undertaken in organizations and suggestions that it should occur are
often felt to be dangerous and anxiety provoking. The response I have often found is
rejection of the suggestion because 'it would open a can of worms'. This is, of course,
true, and opening the 'can of worms' will arouse anxiety and quite possibly lead to
shifts in patterns of power relations. The disadvantage of rejecting the 'technique' of
reflexive inquiry is that the 'can of worms' may stay shut but what it represents will
continue to operate out of sight and understanding. However, developing the 'technique' of reflexive inquiry is far from simple, and many leaders and managers find it very
difficult to practise this 'technique' and therefore need some form of supervision. It is
important not to idealize reflexive inquiry and see it as some kind of panacea which
will lead to success and produce what is good. Expert reflexive inquirers have a greater
capacity to understand the responses of others, and they might use this understanding
for the collective good or they could just as easily use their enhanced understanding
in their own interests; they may become expert manipulators of others.

Leaving, for the time being, the difficulties of practising reflexive inquiry, the next
section goes on to present an understanding of the processes of reflexive inquiry as
essentially participating in conversation.

Participation in conversation: group processes as 'techniques' of widening and deepening communication

Since using the techniques of reflexive inquiry is essentially a collective activity, its
conduct requires social processes of communication which, following Mead, are
understood in the theory of complex responsive processes to be conversation. The
basic structure of conversation is the social act of gestures evoking responses in which
meaning emerges. Engaging in organizational conversations in an effective manner as
the basis of practical judgment calls for an enhanced, expert capacity on the part of
leaders and managers to understand the kinds of responses likely to be evoked by
their gestures at particular times, in particular situations, in particular groups of
people. Practical judgment calls for a wider awareness, an intuitive understanding, of
the thematic, narrative patterning of conversation. A key technique for the development of practical judgment in the interests of the collective is that of opening up
conversation rather than closing down by a hasty jump straight to what is thought of
as a 'solution'. A distinction can be drawn between patterns of conversation which
are simple and highly repetitive and patterns which are more fluid and complex.

Chapter 2 argued that the individual mind, consciousness and self-consciousness, is
social in that it is the activity, the private role play and silent conversation, of a body
directed back to itself, while the social is the same processes publicly directed by
bodies to each other. As an individual, one becomes aware of one's mind when one
recognizes the endless silent conversation one has with oneself. At times of distress
that silent conversation falls into very simple, repetitive, stuck patterns in which one

obsessively goes over the detail of some slight or hurt inflicted by another. To be stuck in this manner is highly distressing and painful and, indeed, this is exactly what happens to anyone who is clinically depressed. It is very hard to get out of this stuck pattern and it usually requires some form of distraction provided by another person or activity. On the other hand, the normal pattern of silent conversation with oneself, where one feels reasonably able to cope with ambiguity and uncertainty, is characterized by regular irregularity, or complexity. In normal patterns we find ourselves jumping rapidly from one idea or thought to another which rapidly triggers yet another thought. Creative insights can emerge in these complex conversational patterns. The public conversations in which people in organizations engage show the same possibilities. People who find themselves trapped in repetitive, jargon-filled conversation cannot produce new ideas or engage in some more creative activities. A key conversational 'technique' of the expert leader and manager is an ability to complexify conversation, often in very simple ways by asking further questions, inviting comment on some idea or requesting an historical narrative of how they have collectively come to be dealing with what they are now dealing with. The technique is to discretely invite others, particularly those who tend to be silent, into the conversation. In more complex conversation, expert leaders and managers are in effect opening up opportunities for further exploration rather than closing them down. Complex conversation widens and deepens communication and meaning through locating situations in a common history and through exploring what we are doing together and why. This forms the basis of more effective practical judgment and since we cannot endlessly open up conversation because we do need temporary closure to act, practical judgment is called for in choosing when to open up and when to close down.

Expert leaders and managers are aware of the difference between the public transcript and the hidden transcripts (see Chapter 3) that pattern conversation in organizations. They are sensitive to the covert ways in which people reveal a little of the patterns of the hidden transcripts. Since these hidden transcripts can either block or support what expert leaders and managers are trying to do, the latter are likely to make more effective practical judgment if they have some awareness of these hidden transcripts, especially bearing in mind that they too are engaged in them.

Another important 'technique' of practical judgment may be described as sensitivity to group dynamics, that is, an ability to interpret what is going on in a group. The inevitable ambiguities and uncertainties of organizational life are bound to make people feel anxious. Paying attention to anxiety and how it is defended against is thus an important 'technique' of practical judgment. This involves a keen awareness of the kinds of anxiety that particular kinds of work and particular kinds of situation are likely to arouse. Anxious groups typically resort to expressions of high degrees of dependency on their leaders and managers, waiting for instruction on what to do, thereby slowing down the responses to ambiguity and uncertainty. Or when the idealization and dependency inevitably fail, they resort to denigration and aggression. Or they may simply distance themselves psychologically from their work. Expert leaders and managers have some intuitive awareness of these patterns and have developed ways of not getting too sucked into such processes themselves, for to do so would be to reduce the capacity for practical judgment. There are also what might be called social defences against anxiety. These take the form of particular procedures or work practices, such as many of the tools of instrumental rationality, which are not accomplishing what they are publicly proclaimed to be accomplishing but are making people feel a little more secure. Another major aspect of group dynamics that experts have some awareness of has to do with patterns of power relations and the way they are expressed in patterns of inclusion and exclusion (see Chapter 3) and hence in patterns of identity. Effective practical judgment reflects the understanding that some actions can threaten identities and disrupt established patterns of relationship that enable work to get done effectively.

A particular 'technique' of conducting group meetings has to do with the nature of the agenda. Overwhelmingly, groups in organizations meet in ways that are highly structured by detailed, often rather mechanistic agendas. The usual consequence is that important issues on the minds of people, issues which are complex, ambiguous and uncertain, are side-lined and covered over. Such highly structured, instrumentally rational meetings cannot provoke, sustain or support reflexive inquiry. However, meetings which have very loose agendas may well be conducive to reflexive inquiry, if the anxiety that tends to be aroused by what looks like a lack of agenda, labelled a talking shop, can be lived with.

This section and the previous one have been concerned with the 'techniques' of reflexive inquiry, interpretation, conversation and sensitivity to group dynamics. What has been stressed is the importance of using the 'techniques' to keep opening the conversation up, although of course there are also often situations where it is important to close down. Practical judgment is knowing when to close down and when to open up. There are certain techniques in the discipline of Organization Development which can also be used to stimulate, provoke and facilitate the process of reflexive inquiry, provided that they are not used in the instrumentally rational way that is quite common. So, for example, open-space techniques used sensitively may well encourage reflexive inquiry and provoke thinking about group dynamics. Here participants numbering from 5 to 2,000 create and manage their own agenda of parallel working sessions around a central theme of importance. This may well prove an effective way of connecting people. However, in my experience, these events are usually conducted in highly orchestrated ways involving exercises which are often gimmicks that have an infanti-lizing effect, and this blocks reflexive inquiry. Similar comments can be made about the use of the well-known action learning groups, which may also provoke reflexive inquiry. However, the problem with action learning techniques is that they were originally formulated in ways that involve following rigid step-by-step procedures with a focus on task and taking action to solve problems and improve a situation. This turns action research into a technique of instrumental rationality which will block reflexive inquiry.

'Techniques' of spontaneity and improvisation

Organizational life has to be much more than the application of rules, procedures and models because none of these can cover every situation that people in an organization are confronted with. People have to interpret rules, procedures and models so that they are appropriate in unique, ambiguous and uncertain situations. In other words, practical judgment is required if we are to be able to cope with unpredictability and uncertainty and, following Bourdieu,[5] this practice can be defined as necessary improvisation. Improvisation is the spontaneous response to a pause, interval and indecision. People do not normally improvise in an intentional manner; they improvise because they have to in order to respond in uncertain situations. However, the spontaneity of improvisation should not be confused with impulse and mindlessness. Spontaneity and improvisation are essential aspects of mature practical judgment, and improvisation itself is a highly expert performance reflecting considerable experience and characterized by discipline. The importance of improvisation has been widely acknowledged in the literature[6] on organizations and is an activity many consultants work with.

Although improvisation is not normally an intentional activity, there are ways of becoming more aware of processes of spontaneity and improvisation in organizational life. One of the fairly widely used 'techniques' for doing this is the use of the theatre.[7] Theatre has always played a part in the way people have understood the relationship between the person and society, between individual experience and socio/political processes. Theatre has been taken into organizations in the last twenty years, particularly in France, Germany, England, Canada, the USA and Scandinavia. There is a considerable literature which tries to identify the particular contribution that theatre can make. Is it a tool for communicating 'messages' or 'reducing equivocality'? Is it a training device for skill development; a mirror in which people recognize the conflicts in which they are caught up; a role-playing rehearsal for future action; a rallying ground for breaking 'oppression'; a useful precursor to other organization development activities? Most approaches to using theatre in organizations sit within the dominant discourse on organizational change in that they see theatre and improvisation used in client organizations as tools for producing particular results.

However, the Danish Dacapo Theatre[8] takes a different approach. It is well known for its ability to engage small and large audiences in live dialogue about change processes taking place in their organizations. The company consists of actors and consultants, and they work together with an audience of managers and other organizational members. When a client organization invites Dacapo to do some consulting work, the actors and consultants spend some time getting to know the people and situation of the organization. They are looking for important stories of life in the organization, particularly those stories reflecting the difficulties people are having. With members of the client organization the actors and consultants then select a story which will be performed as a theatre piece. The piece performed is not exactly the same as the story selected, but it is close enough for organizational members to recognize the situation. The piece is then performed in front of an audience of members of the client organization. After enough of the piece has been performed to give the audience some idea of the situation, the consultant stops the play and asks people what they think is going on and what they think should be done next to deal with the problem emerging in the play. The invitation is to participate in reflexive narrative inquiry. This usually provokes a lively discussion and people come up with solutions to the problem, often stating their case very confidently. The consultant then invites one of the proposers of a solution to take the place of one of the actors and perform his or her recommendation. It is then that the play takes on the unmistakable characteristics of improvisation. None of the performers know what kinds of responses are about to be evoked and they have to carry on dealing spontaneously with what happens, and what happens often surprises everyone. Unlike many, therefore, Dacapo members work in a way that does not split the theatre episode they provide from the reflection on it but has them both happening at the same time as members of the audience take up the roles of actors and improvise on further development. In other words, they have moved from scripted plays to theatre improvisation as a basis for their work, in which changes in thinking and relating take place as people work with theatre not afterwards. This amounts to a 'technique' of reflexivity, an exercise in coming to understand the nature of practical judgment.

The actors and consultants in this company understand the contribution that their form of consulting makes to organizations in terms of Mead's view of communication, which takes the form of gestures made by one person evoking responses from others and it is in this temporal, relational process that meaning emerges. This is an improvisational view of human communication. It follows that improvisation is not a skill located in an autonomous individual but, rather, a relational and spontaneously responsive activity. The Dacapo approach, therefore, is one that deliberately fosters spontaneous interaction between everyone involved in the work, including themselves. Together, they improvise their way forward while continuing to find out what emerges between them. In doing this, they are not following a planned script but, rather, improvising their way forward in the same way as the other participants. What they are trying to do is to bring themselves and others into situations where no one can rely on carefully planned actions, but must risk responding spontaneously to one another. It is in this way that people are able to recognize themselves, each other and their work in new ways. It is in ordinary improvisational, conversational activity that modes of practice and the abilities of practitioners come alive and evolve.

The improvisational nature of organizational life is nowhere more evident than in the practice of ordinary, everyday organizational politics. An essential aspect of practical judgment is the ability to operate effectively in these ordinary political activities, and it is possible to identify what we might call some 'techniques' of ordinary, everyday politics.

'Techniques' of ordinary, everyday politics: rhetoric and truth telling

Members of groups, organizations and societies are all, as interdependent agents, engaged with each other in very serious games which are of great importance because as agents they are invested in these games – each has status, affection, recognition and money to gain or lose depending on how he or she 'plays' the game and also, at the same time, on how all the others are playing. Participating in the game means participating in ongoing processes of communication, understood as conversation, in which emerge patterns of power relations involving inclusion in and exclusion from more and less powerful groupings. As they make their moves in the game, as they choose utterances and actions reflecting their ideologies, they find that because they are interdependent they cannot simply achieve what they desire. Moves in the game always amount to attempts to direct, to persuade, to negotiate and to compromise. It is in this sense that we can say that the games we are invested in are inevitably and fundamentally political, but they are political in an ordinary, everyday sense rather than in the grand, national or party politics sense. It follows that the exercise of practical judgment by expert leaders and managers is a political activity in the ordinary, everyday sense in which they seek to direct, persuade, negotiate and compromise with those they lead and manage, those who lead and manage them, and their peer colleagues. Given the importance of ordinary, everyday politics in the expression of practical judgment, it is sensible to consider whether we can talk about 'techniques' of ordinary politics.

Leaders and managers use particular 'techniques' when they undertake what might be called control acts involving giving directives or instructions, making requests, calling in and granting favours, offering and receiving advice, making prohibitions and issuing invitations. Of course, at the same time, those leaders and managers are responding to the directives, requests and so on, coming from their superiors and peers.[9] In issuing directives to subordinates, leaders and managers use imperative forms of language, for example 'I want' or 'I need'. Holmes and Stubbe have analysed many conversations of the kind in which superiors issue directives to subordinates:

> Speakers exploit a variety of linguistic and pragmatic devices to intensify their directives, increasing the volume of their utterance, using contrastive stress, incorporating intensifiers such as *very*, *definitely*, *just*, making use of deontic modals such as *must* and *have to* and strategies such as repetition, and so on.[10]

Leaders and managers also mitigate the directives they give by using language that reduces the direct explicit force of the directives and sometimes by preceding the directives with praise. It is, of course, a matter of practical judgment whether to intensify or mitigate an instruction, and this will depend upon the context established by, for example, the length and nature of the personal relationship with the subordinate. Instructions are not always direct but can often be indirect when this is judged to be more likely to secure compliance. There is an ongoing negotiation around the pressure to get the job done and the need to take account of people's feelings. Politeness becomes an important 'technique' in securing compliance with directives and the use of humour can soften the impact of a directive. The 'technique' of politeness becomes even more important when trying to get a peer to comply in some way. It becomes important to preserve the dignity of one's equal if one is to secure their cooperation. There are also techniques which leaders and managers deploy in trying to get the cooperation of those who lead and manage them. This may involve making requests in a somewhat hesitant, apologetic way in which what is being asked for is minimized. Deference and politeness are very important 'techniques' here.

An extremely important aspect of practical judgment is the activity of persuading others and yielding to their persuasion. We might look for the 'techniques' of persuasion in the discipline of rhetoric. Rhetoric may be understood as the techniques of prose composition or speech which enable one to influence the judgment or feelings of others. It is the art of using language effectively. An expert leader or manager may use a number of rhetorical devices, which are forms of language use intended to make others receptive to the views of the leader or manager through emotional responses and through rational argument. For example, the rhetorical device of irony, that is, saying one thing while obviously meaning its opposite, may be used to deprecate or ridicule the views of rivals. Irony conveys incongruence to others, often in a humorous way. Another rhetorical device is the use of metaphors to convey new ideas to others by linking them to some idea or meaning that is already familiar. Some other rhetorical devices are: alliteration, which is the repetition of the beginning sound of a word; assonance, which is the repetition of a similar set of sounds to emphasize intensity; antithesis, which is the opposition or contrast of ideas; hyperbole, which is exaggeration for effect.

Rhetorical devices:

- influence the path of conversation by invoking a sense of purpose, as when someone says, 'these are *the* objectives'; or when someone makes silencing moves such as not responding to a point made but rapidly raising another; or when someone makes dismissive moves, such as saying 'this is really Stone Age stuff' or 'there is no appetite for this'; or when someone contracts the line of conversation with remarks like 'let's concentrate on the key points'; or when someone expands the line of conversation with remarks like 'there must be other ways to think about this'; or when someone gives emphasis by saying 'this is the way we must go';
- provide frames of reference as when someone uses other companies as examples of the successful application of their ideas or claims that there is scientific evidence;
- make claims to the truth when someone says 'the latest research shows' or 'customers feel';
- destabilize by using remarks such as 'does that really add anything?' or 'so what?';
- influence beliefs about what is real and possible – examples are making the intangible seem tangible, such as talking about a merger as a 'marriage' or talking about getting into bed with another company, referring to a company as if it were a person, and using statements like 'let me walk you through this'; another example is a move that implies pre-existence, as when people talk about unlocking a company's potential;
- construct urgency with remarks like 'there is a short time window'.

Without even being aware of it, people in ordinary conversation may be using rhetorical devices to dismiss the opinions of others and close down the development of a conversation in an exploratory direction. If this way of talking to each other is widespread in an organization, it will inevitably keep reproducing the same patterns of conversation. The use of some rhetorical devices is therefore one of the most important blockages to free-flowing, flexible conversation and thus the emergence of new knowledge. Other usages of rhetorical devices, however, could have the effect of freeing these blockages.

Chapters 4 and 5 explained why the tools and techniques of instrumental rationality could not possibly produce what is claimed for them. They cannot enable leaders and managers to choose the future and control movement towards that choice. However, when one bears in mind the fundamentally political nature of ordinary, everyday life in organizations, it becomes possible to understand why leaders and managers nevertheless present their arguments in terms of such tools and techniques. They do so because a managerialist ideology discussion of what to do in the terms of instrumental rationality is easily understood and likely to be more persuasive than other forms of argument. In other words, in addition to serving as techniques of disciplinary power, the tools and techniques of instrument rationality are important rhetorical devices. The proclaimed use of the tools and techniques has the effect of covering over how they operate as discipline and how leaders and managers use them as rhetorical devices in the game of organizational politics. This covering over, however, does probably reduce the anxiety people in organizations may feel in confronting matters of power and uncertainty. So the tools and techniques of instrumental rationality, by promising a known future, do operate as social defences against anxiety. However, on the other hand, the covering over also results in repetitive actions and blocks reflexive inquiry.

Foucault[11] contrasted the ancient Greek concept of *parresia*, meaning truth telling, with rhetoric, the art of persuading others. The objective of truth telling is not that of persuading others but that of staying as close as possible to the reality of what it is referring to. This truth telling reflects the being of the one engaged in it, in its simplicity and spontaneity. Truth telling involves standing back and taking a stand. The rhetorical discourse is one in which the speaker claims to know and uses this to persuade others so that they may know what they do not know. The truth tellers do not claim to know but continually test themselves and those they are speaking to. Rhetoric is a way of prevailing over one's rivals rather than telling the truth, although it need not amount to outright lying.

However, it is important to avoid idealizing truth telling. It is quite possible that truth telling, in particular situations, would produce disastrous animosity between people, making it impossible for them to carry on working together. It might be vital for ongoing collective performance to sometimes adopt strategies of avoiding conflict through the use of rhetorical devices. On other occasions, however, such as corruption and exploitation, it is of great importance to a human organization that its members tell the truth. Clearly it is a matter of practical judgment when to tell the truth and when to use rhetoric to avoid breakdowns in relationships. This makes it clear that, in the end, practical judgment is a fundamentally ethical matter.

Conclusion

This chapter picks up on the argument presented in Chapter 5 that instrumentally rational tools and techniques may enable competent leadership and management but they cannot produce proficient, expert leadership and management. Expert leaders and managers act according to practical judgment which they have acquired in the experience of learning how to lead and manage. What this chapter has sought to do is to explore how we might understand the nature of practical judgment and how the capacity for it may be sustained and developed. First, it was argued that the exercise of practical judgment is essentially a social and political activity which should take strong account of the ethics of acting, although, of course, some experts may use their expertise to act in skilfully corrupt and unethical ways. Next it was suggested that the capacity for practical judgment could be enhanced by the 'technique' of reflexive inquiry as members of a group. The 'techniques' of practical judgment encompass a well-developed sensitivity to group dynamics, an ability to judge when to hold ongoing conversation open and when it is necessary to reach temporary closure, an ability to improvise and an ability to engage in the organizational game of politics in persuasive and effective ways. In terms of actual leadership and management performance, these 'techniques' are of far more importance than the tools and techniques of instrumental rationality.

10

CONCLUSION

Frequently asked questions

The theory of complex responsive processes itself does not lead to generalized prescriptions because it describes processes in which generalizations of all kinds emerge. It is in itself not a prescription since it describes responsive processes producing all forms of power relations, including modern disciplinary power which is exercised through particular prescriptive techniques. People paying attention to their own particular responsive processes will formulate their own particular prescriptions for dealing with difference and conflict. In this reflection they will be forming judgments as to whether the techniques of discipline and coercion are ethical or not and what ideologies they reflect. They may, for example, judge that in present times we are taking the techniques of power required for our kind of society to extremes which undermine what we think is our kind of society. We might then conclude that we need to find ways to reverse the ever increasing surveillance. The theory of complex responsive processes is not itself an ideology since it is an account of how all ideologies emerge, but when we reflect on our own particular responsive processes we can glimpse the particular ideologies which they reflect. The theory of complex responsive processes does not produce generalized macro prescriptions but explains how they continue to emerge in the local interactions in which they are made particular.

The key points that I have been trying to make in this book are the following:

- The leadership and management tools and techniques of instrumental rationality cannot enable leaders and managers to choose the future of their organizations; nor can they enable leaders and managers to control the process of realizing whatever choices they make. This is because the assumed 'if ... then' causality required for the tools to do what is claimed for them simply does not apply to human interaction. Furthermore, expert leaders and managers have to move past tools and techniques to exercise practical judgment in ambiguous and uncertain situations.

- However, although the tools and techniques do not enable leaders and managers to control outcomes, they do enable them to control the bodies of others and the activities of those bodies to a considerable degree. The tools and techniques of instrumental rationality are in actual practice the techniques of disciplinary power, namely, surveillance, normalization and examination. The important point, though, is that leaders and managers are themselves subject to disciplinary power in patterns of interaction in which no one is unconstrained.
- The problem is that unreflexive use of the techniques of disciplinary power can lead to extremes of domination, coercive persuasion, bullying and totalitarianism.
- Forms of power and forms of ideology are expressed in institutions and institutional techniques take the form of habits, rules and routines. Leaders and managers have a limited ability to design rules, procedures and routines, but they can never fully control how they are taken up in local situations.
- Finally, expert leadership and management take the form of practical judgment. This pattern-recognizing capacity is developed through experience but it can be sustained and enhanced by using 'techniques' of supervision and mentoring, reflexive inquiry, widening and deepening communication, sensitivity to group dynamics and adroit participation in the ordinary, everyday politics of organizational life, making use of rhetoric and truth telling. In the end, practical judgment is a matter of ethics.

When they are exposed to this kind of reasoning, many leaders and managers experience some distress at the puncturing of grand illusions in which well-meaning individuals can produce improved futures with some certainty. So, by way of concluding, I would like to return to the kind of questions I am frequently and persistently asked when I present the kind of view outlined above.

Which organizations have taken up complex responsive processes and what has been the outcome?

This request is perfectly reasonable if you are coming from the now taken-for-granted understanding that useful literature on organizations provides prescriptions/techniques for how people can secure better outcomes. If one cannot provide 'evidence' of the successful outcomes obtained by thinking about what one is doing as complex responsive processes of relating, then people dismiss what I am saying. However, what I think many find it difficult to see is that I am trying to do something different which does not involve providing tools or producing evidence but which is still of major importance. I am trying to indicate an alternative way of thinking about organizational life which focuses our attention on what we actually are already doing in organizations rather than what we should be doing to achieve outcomes. What I am trying to point to are the processes in which we produce both good and bad 'outcomes'. As we think about these processes of actual daily life in organizations, we come to realize that an 'outcome' is an artificial and static location of events that are simply ongoing. Furthermore, if we take the kind of perspective I am suggesting, we have to accept that complex nonlinear interactions produce unpredictable patterns – they are unpredictable because simple 'if ... then' causal links do not apply. So we can never claim that an 'outcome' was caused by a particular intervention – it is all too complex. This means that 'evidence' for management prescriptions can never be found. What we are left with is judgment on whether some kinds of action are more 'fruitful' in some ways than other actions. I do believe that if people think differently about what they are doing, they will find that in small ways they are carrying out their work differently. So for me there are very few generalized prescriptions, just people making local practical judgments about what they should do next. Asking for examples of successful organizations and successful outcomes makes no sense from the perspective I am trying to present. What makes sense is asking ourselves what we are doing and how we are doing it and why, rather than hoping to find the 'best practice' by looking at what others seem to be doing.

How can one use the insights of complex responsive processes? What do you say to those who claim that there are some easily recognizable laws or principles that could generate a better atmosphere and therefore better outcomes?

I am identifying what seems to me to be going on in all organizations already – I am claiming that people in organizations accomplish whatever they accomplish in complex responsive processes of relating to each other in their local situations. These complex responsive processes are ordinary, everyday conversations between people involving gesturing and responding. These processes are also processes of power relating, and they are processes of people making choices about what to say and do and these choices always reflect ideologies. What I am saying, therefore, is that organizational life is the practice of ordinary, everyday politics in which we seek to dominate and persuade others and also in which we seek to practise both overt and covert resistance. Everyday activities include gossip, hidden transcripts and the strategic poses we strike. So what I am describing is, I think, very clearly identifiable in every organization, no matter how big or small, no matter what sector or country. These are the processes in which we accomplish what is good and what is evil. I resist talking about 'applying' what I am saying to organizations so that they improve. But if I am describing how we together do what we do, both good and evil, both effective and ineffective, both sustainable and not sustainable, then it is already all going on so there is nothing abstract to apply. In another sense you can say that it is already being applied – people are already talking and struggling with each other to get things done so there is nothing new to be taken out of what I say. What is 'new' is that I am directing attention to it, to what we are already doing, and inviting reflection on this – what are we doing and why are we doing it? If you like, this is a general prescription – reflect on what you are doing. There are also others – I am claiming that it would be useful if policy-makers thought more about how people are going to respond to policy directives in their local interactions. I am saying that excessive imposition of targets predictably results in people 'gaming the system'.

So, there are some general types of prescription but they are not about doing things better and this disappoints most people. Of course I want things to improve but I am saying there is no abstract general principle telling us what to do – if there were, we would already have found it, surely. Instead, we have to find ways in our local interactions of improving things and to deal with it if our well-intentioned actions turn out to have unwanted consequences. Instead, I am saying that in our local interactions we are developing more specific prescriptions for the particular context we are in – after all, we have to act. The point is that we can find very few prescriptions which will cover all the unique contexts we find ourselves in. Also, what is being identified is being identified in our experience.

The way we can use the knowledge and insights is by reflecting upon them in the specific contexts we are experiencing. If I am a policy-maker and I notice that hospitals meet their waiting targets but still people wait for long times and I find out that they appear to meet the targets because they bend the rules, then I might start asking if imposing these targets is very helpful in the first place. If I go down this route with others, we might come up with more sensible policy options. So what I am saying, then, is that if you are motivated to attend to certain issues, you will find yourself engaging in the conversational and political activities around these issues and what you and others do might produce more useful activities or your actions may have 'outcomes' that surprise you, even ones you certainly did not want. I am always wary of claims of having found easily recognizable principles for anything in human action. That is not to say, however, that it is useless to choose a certain action and work with what comes of it. Certainly we have to do this but, instead of thinking so firmly in terms of laws, we might do better to think in terms of ideologically driven, ordinary political interaction.

Can organizations which foster healthier social environments, a matter of quality, be identified? Do they produce better outcomes? What fosters something positive among the people? Why are some organizations better able to produce good outcomes?

Clearly, some groups of people, some organizations, achieve more than others do. They may make more money, they may provide more beautiful artifacts and music, good works, first-class health services. Also, clearly, some groups of people, some organizations, change and evolve as innovation and creativity emerge in their interactions with each other, while others seek strenuously to stay the same so preserving tradition (e.g. the Roman Catholic Church), while yet others struggle to change but find themselves stuck. However, it must be borne in mind that as soon as I say that people in this organization do creative things and people in that organization are stuck, I am making a judgment not stating a fact. So when you talk about 'quality' and 'healthier social environments', you are making a judgment too. We always have made such judgments and we always will as part of our striving to improve our lives. It then makes sense to ask what it is that renders some groups of people more, say, creative in our judgment. I think there are some things we can say about this, but trying to link what we judge to be ways of interacting that are, say, more creative to beneficial outcomes is bound to be extremely difficult, I would say even impossible. This is because in complex processes the links between cause and effect are lost as tiny differences can escalate into major outcomes that no one expected or even wants. So in the end we have to act on our collective judgment that some form of interaction is 'good' in itself and then deal with whatever outcomes we produce between us.

So what are the characteristics of forms of interaction that are 'good' in themselves? The basic complex responsive processes are conversation, communicative interaction. If members of a group are conversing in ways that are questioning, fluid, opening up the exploration of meaning, then I would judge that they are capable of changing, while groups stuck in highly repetitive conversation in which they are seeking only closure will find themselves incapable of being creative. Another important form of complex responsive processes is that of the power relations between us. In terms of power relations we are never equal – the power ratio is always tilted towards some and away from others. When the power imbalance is tilted to an extreme, there is a pattern of power relations that we call fascism, which includes communist dictatorships too. History has shown that fascist power structures block change while more equal power distributions enable and constrain change. In fascist power relations where terror is used to block any dissent, the arts of resistance are driven deep underground, making disasters more likely. Power relations are reflections of ideologies, what Mead called cult values. Mead said that in the normal course of events cult values are made functional to specific situations and this always leads to conflict. Where cult values are not functionalized, we have a cult which demands complete conformity. When we interact in cultish ways, we banish the ongoing conflict which gives rise to change and the movement of thought. So there are things along these lines that I think it is possible to say are reflections of our experience. But more equal power relations, more fluid conversation and more functionalizing of our cult values can never be a simple guarantee of some improved outcome and they cannot be regarded as universal prescriptions, tools or techniques.

Is the theory of complex responsive processes postmodern?

The theory of complex responsive processes does not fall into the postmodern camp. In a way it is rather more modernist but not in the sense of an external, objective observer who derives rational rules and principles. However, the theory of complex responsive processes does not present multiple perspectives undistorted by power considerations and so cannot be called postmodern. I do not believe one perspective is as good as another. I am claiming that it is far more useful to make sense of orga-nizational life in the way I suggest than by taking other perspectives. You can never have conversation without power relations. Postmodernists distrust the explanatory power of grand narratives, but in a way I am suggesting a grand narrative in which I am claiming that always and everywhere human interaction is conversation, is power relating, is ideologically based human choice. So I cannot belong to the postmodern camp. However, I also do not belong in a clear way to the modernist camp and I certainly do not follow a positivist method. I guess I would have to say that some aspects of the theory are modernist while others may relate to postmodernism.

As a manager, what could I do with the insight that strategies are emergent patterns of action arising in the interplay of choices made by many different groups of people? Surely there is more to it than just thinking? Surely there are tools and techniques for bringing about improvement?

I think these questions point to the emotional reason that makes it so hard to avoid clinging to tools and this is the whole question of global improvement. If there are no tools and techniques, then how can we improve the whole organization or the whole society? Pointing to the impossibility of doing this in any direct way punctures idealistic grandiosity as well as sincere altruism and so is felt to be depressing. However, understanding that grandiose designs do not work does not mean abandoning any idealistic concern with improving the human conditions of life. It simply means taking a humbler stance and working realistically in our own local interactions to improve what we can. Furthermore, as previous chapters have pointed out, there are techniques of leading and managing: there are the techniques of disciplinary power through which the activities of organizational members are controlled, even though the outcomes of their activities cannot be; there are techniques of policy formation and design of procedures as the expression in organizations of institutions; and there are also ways to support and develop the expert activities of leaders and managers as they exercise the all-important practical judgment.

How can we influence the game so that people play it in more positive ways?

The theory of complex responsive processes problematizes the notion that order and change in society, economies and organizations are the result of the plans formulated by the powerful and applied by hierarchies of managers. Instead, it appeals to the sciences of complexity and to the research done by pragmatist and process sociologists to claim that it is in many, many local interactions that there emerge across whole populations coherent, orderly–disorderly patterns of action which we in our conversation label as credit crunches, poverty, improvement, environmental damage, well-being, resilience or whatever. Although coherent and orderly–disorderly, these population-wide patterns, which are creative and also destructive, constituting continuity and change at the same time, are unpredictable, surprising, unexpected and undesirable and at the same time they are predictable, unsurprising, expected and desirable. If this is the case, then centralized policies, statements and laws can only be gestures whose meaning will emerge in the responses to them in many, many local interactions.

This is a very different way of thinking compared to the dominant discourse, but that dominant discourse will inevitably constitute the way in which people at first try to understand a theory that challenges it. At first they will try to cast the challenge in the very terms of the dominant discourse which the challenge is trying to move from. As a consequence, the challenge will be misunderstood but it is this misunderstanding which provokes the struggle for understanding. From the perspective of the dominant discourse it is natural to conclude that because my explanation encompasses paradox, certain-uncertainty and emergence, that explanation is one which regards human action as arbitrary, transient, not fixed and definite. However, this is not what I am arguing at all. I am arguing that the reality (which is not a 'system') which we create together, the actual reality of our experience not a perception of something outside our interaction that we engage in, is coherent, orderly–disorderly and ongoing in ways that involve understandings from our past and expectations for our futures. These patterns are dynamically iterated over often very long time periods and they are not transient – the pattern called the Roman Catholic Church has been iterated for nearly 2,000 years. I am arguing that continuity and change are dynamically sustained at the same time by the ongoing processes of interaction between us.

Many respond to what I write and say in ways that I often do not recognize as connected to what I have written or said. This is hardly surprising given that meaning emerges in the response to the gesture. When I try to understand these responses, the central point, for me, is the overpowering desire people have to continue thinking that one person, or group of persons, can create the conditions, usually systemic conditions, which will cause other people to produce better outcomes, or, in another expression, influence the game so that others will play it in a more positive way, or, in yet another articulation, design a better system that will produce improved outcomes. This way of thinking naturally links to another closely similar thought, namely, that influencing government policy is the route to better conditions, improved games and more effective systems so as to produce positive improvements. These beliefs are in the service of strong ideologies such as saving the planet, improving human well-being, creating greater resilience and improving local communities in some respect. Given that people are powerfully caught in this way of thinking, it is not surprising that they will respond to what I or anyone else may say by immediately jumping to how it could help to create the system conditions, influence the game, improve the system design, shape the policies of the government so that they can get the outcomes they so strongly believe will be good. When I call this whole way of thinking into question, the responses range from dismissal, bemusement and even outrage to inquiring more deeply into the challenge to dominant ways of thinking.

On what basis am I problematizing the dominant way of thinking that has such a powerful hold on us today? The first basis is our experience. In the 1960s, as an unquestioning positivist economist, I learned how to build mathematical models and use data and statistical techniques to identify macroeconomic regularities that could be used to improve government policy. I focused much of my education and research work on the economics of underdeveloped countries, particularly Africa where I was born, in order to identify ways of aiding their development and improving the lives of their people, all of which I now understand as the expression of a powerful ideology. When I think about my experience since that time I can only conclude that well-meaning actions have often had disastrous consequences. We are still discussing the same issues half a century later and we are still being surprised at the unexpected consequences of our actions and how we continue to produce what no sane person wants. My experience in industry taught me that we cannot forecast what will happen in organizations, economies and society as the result of what we are together doing. Now we can just go on ignoring this experience or we can take a reflexive stance and inquire more deeply into why all this is happening and what it points to about our ways of thinking. I am motivated to take this second course.

The second basis for problematizing currently dominant modes of thinking is the insights coming from the complexity sciences, particularly those relating to inherent uncertainty and the emergence of coherent population-wide patterns in many, many local interactions. The third basis is to be found in pragmatist and process sociology conceptions of agency and society. The second and third bases, I think, provide a way of thinking that helps to make more sense of the experience described as the first basis. This way of thinking involves taking a reflexive perspective on experience, asking what it is that we are actually doing while perhaps using dominant models to cover over what it is that we are actually doing. My argument is that we are actually always engaging in local interactions and that this takes the form of complex responsive processes of relating, that is, communicative interaction (conversation) between us, figurations of power relations which reflect ideologies, which in turn are expressed in our intentions, plans, policies and choices, all of which are constrained in some way or another. In other words, what we are doing all the time is engaging in the ordinary politics of everyday life. If anyone recognizes all of this in their own experience, they will hopefully start challenging their taken-for-granted ways of thinking about what they are actually doing.

So how might we think differently? We can turn to the sociologists Mead, Elias and Bourdieu to understand that what we are doing all day is engaging in various games in which we are invested. Groups, organizations and societies are all games that matter to us because we have stakes in them: money, self-respect, recognition by others, the esteem of others, fulfilment, love, status and so on. Engaging in the game is engaging in the local interactions of conversation, power relations and ideology reflecting intentions and choices, that is, engaging in the ordinary politics of daily life. The games are population-wide coherent patterns emerging in the interplay of local interactions – it is this interplay which produces the patterns and no one can fully know what the interplay is or control what that interplay will be, hence the surprising, the unexpected and the undesired as well as their opposites. In these games people articulate views about the emerging population-wide patterns and form desires for what they should be. These articulations form the basis of policies, laws and guidance issued by centralized legitimate authorities, all of which are taken up in local interactions in which their meaning arises.

If we take up this way of thinking, what do we make of the claim that that one person, or group of persons, can create the conditions which will cause other people to produce better outcomes, or influence the game so that others will play it in a more positive way, or design a better system that will produce improved outcomes?

The first point to notice is that this is a claim that people, particularly in the form of governments, can act on other people from a distance. As the anthropologist James C. Scott points out in his book *Seeing Like a State*, this form of control from a distance is essential to modern social life. We could not have the complex, sophisticated societies we live in without a form of control from a distance. However, the techniques of such control are always and inevitably context-free simplifications and generalizations, and those affected by them will have to interpret and mould them to the specific contingencies of the specific situations they find themselves in. For this reason, the centrally imposed policies will never work in completely the ways expected and indeed if they are simply applied without adjustment, they lead to catastrophes.

The second point to note about the claim that a person can create conditions, influence the game and design the system to bring about improvement is that these are ideological statements. I am using the term ideology here to encompass norms and values, what we feel restricted to do and what we feel voluntarily compelled to do for the good. We can never act without ideology. However, strongly held ideologies also blind us and distort what we see. So as I use it, ideology both helps and hinders, and humans can never act in ideology-free ways, no matter how scientific they are.

The third point to notice is how the claim about conditions, games and designs is made from a position outside of the interaction which is to be conditioned, influenced or designed. So people talk about designing a system which will improve something. However, the idea of 'system' is an abstraction which we reify and anthropomorphize, forgetting that it is simply a conceptual device to think about what we are producing 'as if' it were a system. As soon as we do this, we lose sight of the game. We then talk about influencing the game as if we can stand outside of it and operate on it. However, we cannot step outside of interaction, although we can make mental abstractions from it. In thinking that we can step outside, we lose sight of the fact that in playing the game we are trying to influence other players, not the game, because the game is emerging in our playing it. Some powerful people may create some conditions from afar but how this will affect anything depends on their impact on those who are playing the game in particular situations at particular times. So, if one is being driven by an ideology of saving the planet or improving human well-being, one is engaged in a game with others, businessmen, politicians, scientists and so on. The game will involve lobbying politicians to change laws and policies in the way the lobbyists believe will be best. They may succeed and policy changes may be made, but what effect they will have will depend on how they are taken up in local interaction and this will produce the unexpected and the undesired as well as the expected and the desired.

Some people conclude from what I write or say that I am dismissing all attempts to influence politicians or to formulate policies and make centralized gestures. However, since this is what people actually do, I am interested in what they are doing when they are doing it. So what then causes the difficulty some have with what I am saying? I think it may be difficult, especially in the grip of a powerful ideology, to have to come to terms with the limitations of centralized gestures such as policies and laws. With the very best intentions and the most well-meaning efforts it is not possible in a world of uncertain responses to know in advance that our actions will produce the positive and the good. This is by no means a prescription to stop trying. Instead we could come to understand our ideologies as cult values, after Mead, where cult values are the most precious part of our heritage expressed as generalized idealizations that have to be made functional in particular circumstances and this will always lead to conflict. The alternative is to simply apply the idealization in a conformist manner, in which case we constitute a cult.

My use of the word 'local' may also be understood in a different way from that which I intend. For some, the 'local' relates to local communities, local food supply, local energy supply or local economies. These are all to be distinguished from the national and it is the national that is the determining factor for these local communities and economies. Others interpret 'local' to be equivalent to bottom-up forms of management in which hierarchical impositions are minimized in flat structures or other forms of organization. However, what I am talking about is local *interaction* and hierarchies are also sustained in local interaction so there is no implication of necessarily hierarchically free bottom-up forms of management. People often think that in emphasizing local *interaction*, which is ongoing responsive processes of conversation, power relating, ideology and constrained choice, I am dismissing the national, that is, population-wide patterns. But of course I am not doing this at all. If we think reflexively about what people in cabinets, parliaments, government departments, political parties and other lobbying bodies of one sort or another are doing, they are all engaging in local interaction. Shifting groupings of them engage in conversation, power relations and ideological expressions affecting the choices they make, choices in which they enable and constrain each other. So of course anyone who is motivated to do something that they believe is good for local communities and economies will have to engage in one way or another with the local interactions of people in government departments and other relevant bodies. I have never written anything that dismisses the importance of engaging in political games – I think all organizations and the activities of managing and leading are ordinary political activities. The point to remember is that policies articulated in the local interactions of national politics will only have meaning, will only constitute dynamic knowledge, in the responses of those to whom they are addressed. So I am not dismissing the need to engage in the politics, as some think I am, but I am suggesting that one might play the game better if one reflected on the practical nature of that game rather than being so caught up with one's own ideology. This is not an injunction to abandon ideology because that is impossible, and it would be inhuman even if it was possible.

What about facts and evidence?

Some who listen to me talk are concerned about the implications for causality and positivism. The theory of complex responsive processes amounts to a rejection of positivism as a method of researching human action. There is, however, nothing at all novel about such a position because this rejection is widespread in modern research communities in the fields of organization studies, management and leadership. In these fields it is no longer necessary to critique quantitative methods or positivism to make the case for using qualitative methods such as grounded theory, narrative methods, ethnography and reflexivity because it is now widely accepted that quantitative and positivist approaches do not reveal much about human action and human experience. Positivism is built on a notion of linear, efficient causality with an *if–then* structure, and this is incompatible with phenomena displaying complexity because such phenomena are nonlinear. Complexity sciences are the sciences of uncertainty and they challenge traditional science which is the science of certainty.

Furthermore, the complexity sciences, as well as social constructionism and other sociological and philosophical writings, problematize notions of the 'empirical' and 'evidence'. The complexity sciences also problematize standard statistical analytical techniques such as regression. So I am not saying there is nothing empirical in our lives or that there is never evidence; it is just that we need to question statements claiming to be empirical facts and be sceptical of evidence claims. For example, some say that it is a 'fact' that *if* you have more money, *then* this will not lead to happiness. This is an 'if–then' causal statement and it is highly problematic to make such statements about what is essentially nonlinear interaction. So the 'fact' is actually taking totally for granted what 'happy' means without displaying awareness of the philosophical debate about what 'happiness' is, which has been going on for thousands of years. This statement of 'fact' is also a highly abstract generalization which is made in a completely decontextualized, ahistorical manner, so, not surprisingly, there are immediate counter-examples – if you are poor, some extra money probably does make you happier. Also some people get pleasure, which may or may not be happiness, simply by accumulating masses of money even though they may hardly spend any of it.

APPENDIX

Reflexive narrative inquiry: movements in my thinking and how I find myself working differently as a consequence

Chapter 9 above sought to articulate what one might think of as 'techniques' for developing and sustaining expert leadership and management in the ambiguity, uncertainty and hence unpredictability that characterize, to varying degrees, all the situations that managers and leaders face. The chapter suggested that perhaps the most important of these 'techniques' is what we might call *reflexive narrative inquiry*, the purpose of this inquiry being to develop a greater understanding of what we are doing together and why we are doing it in a particular way. In other words, reflexive inquiry is processes of gaining deeper insight into the practical judgments we are together making in ongoing organizational life as a means of further developing that joint expert capacity. At the time of writing this book, I work as a member of a group of research supervisors on a doctoral programme that colleagues and I initiated eleven years ago, with newer colleagues now continuing to develop it. The Doctor of Management programme is necessarily a part-time research programme in that each researcher is required to research his or her own work in whatever role and whatever organization they work in. The research method of this programme is that of reflexive narrative inquiry and each participant on the programme is required to start the process of reflexive inquiry with an exploration of the major events and ideas which have led them to think and work in the ways in which they now find themselves thinking and working. Since thinking and working are fundamentally social processes, this inquiry must inevitably say something about how one has been formed in the groups, communities and societies one has lived in, and continues to live in, and this also involves an awareness of the history of those groupings and the traditions of thought they reflect. Such reflexive narratives constitute the first chapter of each person's doctoral dissertation.

This book has argued that this method of reflexive narrative inquiry is not simply a professional–academic research method but also the main 'technique' we have available to us to explore what we are doing as expert leaders and managers so as to sustain and further develop the capacity for practical judgment. Given the importance attached to reflexive inquiry in the book, I felt motivated to do myself what we require of our research students and what is also presented as a much more general technique of expert leadership and management. This appendix, then, is an account of the most important events, ideas, work experiences and group memberships that indicate how I have come to think and work in the way that I now do. I want to try to point to how, as I find myself in different groupings of people, I come to think in somewhat different ways which have a great deal to do with what I find myself doing differently in the work that I do.

So, to begin the narrative at what seems like a relevant point, I started studying for a Bachelor of Commerce degree at the University of the Witwatersrand, South Africa, in February 1960. I intended to follow this with a Bachelor of Law degree and so become an advocate. I therefore specialized in legal options in the Bachelor of Commerce curriculum, although I also had to take courses in economics, accounting and marketing. In the first year I did not find economics all that interesting, but then in the second year I attended lectures delivered by Professor Ludwig Lachman. It was only many years later that I realized that he had a considerable world-wide reputation as a leading member of the Austrian school of economics, which included people such as Schumpeter and von Hayek. I found his lectures on macroeconomics and Keynesian models so interesting that I decided to go further in economics even though I was not expected to. I did not want to drop the law subjects so I simply added two or three additional subjects on economics, although they would not count for the final degree. Interaction, at something of a distance, with this teacher and the writers he introduced me to played an important part in redirecting what I wanted to do.

Preparing for a move to London

I completed the Bachelor of Commerce degree in November of 1963, by which time I had decided that I wanted to take a Master of Science degree in economics at the London School of Economics. The term at LSE would only start in September 1964 so I used the six months between ending my Bachelor studies and starting my Masters by attending courses at the university on mathematics and statistics, and I also attended postgraduate seminars on economics. I felt anxious about studying in London with very clever students from around the world – I wondered how I was going to cope and so I read a great deal to try to prepare myself. My interest in macroeconomics had continued and I became interested in theories of economic cycles and in the models that tried to explain them. I also felt that understanding how economies developed would enable me to work in some way that would help with the development of the poorer regions in South Africa, which consisted of what were called the Reserves, later Bantustans, and in which a significant proportion of the Black population lived. Territorial segregation was a significant feature of Apartheid, the stated aim of which was to stop Black people from moving from the Reserves to the industrialized 'White' areas and indeed to reverse the flow, given that the majority of Black people lived in these so-called 'White' areas and in fact constituted about 66 per cent of the total population in those 'White' areas. This attempt at social engineering could only be sustained if the Reserves and their border areas could be developed economically to support larger populations. Having been deeply influenced by reading the book *Naught for Your Comfort* by Father Trevor Huddleston and the novel *Cry the Beloved Country* by Alan Paton, both of which described the iniquitous ways in which Black people were being treated, I regarded the whole policy of moving people against their will to the Reserves as both evil and totally impractical. I was convinced that there would be a revolution in my lifetime and that it would be a highly destructive blood bath in which Whites would be wiped out, irrespective of whether they had agreed with Apartheid or not. Being no hero, this belief and my growing dismay at the government's policies played a big part in my switch to economics and my desire to study in London – I would not be trapped in South Africa in career terms if I took an international economics degree rather than a South African law degree.

However, before going to London and pursuing my interest in economic models of growth and cycles, I studied, in great detail, about three or four papers written by the Cambridge economists Hahn and Harrod. I found them very difficult to understand but felt that I had to understand them – failure to do so would indicate that I would never survive at the LSE. I spent days and days poring over these papers and eventually gave a paper to the postgraduate seminar I mentioned above which set out my understanding. This paper included a section on cobweb theory, also known as the hog cycle. This is a mathematical model where the essential feature is that of taking account of lags between changes in one variable and changes in another. What these models show is that within some range of parameters any disturbance to the equilibrium state of the model quickly dies out and there is a return to the stable equilibrium state, a point attractor. At yet other parameters, any disturbance has an exponential effect and explodes off to infinity. But between these extremes the model produces a perfectly regular cycle of peaks and troughs – stability took a cyclical form, a period two attractor. This was interesting because it showed that economic cycles could be arising endogenously as a property of the economic system itself. Of course, real economic cycles were not regular but this irregularity was assumed to be due to random exogenous shocks to the system. I was interested in this because I thought it could be very useful in forecasting movements in the economy and so enable policy-makers to improve economic performance. Many years later I would again take up ideas like this when I came across the discovery of mathematic chaos – this simple model had much more surprising patterns than any economist of the time realized.

My interest in economic growth led to me reading the work of Professor Chenery at Stanford. He had developed what was called an input–output model of an economy in which measures of various inputs could be related to outputs. This meant that you could calculate what investment expenditures would be required to produce particular rates of growth in outputs and jobs. I began to think that this model could be used to identify just what size of investment the government's territorial segregation policy would require – I had the feeling that when people realized just how much it would cost, they would have to conclude that it was not feasible. I then learned that the

J. B. Ebden Prize was to be offered for the best essay on economics by a new graduate and I decided to enter the competition. So, I gathered the large amount of statistical data required to use Chenery's input–output model as a tool to predict the size of investment that would be required to make the Reserves and their border areas economically viable. The model calculations showed that even stopping the flow of people out of the Reserves would require the diversion of nearly 20 per cent of the current investment in existing industrial areas. Even if this happened, it would still leave Whites in the minority in the areas they arbitrarily called 'White'. I wrote this in early 1964, when the huge flow of laws establishing Apartheid was reaching its peak. When I got to London in August 1964, I learned that I had won the prize. I shortened the essay for publication in the *South African Journal of Economics* in March 1966.[1]

In reflecting on what I was doing during this first half of 1964, I can see how totally immersed I was in the ideology of the scientific method. I was clearly following positivist methods, and it never even occurred to me that there were taken-for-granted assumptions in doing what I was doing. I never questioned the supposed value-free statements of facts that I was making but simply accepted the method of the group of economists I had in effect joined. I can also see how the ideologies of Apartheid, and those of the Communist Party and the Progressive Party, of which I was a member, were affecting how I thought and indeed in some ways exercised a silencing effect. I had the experience of being on the margin, not quite belonging on either side of the racial divide but feeling unable to speak out too much in a community which would reject me if I did, perhaps even imprison me. I would later find the work of Elias on power and ideology very illuminating of this early experience. I also uncritically accepted the ideology of improvement; indeed, it would never have occurred to me that it was an ideology – I simply thought it was obviously and factually the right thing to be looking for. Also by this time it was clear that my interests lay in building models of economic systems and using them to make forecasts in order to bring greater control and so improvement. It was the era in which governments were beginning to make national plans and I was very much for this as an activity to supplement and improve the functioning of the market system.

Studying at the London School of Economics: my doctoral thesis

In September 1964 I started the MSc in economics and completed it one year later, having taken many courses on mathematics and statistics as well as one on the economics of underdeveloped countries. The LSE was then one of the most notable centres of econometrics and this is what I specialized in. Then I decided to carry on and do a PhD.

My thesis consisted of testing Chenery's hypothesis that the sectoral composition of national output followed a uniform pattern across time in all countries: increases in income per capita and population caused shifts from agriculture to manufacturing and services and also produced particular sub-sectoral patterns within the manufacturing and services sectors. It would be useful if such patterns could be identified because it would then be possible to calculate what inputs of labour and capital would be required to sustain each stage in the development of the poor economies and the rich as well. Governments could make policy changes if they discovered that there would not be sufficient labour available, for example, to sustain a particular development. Identifying the pattern would therefore provide a useful tool to help formulate the right national plan. At that time the Labour Party under Wilson won the election in the UK and the new government set about preparing its national plan. Chenery had presented a nonlinear mathematical model of sectoral growth which took the form of an exponential equation that was linear in its logarithmic form. The statistical method of linear regression could then be used to fit the equation to statistics on output composition in a large sample of countries. He found that his model provided a reasonable statistical fit to the data, certainly a better fit than a straightforward linear equation and so he recommended it be used for forecasting. The United Nations did a much larger study and produced similar equations with an additional variable.

My thesis was that although the statistical fit of these equations was reasonable, they were derived from a cross-section sample and no one had used them to generate predictions over time or to analyse their accuracy. My research, therefore, consisted of collecting detailed data on sector outputs, per capita income and population for a sample of sixteen countries over periods of two to sixteen years. The Chenery and UN equations could then be used to make predictions which could be compared with this data. The conclusion was that they each displayed much the same level of accuracy, which was only slightly better than a naïve predicting rule of simply projecting the past, but even then they were not much good. So I suggested that using an exponential equation was not realistic because it produces continuously accelerating growth, implying that a sector's output would carry on growing forever. Instead, the logistic equation could be used because it has an S-shaped graph in which output would grow increasingly rapidly at first and then slow, eventually reaching a plateau. This is also a nonlinear equation which can be linearized by using its logarithmic form, and I laboriously used the computer to fit various forms of the equation to the data. At the time, I had no idea of the interesting dynamics that this simple equation displays; it was not until many years later that I found it in the literature on mathematical chaos theory. The logistic equations gave a less good fit to the cross-section data than the exponential function, but nevertheless I went on to test them for forecasting accuracy and found that they produced only marginal improvement over either the Chenery or UN models. Instead of finding uniformity in output growth patterns, I found only difference. I concluded that we would have to do a lot more research to find a better model and did not question the belief that we would eventually find it; I was simply disappointed that I had not done. Anyway, the thesis was good enough for a PhD in economics at that time.

So, reflecting on this period at the LSE, I can see how my interest in modelling and forecasting economic systems intensified and how I noticed we were not good at forecasting but never dreamt of questioning whether it was possible or not. I never questioned processes of national planning either – I took them to be a good thing. When I failed to identify uniformity and found only difference, I did not explore why this should be – I accepted that one day we would find some kind of macro regularity. Of course, given that I was a member of the community of positivist economists who certainly did not engage in reflexive inquiry, it was perfectly natural that I would take all these matters for granted.

Then in December 1967, having passed the PhD viva in June, I returned to South Africa to take up a post as lecturer in applied economics at the University of the Witwatersrand where I had been an undergraduate. My interest in modelling and forecasting continued, and I used my thesis to prepare a journal paper which was published in the *South African Journal of Economics* in March 1969.[2] This came just after another paper was published in September 1968,[3] in which I did tests on the forecasts made by a prestigious research centre at Stellenbosch University. These were forecasts based on opinion surveys, and the tests showed that the forecasts were consistently poorer than simply assuming that tomorrow would be the same as yesterday. I concluded that we needed an econometric model to make better forecasts and around this time I was invited by the head of research at the Netherlands Bank in South Africa to construct an econometric model of the economy. I set about estimating a 12-equation macroeconomic model of the South African economy and found that this model was better at forecasting than the Stellenbosch one but still no better than the naïve prediction rule. I concluded that we needed to do much more research to find a good model, but the man who had commissioned the model moved to another job and his successor was not interested in publishing the model or taking it any further. I returned to the UK in February 1970.

During this period, however, much of my time was taken up with teaching applied economics to undergraduate students. They repeatedly asked me if anyone in 'the real world' used all the theories I was explaining with the aid of blackboard diagrams. Since I had so far spent all my life in universities, which at the time I accepted as 'not the real world', I had to admit that I had no idea whether practical people used the theories or not. Looking back, I now think that we were together engaging in reflexive inquiry. We were asking what we were doing and whether it was worthwhile doing it. The fact that I did not know led me to the conclusion that I should take a job in industry for a few years to find out what happened in the 'real world'. For me, this is an example of how reflexive inquiry can lead one to do something different: I found myself changing the focus of my work.

Coming to live in the United Kingdom

On returning to the UK, I took a post as an economist at British Steel, working as part of an enormous team of economists predicting steel demand. I remember that it was a regular part of my job to go to the government Treasury office to extract data from their econometric model forecasts to use in our models of steel-demand forecasting. I remember noticing at the time that the forecasts produced by the model were subject to the scrutiny of a forecasting committee and, on looking at the minutes of their meetings, I was surprised at how frequently the committee amended the forecasts on the basis of their obviously subjective judgment. I began to wonder why they bothered with the expensive model; they might as well just guess instead. However, this observation triggered no further thinking on my part.

I found this job incredibly boring and so moved to a post in the planning department of John Laing, the construction company, in 1972. At Laing I was also engaged in gathering data and forecasting but became more and more involved in forming judgments and giving advice on what to do in the light of the data and other factors. Early on in my career, a new CEO was appointed and he appointed a new board director to whom the corporate planning manager, my boss, would report. The corporate planning manager retired soon after this and I now had to report to the new director until a new corporate planning manager was appointed. The new director had the idea of constructing a financial model of the business that could be projected onto the walls of the boardroom, enabling the directors to make forecasts of the outcomes of the various strategic options facing them. Although still believing that one had to try to forecast, I also knew how bad we were at it and I could see that what he was doing would never work. Looking back, I think this is another example of how reflection, if not really reflexive inquiry in this case, leads to changes in how one thinks and acts. I had clearly moved some way from the earlier taken-for-granted belief in our ability to forecast the outcomes of our actions due to the experience of engaging with managers in both the steel and construction industries who were finding it impossible to do so.

This shift in thinking resulted in an enforced change in the work I found myself doing. As a result of my lack of enthusiasm for the financial model, I never really got on with my new boss and he brought in his own people, so sidelining me. Fortunately, the Chairman had nominated me as the company representative on the government's Aggregates Advisory Committee chaired by Sir Ralph Verney, and this took me away from the office for much of the time. I contributed a chapter to the Verney report which analysed the impact on transport of different options for mining sand or crushed rock for use in making concrete. In the meantime, a new corporate planning manager was appointed who also did not agree with the idea of the financial model and so I now found that I was no longer at the margins of power. The new corporate planning manager was a skilful politician and he soon helped to activate a group of other powerful board directors who also disagreed with the financial model. This group acted and the new director was effectively sidelined. I found working with the new corporate planning manager to be a very instructive pleasure; he was an important mentor, and I eventually succeeded him as corporate planning manager. During this latter period, I was still engaged in forecasting, especially in the period of accelerating inflation and fixed-price contracts when making money depended more on getting inflation forecasts right than on the construction work. I no longer thought national plans were such a good idea but I still thought company ones were. However, analysis and forecasting ceased to be the main focus of attention for me and even formal planning took up little of my time – working with my new manager, I came to understand my work as primarily a political activity involving the backing or blocking of proposals made by subsidiary company managing directors for investments. I now think that what I have described above is a further example of reflexive inquiry leading to different ways of thinking and different ways of working. Clearly the mentoring I received played an important part in any capacity for practical judgment that I may have developed.

I eventually became the manager of the department, before leaving in early 1984 to take up a role as investment strategist for a stock broker and fund manager. As investment strategist, I was supposed to report each morning to assembled brokers and fund managers on what was likely to happen in the financial markets of the UK, Germany and USA. I found this incredibly stressful because I had no idea what was going to happen that day, let alone the next one. All I could do was summarize what I had just read in the newspapers. It all felt very unsatisfactory and rather fraudulent, but I am afraid this experience did not prompt me to think about what we were trying to do, whether forecasting what would happen was possible and what my job really was. Fortunately, I was made redundant. After a brief period with a management consultancy firm I returned to academia, having spent 14 years in industry and finance. The management consultancy firm invited me to continue to work for them as an associate involved in working with top executive teams on strategy formulation.

Looking back on how my way of thinking had changed, reflecting my participation in the group of managers I worked with, I can see that I gradually dropped the interest in forecasting, model building and analysis and became much more interested in how to go on each day in a senior position with others. I did come to act in a highly political manner and must have been fairly good at it because I survived a number of changes in the top executive team. However, I never really reflected on my loss of interest in forecasting and planning, and nor did I reflect on why we spent so little time on corporate planning while proclaiming how important it was. I did not ask myself what we were really doing; I just got on and did it.

My first book

In September 1985 I joined the Business School of Hatfield Polytechnic (to become Hertfordshire University in 1992) and, since I had experience in strategic management in industry, I was allocated to teach strategic management to undergraduates and then to the part-time students who had enrolled on our new MBA in 1987. In order to do this teaching I had to engage with the textbooks and other literature on strategic management, which I found to have very little relationship to what I had been doing in industry. Although continuing to use the textbooks, I also began to engage the MBA students in discussions about our experiences – mine as a former industrial strategist and theirs in their current management positions. This, of course, required all of us to reflect on our experience and so I began to review what I thought had been going on in my work as a strategist. This was another, this time much fuller, experience of reflexive inquiry, and we all engaged in it and began to experience the movement in thinking that it provoked. I also found myself teaching in a much more participative way; instead of simply lecturing the students, we spent much of our time together discussing our experiences. Also, this movement of thinking motivated me to start writing my first book in 1987, which was eventually completed in mid-1989. It was published in 1990,[4] and I never read it again until coming to write this appendix.

This book, *Dynamic Strategic Management for the 1990s*, rather stridently rejected conventional strategic management views which focused on an orderly 'grand design' involving missions, long-term plans based on analysis, quantification and forecasting. Instead it proposed the view that, in practice, strategic management is about handling the unknowable and that the conventional caste of mind is a hindrance to this. Managers might talk the language of rational planning but actually, at their most effective, they are engaged in opportunistic action and trial-and-error learning. This argument was based on a distinction between three different change situations: closed, contained and open-ended change. At the time I was thinking of change as being determined by mathematical relationships in which changes in variables, such as prices, affected outcomes in ways that depended on the parameters of the equations. Closed change was defined in terms of stable variable sets and stable parameters – in effect constituting stable 'if ... then' causality which made it possible to forecast the outcomes of actions. Conventional views on strategic management were applicable in conditions of closed change. Contained change was where variable sets and parameters were more volatile and could only be specified as probabilities. This kind of situation called for a much more flexible use of conventional management ideas. Open-ended change, however, was where variables were highly volatile and difficult to identify and the parameters were also highly volatile. In this situation the future is unique and unknowable and the only way to deal with this kind of change situation is to try things out and learn from mistakes. These activities were described as experimenting, playing games and taking opportunistic action. In this kind of change situation, conventional strategic management is simply no help whatsoever and since managers are always encountering this kind of change, that is why they do not actually follow the conventional prescriptions for strategic management, although they give the appearance that they do.

In addition to the framework of change situations, a great deal of significance was attached to the need for control, defined as the activity of directing and guiding and composed of three elements: goal and path selection, progress checks and corrective action. However, these three elements had different meanings in different change situations, making it necessary for the type of control being practised to match the change situation. Control in closed change situations, relating to the very short term, takes the form of setting precise objectives and attending to detailed planning. It constitutes a management information and control sub-system. In contained change situations, goals become less detailed and attention is focused on a 'grand design'. In open-ended change, which applies to the long term, control has to cope with tentative purpose, an inability to define the path to the goal and the impossibility of planning. This means that attention has to be directed to significant single issues and that action is opportunistic and involves trial and error, all carried out in the political subsystem characterized by the inevitable conflict to be found in organizational life. These two overlapping subsystems operate at the same time and it is not possible to choose between them – both are essential and it is not a matter of now using one and then using the other. Instead, management is a paradoxical activity. This notion of paradox would become more and more important in what I subsequently wrote. I drew on my experience as a planner at the construction company to describe how various strategies had emerged in the daily political interaction of the executives concerned.

This book referred to only a very narrow range of work from the literature on organizations and management. The key authors referred to were Drucker,[5] Goold and Campbell,[6] Mintzberg,[7] Pascale[8] and Quinn.[9] No appeal was made to literature on psychology or sociology at this stage.

So at this time I was thinking that an organization is a system with subsystems required to deal with different change situations, one of them being the political subsystem in which managers dealt with the inevitable conflict they generated between themselves. I thought that it was in the political subsystem that managers actually conducted strategic management and, given our experienced inability to forecast outcomes of actions, events were not caused by long-term plans. I still agree with much of this, although the way of making sense of it has evolved considerably, leading eventually to completely dropping the taken-for-granted view that an organization is a system. At the time, I very clearly thought in terms of 'if ... then' causality, and there was much else that I took for granted, for example in the conventional way in which I used the terminology of management tools. Apart from a rather dogmatic injunction to abandon all long-term planning and apply tight short-interval control to day-to-day activities, the other recommendations in the book were not much different from those to be found in what I was calling the conventional literature.

Encountering chaos theory

Once I had sent the manuscript to the publisher, I was left with a disturbing question: why are we not able to forecast what will happen in companies or economies? Why are variables and parameters so volatile? I had described open-ended change but had not been able to explain how and why it occurred. I also wondered why people carried on planning, or at least claiming that they were planning, when they did not use the plans. All my education had led me to believe that ultimately we could, and we should, be able to forecast the outcomes of actions and none of the theories or models I had ever come across could help me to understand the failure to do so. It was then, by chance, that I came across the book *Chaos: Making a New Science* by Gleick. This prompted me to read more widely about chaos theory, which was often explained using the logistic equation that I had used in my PhD thesis. At that time I did not know that this equation displays the properties of uncertainty, which makes it clear why we had failed to forecast accurately – the reason is quite simple; it is not possible. But does this apply to human action? If it does, what would that mean for how we think about planning and managing? If we cannot forecast and our plans are rarely achieved, just what is it that we are doing to get things done? This was the beginning of an inquiry that has gone on for 20 years and is still going on.

Just before discovering chaos theory, I had become involved in short group relations events conducted by the Tavistock Institute for the MBA course at Hertfordshire University. I became fascinated by these events and was puzzled by the strange behaviour they evoked and what this meant. I came to see that what we are actually doing to get things done in organizations has something to do with the kind of dynamics I was experiencing at these events. My growing interest in groups led me to the Institute of Group Analysis (IGA), where I was ultimately to qualify as a group psychotherapist. Group dynamics and chaos theory seemed to me to be linked.

I read about chaos theory in the months before the proofs of my first book were sent to me for correction. I could see how I would have written it differently, had I known about chaos theory but, given the stage the book had reached, all I could do was insert a sentence mentioning it and two footnotes.

As I started reading about mathematical chaos, the explanation provided using the logistic equation was strangely familiar and not at all familiar at the same time. From cobweb theory I knew that at certain parameter values the time path produced by the equation would converge on an equilibrium point and that for other parameter values the time path would be one of exponential growth. The fascinating 'discovery' for me in my early twenties was that for yet other parameter values the time series would follow a regular cycle. What I did not know until I read about chaos was that there were many other possibilities: many kinds of regular cycles and also recurring chaos. The key point about mathematical chaos is that it is a dynamic in which tiny changes can escalate to yield completely different time series, making any long-term prediction impossible. Mathematical chaos is a paradoxical dynamic, a pattern of movement over time which is predictably unpredictable or unpredictably predictable. It is not utter disorder. There is a border between stability and instability and it takes the form of a strange attractor called chaos. Of course I found this such a revelation because it gave me a new way of thinking about the possibility of prediction. We do not get our economic forecasts right because the dynamics of economic systems are such that forecasting over any long time period is impossible.

I was drawn to these models because of the insights they gave, but I could not see much use in trying to model people or organizations using such equations. Instead I wanted to take the insights across to human action and consider what implications they might have. I still thought an organization was a system but I could now see how taken-for-granted views of control would make little sense. So by then I was moving away from the idea of directly applying quantitative mathematical models, as I had done earlier in my research career, and was thinking in terms of much more qualitative models, of the kind to be found in some of the organizational literature and increasingly, for me, in psychoanalysis. I became interested in the impact of anxiety on organizations and explored group dynamics, both reflections of my continued engagement with the Tavistock work on group relations and my reading of psychoanalytic writers.

I now began to link chaos theory, groups and power and published the book *The Chaos Frontier: Creative Strategic Control for Business* in 1991.[10] I wrote *The Chaos Frontier* between the summer of 1989, when I first read Gleick's book, and the summer of

1990. In addition to reading this book, I read a number of other books and papers on the theory of chaos,[11] and also on the theory of dissipative structures.[12] I turned to the economics literature and found a number of economists who had written about chaos and the economy.[13] Then there were a few studies of chaos in stock and foreign exchange markets.[14] The only publication I could find on chaos and organizations at that time was by Nonaka,[15] although I now see that there was a very small number of others that I missed at the time.[16] The literature drawn on in my first book was very limited but it was extended significantly in *The Chaos Frontier*. The key authors used from the organizational literature, either to clarify the difference between the most prominent approaches and the position taken in the book or to support the argument in the book, were Ansoff,[17] Burns and Stalker,[18] Drucker,[19] Hamel and Prahalad,[20] Moss Kanter,[21] Mintzberg,[22] Ohmae,[23] Peters and Waterman,[24] Quinn[25] and Simon.[26] The work of Lindblom on muddling through was useful,[27] as was that of Cohen, March and Ohlsen[28] on garbage can decision-making, in setting out the argument. Weick's[29] work on social psychology was taken up and, in introducing some ideas from psychoanalysis on groups, I referred to Bion,[30] as well as Miller and Rice.[31] Chapters on power and politics in organizations referred to Bacharach and Lawler,[32] Pettigrew,[33] Pfeffer,[34] as well as Zaleznik and Kets de Vries's psycho-analytically informed perspective.[35] The work of Argyris,[36] Penrose[37] and Schön[38] was used to explain the cognitivist perspective on human psychology.

The Chaos Frontier continued the kind of analysis presented in *Dynamic Strategic Management for the 1990s* and set out the key features of organizational change that should be addressed by a useful explanation of management. The first of these features had to do with the nature of the change situation an organization was facing. The notions of closed, contained and open-ended change were developed further, stressing that all three kinds of change are simultaneously present in all time frames, past, present and future. We act in the present on the basis of the past but we do not know everything that has been done and everything that is still flowing from those actions. In the present, therefore, we are addressing open-ended change arising from the past as well as from the future consequences of our actions. Managers have no option but to address all three change situations at the same time and since they require different, indeed contradictory, forms of 'control', this will create tension and management is also the activity of dealing with, or resolving, that tension. This was a paradoxical formulation of control situations but it was claimed that it was the manager's role to resolve the paradox – a view that would eventually change.

The book argued that managers follow a process that has distinctive phases of discovery, choice and action leading to further discovery, a view that was questioned by colleagues, leading me to drop it later on. These phases had different meanings in different change situations: tight short-interval control for closed change; a loose form of long-term planning for contained change; creative exploration, trial-and-error action, organizational learning and spontaneous political choices in open-ended situations. The latter is the diametric opposite of the other two forms and since they must be applied at the same time, tension and conflict are inevitable.[39] One chapter of the book was concerned with 'the mechanisms driving business development', the kind of formulation that I would later drop altogether. It was argued that these mechanisms were complex feedback loops of both the damping and amplifying type, in which small changes could be observed to escalate. When operating far from certainty, it was necessary to operate through these loops to discover what was changing, pressing these discoveries on the attention of the powerful, so gaining an arena to discuss them in and finding a place to strive for putting them on strategic agendas, and then undertaking creative exploratory action.

An analysis of the prescriptions of conventional ideas on management concluded that they provided little explanation of what managers actually do when they have to deal with open-ended change. The need for an explanation of what managers actually do, rather than rushing to prescriptions, was emphasized. Indeed, the nature of open-ended change is such that no universal, general techniques can be prescribed – the techniques break down in open-ended change and part of the creative exploration of managers is identifying what works in the unique situations encountered.

The book briefly reviewed the theories of mathematical chaos and fractal geometry, as well as Prigogine's[40] far-from-equilibrium theory of dissipative structures and what the implications of these sciences were for managing in open-ended change. On now reading my explanations of chaos, I notice how I said that chaos was not utter confusion but pattern where we thought there was none, but in other places I referred to chaos as random events. This is clearly wrong because if chaos is a paradoxical pattern of regularity and irregularity, regular irregularity, as I claimed, then the events cannot, by definition, be random. Also, in reviewing my account of dissipative structure theory, I described how far-from-equilibrium, nonlinear systems go through phase transitions from a current state, through symmetry-breaking chaos, or disorder, to bifurcation points where the system displays self-organization, that is, it 'chooses' one path rather than another and this path may lead either to further chaos or some new order which has to be sustained by the input of energy. I used descriptions from the literature which tell us that self-organization is a process of communication across a distance between entities, such as molecules, and at some critical point they 'choose' a new form of alignment as a higher pattern of order. But this is a precarious state which remains only while sustained by ongoing inputs of energy. I then simply used this sequence of phases to explain the political phases of action in an organization. With hindsight, I do not think this rather mystifying account of self-organization is all that helpful and I would later come to realize that much simpler accounts were available – it simply means local interaction.

The book claimed that managers should sustain their organization in the border between stability and instability, in effect creating the conditions in which people could learn. In later discussions with colleagues we came to see that this formulation subtly retains the position of the objective observer, a view we were to replace with the claim that there is no objective observer, only participants trying to make sense of their experience from within that experience. The book advised managers to forget their long-term plans and visions because they are illusions, and it advised them to stop trying to get everyone to share the same values. Instead, they should create the conditions in which they can explore their differences on the grounds that it is not consensus but the lack of it that generates creativity. The book advised against rigid forms of control and excessive formal order because innovation depends on the spontaneity of people, and the use of workshops with loose agendas was recommended to enable reflection on, and discussion of, issues that were far from being clear.

In going through *The Chaos Frontier* for the first time in twenty years, I noticed that it expressed many of the themes that I would continue working with over those twenty years:

- the need to inquire into what managers actually do rather than what they, consultants and academics say they should do;
- the experience of uncertainty and unpredictability which could now be explained as properties fundamental to nonlinear relationships, involving the escalation of small differences;
- the link between this uncertainty, creativity and destruction;
- power, understood as a relationship, as essential to organizational life;
- processes of political activity tied into exploration as the mode in which managers actually decide and act;
- conflict, tension and contradiction as essential aspects of organizations;
- politics, learning and reflection as modes of managing.

However, the ways in which these themes are presented and understood were to change substantially over the years after publication of *The Chaos Frontier* in the following areas:

- I took it totally for granted that the brain is an information-processing device which builds mental models. I did not notice any differences between this cognitivist psychology and psychoanalytic understandings of the mind which I was also using. I would later move away from cognitivism altogether and adopt a somewhat critical attitude to psychoanalysis.
- I presented my argument in terms of systems, claiming that organizations are sets of amplifying and damping feedback mechanisms and talking about business as systems driven by feedback. Colleagues and I would later move away from thinking of organizations as systems.
- I did not notice how thoroughly people disappeared from the explanation couched in systems terms. We would later focus much more clearly on the interactions between people.
- I did not notice any contradiction in turning from this highly abstract reasoning to paying attention to people and what they did, drawing on psychology and a little sociology to talk about personality, groups and politics. We would later abandon the notion of systems altogether and try to focus just on people and their interactions.
- I presented the argument very much from the view of the external observer, another position that colleagues and I would later abandon in favour of trying instead to understand experience as a participant in that experience.

- The way in which I dealt with self-organization was inadequate and I had not taken up the notion of emergence at all. These ideas would become important in later work.

The Chaos Frontier came out in 1991 and it led to an invitation to attend a restricted membership symposium in Canada. At this meeting I found that a few other people were also exploring the connection between chaos theory and organizations, for example Brenda Zimmerman who was doing her PhD on the subject and had already delivered a conference paper, to be followed by a book chapter published in 1992.[41] I also discovered that others interested in the subject had formed a Chaos Network, and I joined and started going to their annual conferences. There I met a number of others writing on chaos and organizations, for example Meg Wheatley,[42] whose book on leadership and the new sciences was published in 1992, Jeff Goldstein[43] and Stephen Guastello.[44] Several others started to have their work published in 1992 and 1993.[45]

The two books I have just been discussing attracted some interest, and I began to receive invitations to address conferences and also to conduct workshops on management development programmes. This led to quite a lot of travelling, at first to the USA, Hong Kong and Sweden, and later to many more countries. Two responses to what I had to say gave me cause for much reflection. First, the groups of managers I was working with frequently formed three recognizable subgroups. The first subgroup consisted of those who immediately recognized the reality of their own experience in what I was saying, finding it both interesting and often amusing to reflect upon what they actually did. Another subgroup, usually the largest, expressed feelings of some confusion and depression since they felt that how they understood things was being undermined and they were being invited to consider that they might be able to do less than they thought they could. The third subgroup rejected totally what I was saying and often got angry, sometimes very angry, which of course I found both puzzling and distressing. I will come back to how I began to think about this later. The other very frequent response to what I was saying took the form of great pressure by people to exclude their most cherished techniques from criticism or at the very least specify what they should be replaced with. This demand was to continue for the next twenty years and no matter how much I explained that providing general techniques to deal with open-ended change was impossible, they simply continued pressing for them. The chapters above are my attempt to deal with the question of techniques in some detail.

In between teaching at the Business School and travelling, I turned to another project. Some had critiqued *The Chaos Frontier* for being too difficult and called for a simpler exposition, and this became my next project. From late 1990 to mid-1991 I worked on this simpler version, which was published in 1992 under the title *Managing Chaos: Dynamic Business Strategies in an Unpredictable World* in the UK and Europe and *Managing the Unknowable: Strategic Boundaries between Order and Chaos in Organizations* in North America. These books paid more explicit attention to anxiety in organizations and the impact it has on how organizations change or fail to change. They presented strategy as patterns of action emerging in processes of self-organization between people. However, it was claimed that managers should let, or allow, emergence to take place and that they should intentionally use self-organization and feedback loops to manage their organizations. Later I came to see, with colleagues, how all of this is a misunderstanding of the concepts of emergence and self-organization, essentially re-presenting the kind of direct management control that I was critiquing. Later discussion with colleagues would bring this out and lead to an understanding in which self-organization is conceived as processes of local interaction which produce emergent global patterns and they cannot be intended, controlled or conditioned by some outside observer. These books shed no further light on the meaning of self-organization, other than claiming that it was different from self-managing teams. Senge's thinking on the learning organization was uncritically incorporated into the argument of these books. They presented prescriptions that were much the same as those in *The Chaos Frontier*.

From mid-1991 to mid-1992 I worked on the first edition of my textbook *Strategic Management and Organisational Dynamics*, published in 1993. This book drew on Kuhn's[46] distinction between ordinary and revolutionary science to differentiate between ordinary and extraordinary management. Ordinary management was defined as the practice of rationality in reasonably certain situations, which was equated with the conventional wisdom on management. Extraordinary management was what managers did when they were in uncertain and ambiguous situations, and this was equated with trial-and-error learning, political choices and creative exploration. The book went into more detail on what self-organization in human organizations might mean and continued to refer to the notion of emergence. Additional psycho-analytic writers were introduced, such as Melanie Klein,[47] and much more was made of what paradox and dialectic meant and why they were important notions in trying to understand management. Strategy was described as a game and pointed to how managers justify their existence when they apply their intuition and judgment to open-ended situations in which techniques, procedures, rules and structures are inadequate. However, this book did not represent any significant addition or change to how I was thinking – it simply clarified a little what I was trying to say and located this in a much more detailed look at, and critique of, conventional management theories.

Looking back, I can remember thinking that if planning is not the cause of what happens, then what is? In reflecting on this with those I worked with, I began to think that the answer to this question had something to do with what we do in groups. Since I had little formal education on group dynamics, I sought out ways of increasing my understanding which led me to the Institute of Group Analysis. I think this is another occasion in my life where shifts in thinking were leading me to shifts in how I worked.

During this period I continued working as a staff member with consultants from the Tavistock Institute on small group relations conferences for our MBA students, and I also went as a member on two twelve-day-long group relations conferences. From September 1992 to September 1993 I took the introductory course in group analysis at the IGA. It was what I learned about group dynamics from these experiences that helped me understand the aggression that my presentations aroused in some group members. Being confronted with a direct challenge to their ways of thinking, especially if the challenge presented is couched in terms of unpredictability where no one is in control, arouses considerable anxiety in some people, and the attack is a defence against this anxiety. Understanding this made my work less puzzling and distressing; indeed, I came to be able to use the angry pattern to explore what was going on. I noticed that if all the participants in a workshop were from the same company and that company was reducing costs by making people redundant, the likelihood of angry responses was much greater, which I took to be further support for the hypothesis about anxiety. This is another example of how reflexive inquiry leads to shifts in thinking and so in working.

Taking account of the complexity sciences

As far as I can remember, I attended the third annual conference of the Chaos Network in the USA in 1993. This Network was a group of people who were working at the interface of social systems and chaos theory, and I was informed of its existence at the symposium meeting in Canada which I referred to above. It must have been at this meeting that I heard people talking about the complexity sciences, a field I had never heard of. When I got home from the conference, I began to read about the complexity sciences and found the publications of the Santa Fe Institute in New Mexico a rich source of information. I also came across Waldrop's book *Complexity: The Emerging Science at the Edge of Order and Chaos*,[48] which presented a history and summary of the complexity sciences. This led me to work on a journal paper, 'The Science of Complexity: An Alternative Perspective for Strategic Change Processes', from late 1993 to early 1994, which was published in 1995.[49]

This paper mistakenly argued that organizations are systems driven by deterministic laws which, however, also allowed free choice. Clearly this is confused thinking for if there is free choice, there is no determinism. The paper then went on to incorporate some ideas from the complexity sciences. It explained what the concept 'the edge of chaos' meant in organizational terms, using the well-known distinction between formal and informal systems in an organization to argue that the formal system operates in a negative feedback manner, that is, according to principles of integration which move it to stability, while the informal system operates in a positive feedback manner, according to the principles of division which pull the organization to instability. At the border between the two, that is, the edge of chaos, the whole organizational system flips between negative and positive feedback, generating the paradoxical dynamics of stability and instability at the same time. The formal system is producing stability while the shadowy informal system tries to produce change, and it is the tension between the two which generates the edge-of-chaos conditions necessary for the unpredictable emergence of innovative patterns. This dynamic is one of contention, political activity and dialogue as managers handle ambiguous strategic issues. The paper also introduced Kauffman's[50] work on Boolean networks to explain how the edge of chaos is generated by critical degrees of connectivity between organizations.

I used the notion of self-organization, again without carefully defining it, to describe the political and learning processes in organizations and suggested that managers continued to use planning in uncertain situations as a defence against anxiety.

During 1995 I worked on my book *Complexity and Creativity in Organizations*, which was published in 1996. This book was basically an elaboration of the key ideas presented in the above paper. The book devoted attention to the tension between the legitimate system and the shadow system and introduced the terms 'close to certainty and agreement' and 'far from certainty and agreement' to indicate the situations in which conventional management ideas were useful and the situations where they were not. The book claimed that the brain, the individual mind, the group, the organization, the society were all complex adaptive systems nesting into each other. Cognitivist psychology was taken for granted in claiming that humans behave according to rules, schemas and mental models, a view I would change substantially later on. A number of chapters were concerned with what was called the space for creativity. In the simulations of complex adaptive systems, the space was the edge of chaos. For understanding the individual 'space for creativity', psychoanalytic object relations theory was drawn upon to argue that Melanie Klein's[51] depressive position and Winnicott's[52] transitional object or transitional phase constituted the space for individual creativity. For the group, Bion's work was used to argue that the space for creativity in a group was constituted by the tension between task and highly defensive basic assumption aspects of a group. For the organization, it was suggested that the space for creativity lay in the border between the legitimate and shadow systems.

Looking back on the journal paper and the book, I now feel that they did not add all that much to what I had already said about organizations. The incorporation of notions from the complexity sciences led to some additional points but did not represent any significant shift in how I was thinking about organizations. Any shift was generated mainly by my growing interest in psychoanalysis. I can now see how, particularly in the book, I had lost sight of the question of what managers actually do and presented a rather abstract account of creativity in organizations. The emphasis on spontaneous political activity had largely disappeared, but I would return to this later.

During 1995 I also completed the second edition of my textbook and this too was published in 1996. This second edition incorporated what I had already written about complexity and complex adaptive systems, and it also included additional material on neurotic forms of leadership. The main change in this edition was not, therefore, the addition of new material but the reorganization of the structure of the book to reflect comments received on the first edition. The book set out a conceptual framework which was much the same as those in previous books: different models of decision-making and control are appropriate for different change situations defined in terms of conditions close to and far from certainty and agreement, and organizational dynamics was understood in terms of feedback systems. A distinction was drawn between extraordinary management, which made use of the notion of the shadow systems and did pay attention to politics, covert politics and unconscious processes, and ordinary management, which was essentially the same as that found in conventional views on management. The different forms of ordinary and extraordinary management had to be applied at the same time and since they are opposites, this generates tension.

The book introduced a diagram which I have since come to regret. The y axis of this diagram indicated movement from situations close to certainty to situations far from certainty, while the x axis indicated movement from situations in which people were close to agreement with each other to situations in which they were far from agreement with each other. It was then argued that in conditions close to certainty and agreement, that is situations of regularity, stability and predictability, it was possible and useful to use the standard tools and techniques of management. In intermediate situations, where the situations are close to certainty but there is a high degree of disagreement, political decision-making was required, while in conditions close to agreement but some way away from certainty, judgmental forms of decision-making were required. These possibilities were described as the ordered zone. It was also suggested that in conditions very far from certainty and agreement there would be old-fashioned chaos and anarchy, the disordered zone. However, between the ordered and disordered zones there was a zone of complexity with the paradoxical dynamic of regularity and irregularity, predictability and unpredictability, at the same time. It is in the dynamics of complexity, the only dynamics in which the new and the creative can emerge, that the standard tools and techniques of management cannot be used. Instead, we would find that decision-making was unprogrammed, having the form of muddling through and garbage-can decision-making. Here we would search for error and engage in the kind of agenda-building politics that the book had described. Of course, presenting things in this way suggests that managers can decide which kind of situation they are in and then choose the appropriate tools. This is typical of a number of contingency approaches to tools and techniques. The diagram proved to be very popular and a number of writers took it up and amended it in various ways – it came to be referred to as the Stacey Diagram, which is unfortunate because, as I describe below, I came to see how problematic this kind of contingency approach is. I no longer use the diagram because it is simply interpreted in a way that sustains the dominant discourse while using the alternative jargon of complexity.

These post-1993 books took up psychoanalytic ideas and developed further the focus on groups. During this five-year period my thinking about chaos and then complexity did develop, increasingly by bringing in a psychological dimension which I felt was fundamentally necessary if we are to talk about models of human agents. But all of these books also had certain features in common. I took it for granted that individuals were autonomous, that their minds processed information and built models, and that an organization is a system. I continued to think to a significant extent in terms of models, and I was also concerned to integrate what I thought were radical new insights coming from the complexity sciences with the traditional approaches found in most of the literature. All of these assumptions would be questioned in new groups of colleagues.

Participating in two new challenging communities

Teaching on the MBA had been my major role at the Business School, but by 1995 my involvement in it had diminished and I became interested in supervising research students. I still remembered what a lonely experience my own PhD had been and this, together with my ongoing experience with experiential and therapy groups, led to my desire to set up a PhD group at the Business School, which I did in the early part of 1995. Other colleagues agreed to be involved as supervisors. It was very unusual at this time for PhD students to be supervised in groups and it had never happened before at the University of Hertfordshire. The proposal to set up the group led to some discussion, and I had to justify it to the members of the committee responsible for overseeing research degrees. However, the proposal was supported, albeit with some scepticism. Chapter 9 of this book on tools and techniques of management and leadership argues that reflexive inquiry constitutes a 'technique' which fosters practical judgment. It claims that those who engage in reflexive inquiry will find themselves working in a way that is somewhat different from what they usually did. During the early 1990s I had become more and more involved in the experiential and therapeutic activities of members of the Tavistock Institute and the Institute of Group Analysis. These activities amounted to reflexive inquiry; in effect I had become a member of a number of groups engaging in reflexive inquiry. I would argue that it was because of this engagement in reflexive inquiry that when it came to working as a PhD supervisor, I wanted to do so in a group in which the research students would engage in an inquiry into their own work experiences. I think this is an example of finding oneself working in a different way.

Over the following three years something like fifteen people passed through the PhD group and seven of these completed their research and were awarded the PhD. Two of these graduates were Patricia Shaw and Doug Griffin. We soon found that we had much in common and started to do consulting and management development work together. This rapidly developed into a strong friendship involving lengthy, sometimes turbulent, conversations in which we discussed our sometimes very different understandings of complexity, organizations, management, thought processes, the nature of knowledge and many more topics. What we found ourselves engaged in was an intense reflexive inquiry into who we were, what we were doing together and why we were doing it. As a small group of colleagues and friends we found ourselves supervising each other, although I was formally supposed to be the supervisor and they were supposed to be the supervisees. An example of this was Doug's often-repeated criticism of the diagram I had included in the second edition of *Strategic Management and Organisational Dynamics* which located different modes of decision-making in different situations either far from or close to certainty and agreement. I used this diagram often in presentations I gave and people usually responded very positively to it. Doug kept telling me that this was because I had collapsed the paradox of certainty and uncertainty and that doing so enabled people to carry on thinking as before when I thought I was challenging them to think in a different way. I resisted his criticism for some time but then eventually saw the point and dropped the diagram altogether, only to find that it had developed a life of its own whether I liked it or not, as others adapted and used it. However, I had to continue using it, although sceptically, for some time until I could articulate alternative ways of explaining what I was trying to explain. I think this is another example of how engagement in reflexive inquiry changes the way one finds oneself thinking and working and how one cannot simply move from one way of thinking to another – we cannot simply change the lenses through which we see things.

Around mid-1995 I told Doug and Patricia about the pressure being applied to me to set up a research centre at the Business School where researchers could work on ideas of complexity and organizations. I explained how I was doing my best to avoid this because I did not want to get involved in what I thought would be the inevitable bureaucracy. To my surprise they both said that I should set up such a centre, and they enthusiastically undertook to do it with me. On that basis I submitted to the pressure and the three of us set up the Complexity and Management Centre to research into developing a useful complexity perspective on organizations and on appropriate ways of working through involving not only academics but also members of other organizations in our activities. It was in these communities of the PhD group and the Complexity and Management Centre (CMC), as well as in the ongoing inquiry between the three of us, that we gradually developed what we now call the theory of complex responsive processes, which relies on taking abstract relationships from the complexity sciences to provide analogies of human interaction which have to be clothed in the attributes of human agency. In coming to describe these attributes, we drew on certain key writers in psychology, sociology and philosophy. Doug introduced the thinking of the American pragmatist George Herbert Mead,[53] as well as that of key philosophers such as Kant and Hegel. Patricia emphasized the importance of conversation and introduced the work of social constructionist Shotter,[54] while I introduced the work of Elias[55] into our discussion, my interest in this having been stimulated by Farhad Dalal, one of my supervisors at the IGA. Doug, Patricia and I worked on two joint papers published in 1998 and 1999,[56] which gave some indication of how we were together developing a different complexity perspective on organizations.

Not long after the start of the PhD programme, I embarked on the Qualifying Course at the Institute of Group Analysis, having completed two years in a twice weekly therapy group as a patient. The Qualifying Course required that I continue as a patient in this group for another three years and in addition run two weekly groups as group therapist, each of which was supervised on a weekly basis by an expert group therapist. For me, this was an intense experience of developing practical judgment as the conductor of a therapy group, or any other group for that matter, through closely supervised in-depth reflexive inquiries. Once again, during and after this reflexive inquiry, I found myself working in groups in different ways and this was as true of working with groups of managers and leaders in organizations as it was of working with people suffering from some form of mental illness. The reflexive inquiry I engaged in through participating in the community of group analysts enabled me to live with the anxiety of not knowing what is going on in a group for long enough to begin to get some sense of what might be happening and then offering some idea to the group in the hope that it would be found helpful. The way of working I came to learn involved following the themes emerging in the group conversation, trying to keep opening the conversation up in the interest of the emergence of new meaning, rather than closing down the conversation by seeking to direct it to the kind of problem solution I thought should be found. This way of working also enables one to endure aggression without immediate retaliation. These 'techniques' of reflexive inquiry offer the potential, but not the guarantee, of the emergence of new meaning and thus of some kind of creativity and innovation.

A major shift in thinking: complex responsive processes

During the first half of 1999 I completed the third edition of *Strategic Management and Organisational Dynamics*, adding as a subtitle *The Challenge of Complexity*. This was a major rewrite which involved abandoning the distinction between ordinary and extraordinary management. This decision arose in the discussions between Doug, Patricia and me and in my experience, over the previous seven years, of working with groups of managers on how they might think about their work from the perspectives of chaos and complexity. I was originally attracted to the theories of chaos and complexity because of my dissatisfaction with orthodox management theory; it simply did not help me make sense of my experience of the unexpected and the creative in organizations. More important was the deep feeling I had that there were radical implications in chaos and complexity for understanding the nature of management. However, I discovered that my ways of trying to express this intuition were far from adequate. I was trying to hold on to the paradoxical nature of complexity theory and of life in organizations. I attempted to do this in the distinction I made in the second edition between ordinary and extraordinary management, arguing that complexity theory enabled a deeper understanding of the latter. However, although I stressed the paradoxical nature of ordinary and extraordinary management, namely, that they were practised at the same time even though they were directly contrary to each other, the concepts were usually interpreted in a sequential manner. Managers talked about practising ordinary management most of the time and occasionally finding that they had to move into the dangerous practice of extraordinary management. I found it difficult to explain why this was not the case. Other experiences in the previous few years had given me some insight into the inadequacy of the explanations that I was putting forward.

First, I came to realize that I had been trying to explain paradoxical complex human processes in language taken from a mixture of cognitive psychology and psychoanalysis. Both of these psychologies start from the position of the autonomous individual. For the former, group and society are simply formed by individuals who are then influenced by what they have formed. In the latter, group and society play a much more important role in that the individual mind is structured by the clash between individual drives and social prohibition. The social then has a much more formative impact on the individual but the motivation and energy for behaviour still come from drives located in the individual. This questioning of the relationship between the individual (agent) and the society (structure) is, of course, a major question in sociology and it certainly featured strongly in the conversations and arguments with Doug and Patricia. We began to connect with another way of thinking about human nature to be found in process sociology and in group analytic theory. From this perspective, the individual is social through and through to the core. The individual mind and social relations are simply two different perspectives on the same phenomenon, namely, interdependent people.

When I wrote the first two editions of *Strategic Management and Organisational Dynamics*, my underlying, although poorly expressed, interest was not in how to understand complexity as an objective property of an organization, but in how to understand complexity from within the system. I was interested in what it was like to be a human complex system and what it was like to be a member of a group that is a complex system. This did not come out at all clearly. I came to realize that this was because I was not being clear about the methodological position I was taking. My second realization, then, was just how fundamental is the methodological stance one takes. Individual-centred cognitive psychology and the scientific origins of systems theory make it feel natural to take the methodological position of the objective observer. The implicit prescription is that this is the position that managers should take. In this they stand outside the organizational system and either manipulate it or understand it from a distant, uninvolved position. An alternative methodological position is a reflexive one, and this distinction between the external objective observer and the participant understanding from within the experience was another, sometimes fraught, topic of conversation between Doug, Patricia and me.

These two distinctions, namely, the distinction between an individual-centred and a relationship-focused psychology, and the distinction between the methodological position of the objective observer and the participative inquirer, provided the basic structure of the third edition. The first part of the book reviewed orthodox theories of organization and management. The criteria for orthodoxy were the use of the first wave of systems theories (cybernetics, systems dynamics, open systems) in combination with individual-centred psychology and the methodology of the objective observer. The second part explored a radical approach. The first criterion for potentially radical theories is that they take the perspective of chaos and complexity on systems. However, if they do this in a way that retains individual-centred psychology and the position of the objective observer, they implicitly subsume chaos and complexity theory into a cybernetic framework. The result is a collapse back into management orthodoxy. In place of this, a relationship psychology complexity perspective on organizations would put the self-organizing conversational life of an organization at the centre of the processes through which strategies emerge. These were called complex responsive processes, a term developed in the discussions between Doug, Patricia and me in order to avoid the term complex adaptive system that had become so associated with the autonomous individual and the objective observer. The term complex responsive processes signals the danger of treating an organization as a system, as a thing, and suggests that it would be more helpful to avoid describing organizations as systems altogether and to understand what goes on in organizations as responsive processes.

I said earlier that Doug introduced the work of Mead into our discussions and the impact of Mead's thinking is evident in the last few chapters of the third edition. Also, all the other members of the PhD group worked on themes to do with how they might understand their experience of life in organizations from a complexity perspective, as I did in my training as a group analyst at the IGA. At the end of that training I read Farhad Dalal's book *Taking the Group Seriously*,[57] and its impact on this edition is evident in the last few chapters, particularly because the book introduced me to the work of Norbert Elias, the process sociologist.

Then, for most of 1999 and I think the early part of 2000, Doug, Patricia and I worked on the first of a series of books we had undertaken to produce in the series *Complexity and Emergence in Organizations*. This first book was published in 2000 under the title *Complexity and Management: Fad or Radical Challenge to Systems Thinking?*[58] In this book, we made a decisive shift from thinking in terms of systems to thinking in terms of responsive processes, and we introduced the notion of transformative causality which was different from the formative causality of systems thinking, the efficient causality of traditional science and the rationalist causality of the autonomous individual. We also moved from the assumption of the autonomous individual to understanding individuals as essentially interdependent, pointing to the paradox of individuals forming the social while at the same time being formed by it. We also brought in the notion of the living present. Doug underpinned our argument by bringing in the philosophical positions of Kant and Hegel. This book, then, represented a radical shift in our thinking and established the foundations that we are still developing. During 2000 I completed the second book in the series, *Complex Responsive Processes in Organisations*,[59] which was published in 2001. This book worked out in more detail what we meant by the theory of complex responsive processes. During the course of 2001 and 2002 four additional volumes by graduates from the PhD group were published in the series, all further developing the theory of complex responsive processes – these were *The Emergence of Leadership* by Doug Griffin,[60] *The Paradox of Control in Organizations* by Phil Streatfield,[61] *Complexity and Innovation in Organizations* by Jose Fonseca,[62] and *Changing Conversations in Organizations* by Patricia Shaw.[63] This development of ideas continues, and more recently Chris Mowles published *Rethinking Management*.[64] I will not say anything further about these books because the ideas developed in them are summarized in Chapters 2 and 3 above.

The Doctor of Management programme

In 1998 CMC members explored the possibility of setting up a Master of Science degree programme for managers at IBM. A number of meetings were held with the European director of HR in Italy and a possible joint venture with an Italian university was explored. For a number of reasons, one of which was disagreement over what an innovative MSc would look like, the talks fell through. However, the idea remained and when colleagues at the IGA expressed interest in some kind of degree which would include group analysis relevant to organizations, meetings were held with CMC members. These progressed and the University of Hertfordshire approved an MA in organizational change in association with the IGA. This was designed as a two-year part-time research degree in which participants working in organizations would be researching into their own work experience as leaders, managers and consultants. Students were recruited, and in February 2000 eighteen leaders, managers and consultants from a wide range of organizations in the USA, Ireland, Norway, Germany and the UK attended the first residential meeting. The head of research degrees at the university then drew our attention to the movement to develop professional doctorates, two of which had already been set up at the university. Within a short time an additional year and further research requirements were added and the MA became the Doctor of Management programme, with a research MA as a drop-off point. The supervisors on this new DMan programme were Doug, Patricia and me, as well as two colleagues from the IGA, Wil Penny-Cooke Grieves and Chris Rance. This programme has become the key community in developing the thinking around complex responsive processes of relating as a way of understanding organizations, leadership and management. Fifteen of the first eighteen participants graduated with either an MA or a DMan and to date there have been 51 graduates, 39 being at the doctoral level. The programme continues and, in addition to the countries mentioned above, graduates come from New Zealand, South Africa, Israel, Canada, Denmark and Portugal. With a new director, Chris Mowles, the programme will hopefully continue for many years.

I think this programme, the way we are working as supervisors and the research method the students employ are all examples of how people find themselves working in ways different from those they used to work in as a reflection of ongoing, exploratory, reflexive inquiry. The participants also report that they find themselves working differently in their own organizations.

Further publications

During the first half of 2002 I completed the fourth edition of my textbook, which was published in 2003. This edition made a sharper distinction between systemic and process thinking than the third edition had done, particularly by including new chapters on the philosophical origins of systems and process thinking and by adding chapters on second order and critical system thinking. New material was also included on the theory of complex responsive processes, particularly to do with control, leadership and ethics.

In 2002 I worked on another book, *Complexity and Group Processes: A Radically Social Understanding of Individuals*,[65] which came out in 2003. This was addressed to the community of group therapists and it distinguished between a tradition of thought which led to the psychoanalytic emphasis on intra-psychic processes of the individual who strives for autonomy and another tradition which led to the emphasis on interdependent individuals in which the individual and the social are the same processes. This book marked a shift in my thinking away from psychoanalytic thinking to a complex responsive processes view of individuals who are thoroughly social beings.

By 2005 two cohorts of researchers had graduated from the Doctor of Management research degree programme mentioned above and, in various combinations, Doug, Patricia and I edited the series *Complexity as the Experience of Organizing* which consisted of six volumes,[66] containing chapters drawn from the theses of the programme's graduates. These came out in 2005, 2006 and 2008. The work of the graduates made a significant contribution to the further development of complex responsive processes as a way of thinking about what people did in organizations.

In the first half of 2006 I did the fifth edition of my textbook, published in 2007. The structure of this edition was the same as that of the previous edition. The chapters dealing with the theory of complex responsive processes were significantly expanded to bring in more recent developments of the theory to do with values, ideology and the link between local interaction, the micro, and population-wide patterns, the macro. These developments reflected a growing literature on the complex responsive processes perspective, mainly coming from graduates of the Doctor of Management programme.

In 2009 I worked on *Complexity and Organizational Reality: Uncertainty and the Need to Rethink Management after the Collapse of Investment Capitalism*, published in 2010.[67] This book was something between a second edition of *Complexity and Management* (2000) and *Complex Responsive Processes in Organizations* (2001) and a new book which introduced more material extending the theory of complex responsive processes.

In the first half of 2010 I did the revisions for the sixth edition of my textbook, published in 2011. The general structure of this edition was the same as that of the previous one but there was a new introductory chapter which attempted to clarify why this was a book about thinking and why it did not present prescriptions for success. Another new chapter reviewed where the dominant discourse had got to and what evidence there was for the success of its prescriptions, concluding that there was no reliable scientific evidence supporting the prescriptions and yet it continued to be the dominant discourse. Yet another new chapter incorporated material about second order systems thinking and communities of practice from the previous edition and added material mainly on social constructionist approaches and labour process theory. The last three chapters of this edition were substantially rewritten, with one of them focusing specifically on what strategic management might mean from the perspective of complex responsive processes.

Many of the same themes of interest have run through the publications by colleagues and me, as described in this appendix. These themes have to do with trying to understand what leaders and managers actually do rather than what they are supposed to do, and that means focusing attention on conversation, power, ideology and the daily politics of organizational life. However, the way of thinking about and explaining these themes has shifted radically. Prior to 2000 organizations were understood as systems, while after 2000 they were understood as responsive processes of interacting between interdependent people. Before 2000 a taken-for-granted assumption was made of the autonomous individual, understood in terms of cognitivist psychology, but after 2000 our thinking moved to understanding individuals, groups, organizations and societies as interdependent people. Before 2000 there was an implicit assumption of the external objective observer, but after that we moved to thinking in terms of participative inquiry, that is, a method of inquiring into experience from within experience. This shift in thinking is reflected in how we work as supervisors of research degrees and as consultants to organizations.

So after a major shift around 1999 to 2000 in the way my colleagues and I were thinking, the period since then has been one of extending and refining this way of thinking. Although this appendix is about shifts in my own thinking, I think it is evident that my thinking is inextricably intertwined with the thinking of my closest colleagues, other members of the staff group of our Doctor of Management programme, the students doing research on the programme, colleagues at the Institute of Group Analysis, others I have been corresponding with and also those I have worked with in seminars and workshops. Movements of individual thought are always social movements and none of us can change how we think all on our own; nor can we know in advance just how these changes in thinking will change how we find ourselves working.

NOTES

1 Introduction

1 Fonseca, 2001; Griffin, 2002; Griffin and Stacey (eds), 2005; Shaw, 2002; Shaw and Stacey, 2006; Stacey, Griffin and Shaw, 2000; Stacey, 2001; Stacey, 2003; Stacey and Griffin (eds), 2005a; Stacey (ed.), 2005; Stacey and Griffin (eds), 2005b; Stacey and Griffin (eds), 2008; Stacey, 2010; Stacey, 2011; Streatfield, 2001; Mowles, 2011.
2 Khurana, 2007.
3 Zaleznick, 1977.
4 Schein, 1985.
5 Foucault, 1977.
6 Schein, 1985.

2 The theory of complex responsive processes: understanding organizations as patterns of interaction between people

1 Gleick, 1988.
2 Lorenz, 1963.
3 The geometric equivalent of chaos is what are called fractals. See Mandelbrot, 1982.
4 Stewart, 1989.
5 Goldberger, 1997.
6 Maguire and McKelvey, 1999.
7 Freeman, 1994; Freeman, 1995; Freeman and Schneider, 1982; Freeman and Barrie, 1994.
8 Elias, 2000 [1939].
9 Elias, 1991, p. 480.
10 Elias, 1991, pp. 5–6.
11 Elias, 1991, p. 456.
12 Elias, 1991, p. 12.
13 Elias, 2000 [1939].
14 Elias, 1991, pp. 146–7.
15 Elias, 2000 [1939], p. 365.
16 Elias, 2000 [1939], p. 366 (original italics).
17 Mezrich, 2009.

3 Understanding organizing activities as the game: implications for leadership and management tools and techniques

1 Mead, 1934.
2 Mead, 1964, p. 130.
3 Boje, 1991, 1994, 1995.
4 Elias and Scotson, 1994.
5 Elias and Scotson, 1994.
6 Elias, 2000 [1939].
7 Dewey, 1934.
8 Mead, 1914.
9 MacIntyre, 1998.
10 Honneth, 2007.
11 Mead, 1938.
12 Elias, 2008; Bourdieu, 1990.
13 For example, Elias, 1997.
14 Bourdieu, 1990.

4 The leadership and management tools and techniques of instrumental rationality: rules and step-by-step procedures

1 Johnson, Whittington and Scholes, 2011.
2 Porter, 1980.
3 Johnson, Whittington and Scholes, 2011.
4 Porter, 1985.
5 Johnson, Whittington and Scholes, 2011.
6 Mintzberg, Theoret and Rainsinghani, 1976.
7 For example, Churchman, 1968, 1970; Ackoff, 1981, 1994; Checkland, 1981, 1983; Checkland and Scholes, 1990; Flood, 1990, 1999; Jackson, 2000; Midgley, 2000.
8 Ackoff, 1981, 1994.
9 Churchman, 1968, 1970.
10 Checkland, 1981, 1983.
11 Midgley, 2000.
12 Jackson, 2000.
13 Snowden, 2000.
14 Stacey, 2010.
15 Grimshaw and Eccles, 2004.
16 Taylor, 1997.
17 Taylor, 1997, p. 170.

5 The limitations of the tools and techniques of instrumental rationality: incompatibility with expert performance

1 Dreyfus and Dreyfus, 1986.
2 Although Dreyfus and Dreyfus did not focus on leading and management, their model can be used to understand the development of the skills required.
3 Dreyfus and Dreyfus, 1986, p. 35.
4 For example, Flyvbjerg, 2001; Taylor, 1997.
5 Alvesson and Sveningsson, 2003a.
6 Alvesson and Sveningsson, 2003a, p. 1436.
7 Alvesson and Sveningsson, 2003b.

8 Orwell, 1949.
9 Tobin, 2005a, 2005b.
10 Taylor, 2005a, 2005b.

6 The leadership and management techniques of disciplinary power: surveillance and normalization

1 Foucault, 1977.
2 Foucault, 2004, p. 2.
3 Foucault, 1977, p. 148.
4 Foucault, 2004, p. 245.
5 Foucault, 2004, p. 245.
6 Foucault, 2004, p. 249.
7 Foucault, 1977, p. 164.
8 Foucault, 1977, p. 170.
9 Foucault, 1977, p. 175.
10 Foucault, 1977, p. 177.
11 Foucault, 1977, p. 184.
12 Foucault, 1977, p. 194.
13 Foucault, 1977, p. 215.
14 Foucault, 1977, p. 224.
15 Foucault, 1977, p. 220.
16 Foucault, 1977, p. 220.
17 Billing, 2008.

7 Taking the techniques of disciplinary power to the extreme: domination and coercive persuasion

1 Foucault, 1977.
2 Schein, 1985.
3 Senge, 1990.
4 Argyris and Schön, 1978; Argyris, 1990.
5 Schein, 1999, p. 169.
6 Ofshe, 2000.
7 Ofshe, 2000, p. 149.
8 Scott, 1990.
9 Foucault, 2004, p. 194.
10 Scott, 1990.

8 Institutions and the techniques of leadership and management: habits, rules and routines

1 Veblen, 1909, 1989 [1934]; Mitchell, 1937; Commons, 1934, 1957.
2 North, 1981, 1990, 1991; Hodgson, 2006.
3 Hodgson, 2006.
4 North, 1990.
5 Hodgson, 2006.
6 Hodgson, 2006.
7 Nelson and Winter, 1982.
8 Egidi, 1996.
9 Egidi, 1992.
10 Nelson and Winter, 1982.

11 Coase, 1988; North, 1981; Williamson, 1975, 1981, 1985, 1994, 2000.
12 North, 1991.
13 North, 1991.
14 Hodgson, 2006.
15 Lawson, 2003.
16 Nee, 2003.
17 Granovetter, 1985; Nee, 2003; Fligstein, 1996, 2001; Swedberg, 1994, 1998, 2003.
18 Nee, 2003, pp. 23–4 (original italics).
19 Burns, 2000.
20 Feldman, 2000.
21 McKeown, 2001.
22 Searle, 2005.
23 Feldman and Pentland, 2003; Pentland and Feldman, 2007.
24 Lawson, 2003.
25 Feldman and Pentland, 2003.
26 Feldman and Pentland, 2003.
27 Granovetter, 1985; Nee, 2003; Fligstein, 1996, 2001; Swedberg, 1994, 1998, 2003.
28 Feldman and Pentland, 2003, and Pentland and Feldman, 2007, make much the same point in underscoring reflexive and narrative understandings of routines.
29 Some writers in the literature on routines make a very similar point in directing attention to context and the need to interpret what the routine means in different contexts – see Feldman and Pentland, 2003.
30 For example, Feldman and Pentland, 2003.
31 For example, Hodgson, 2006.
32 Elias, 1987.
33 Feldman and Pentland, 2003, make much the same point when they talk about objectivity and subjectivity as mutually constituted.
34 Geertz, 1973.
35 Foucault, 2009, p. 116.
36 McKeown, 2001.

9 The leadership and management 'techniques' of practical judgement: reflexive inquiry, improvisation and political adroitness

1 Schön, 1983, 1987.
2 McDonald and Robinson, 2009.
3 Kolb and Kolb, 2005.
4 Schön, 1983, 1987.
5 Bourdieu, 1990.
6 Crossan and Sorrenti, 2002; Keefe, 2003.
7 Boal, 1979, 1992, 1995, 1998; Boje, 2002; Clark and Mangham, 2002, 2004; Johnstone, 1979, 1999; Meisiek, 2002; Oswick, Keenoy and Grant, 2001.
8 Larsen and Friis, 2006.
9 Holmes and Stubbe, 2003.
10 Holmes and Stubbe, 2003, p. 343.
11 Foucault, 2010.

Appendix: reflexive narrative inquiry: movements in my thinking and how I find myself working differently as a consequence

1 Stacey, 1966.
2 Stacey, 1969.

3 Stacey, 1968.
4 Stacey, 1990.
5 Drucker, 1985.
6 Goold and Campbell, 1988.
7 Quinn, Mintzberg and James, 1988.
8 Pascale, 1988.
9 Quinn, Mintzberg and James, 1988.
10 Stacey, 1991.
11 Lorenz, 1963; Stewart, 1989.
12 Prigogine and Stengers, 1984; Davies, 1987.
13 For example, Baumol and Benhabib, 1989; Arthur, 1988.
14 Shenkman and Le Baron, 1989; Hsieh, 1989.
15 Nonaka, 1988.
16 Smith, 1986; Rasmussen and Mosekilde, 1988; Bygrave, 1989; Priesmeyer and Baik, 1989; Goldstein, 1989; Zimmerman, 1990.
17 Ansoff, 1965.
18 Burns and Stalker, 1961.
19 Drucker, 1967.
20 Hamel and Prahalad, 1989.
21 Moss Kanter, 1985.
22 Quinn, Mintzberg and James, 1988.
23 Ohmae, 1990.
24 Peters and Waterman, 1982.
25 Quinn, Mintzberg and James, 1988.
26 Simon, 1970.
27 Lindblom, 1959.
28 Cohen, March and Ohlsen, 1972.
29 Weick, 1979.
30 Bion, 1961.
31 Miller and Rice, 1967.
32 Bacharach and Lawler, 1980.
33 Pettigrew, 1973.
34 Pfeffer, 1981.
35 Zaleznik and Kets de Vries, 1985.
36 Argyris, 1982.
37 Penrose, 1988.
38 Argyris and Schön, 1978; Schön, 1983, 1987.
39 The notion of organizational learning was based on the work of Argyris and Schön, 1978. What was to become the famous *Fifth Discipline* by Senge was published in 1990 while I was writing the *Chaos Frontier* and so it was not referred to.
40 Prigogine and Stengers, 1984.
41 Zimmerman, 1992.
42 Wheatley, 1992.
43 Goldstein, 1989.
44 Guastello, 1992.
45 For example, Young, 1992; DeShon and Svyantek, 1993; Levy, 1994.
46 Kuhn, 1970.
47 Klein, 1975.
48 Waldrop, 1992.
49 Stacey, 1995.
50 Kauffman, 1995.
51 Klein, 1975.
52 Winnicott, 1971.
53 Mead, 1934.

54 Shotter, 1993.
55 Elias, 2000 [1939].
56 Stacey, Griffin and Shaw, 1998, 1999.
57 Dalal, 1998.
58 Stacey, Griffin and Shaw, 2000.
59 Stacey, 2001.
60 Griffin, 2002.
61 Streatfield, 2001.
62 Fonseca, 2002.
63 Shaw, 2002.
64 Mowles, 2011.
65 Stacey, 2003.
66 Stacey and Griffin, 2005a; Griffin and Stacey, 2005; Stacey, 2005; Stacey and Griffin, 2005b; Shaw and Stacey, 2006; Stacey and Griffin, 2008.
67 Stacey, 2010.

BIBLIOGRAPHY

Ackoff, R. L. (1981) *Creating the Corporate Future*, New York: Wiley.

——(1994) *The Democratic Organization*, New York: Oxford University Press.

Alvesson, M. and Sveningsson, S. (2003a) 'Managers Doing Leadership: The Extra-ordinarization of the Mundane', *Human Relations*, 56(12): 1435–59.

——(2003b) 'Good Visions, Bad Micro-management and Ugly Ambiguity: Contradictions of Non-leadership in a Knowledge-Intensive Organization', *Organization Studies*, 24(6): 961–88.

Ansoff, I. (1965) *Corporate Strategy*, New York: McGraw-Hill.

Argyris, C. (1990) *Overcoming Organizational Defenses: Facilitating Organizational Learning*, Boston, MA: Allyn & Bacon.

Argyris, C. and Schön, D. (1978) *Organizational Learning: A Theory of Action Perspective*, Reading, MA: Addison-Wesley.

Argyris, J. (1982) *Reasoning, Learning and Action*, San Francisco, CA: Jossey-Bass.

Arthur, W. B. (1988) 'Self-Reinforcing Mechanisms in Economics', in Anderson, P., Arrow, K. and Pines, D. (eds) *The Economy as an Evolving Complex System*, Reading, MA: Addison-Wesley.

Bacharach, S. B. and Lawler, E. J. (1980) *Power and Politics in Organizations*, San Francisco, CA: Jossey-Bass.

Baumol, W. J. and Benhabib, J. (1989) 'Chaos: Significance, Mechanism and Economic Applications', *Journal of Economic Perspectives*, 3(1): 77–105.

Billing, S. (2008) 'The Role of Propaganda in Managing Organizational Change: Ethics, Conflict and Compromise in Consulting', in Stacey, R. and Griffin, D. (eds) *Complexity and the Experience of Values, Conflict and Compromise in Organizations*, London: Routledge.

Bion, W. (1961) *Experiences in Groups and Other Papers*, London: Tavistock.

Boal, A. (1979) *Theatre of the Oppressed*, New York: Theatre Communication Group Inc.

——(1992) *Games for Actors and Non-actors*, London: Routledge.

——(1995) *The Rainbow of Desire – The Boal Method on Theatre and Therapy*, London: Routledge.

——(1998) *Legislative Theatre: Using Performance to Make Politics*, London: Routledge.

Boje, D. M. (1991) 'The Storytelling Organization: A Study of Performance in an Office Supply Firm', *Administrative Science Quarterly*, 36: 106–26.

——(1994) 'Organizational Storytelling: The Struggle of Pre-modern, Modern and Post-modern Organizational Learning Discourses', *Management Learning*, 25(3): 433–62.

——(1995) 'Stories of the Storytelling Organization: A Postmodern Analysis of Disney as Tamara-Land', *Academy of Management Journal*, 38(4): 997–1055.

——(2002) 'Global Theatrics and Capitalism', *Academy of Management Journal*, conference paper.

Bourdieu, P. (1990) *The Logic of Practice*, Cambridge: Polity Press.

Burns, J. (2000) 'The Dynamics of Accounting Change: Interplay between New Practices, Routines, Institutions, Power and Politics', *Accounting, Auditing and Accountability Journal*, 13(5): 566–86.

Burns, T. and Stalker, G. M. (1961) *The Management of Innovation*, London: Tavistock Publications.

Bygrave, W. (1989) 'The Entrepreneurship Paradigm II: Chaos and Catastrophes among Quantum Jumps?', *Entrepreneurship: Theory and Practice*, 14(2): 7–30.

Cartwright, T. J. (1991) 'Planning and Chaos Theory', *Journal of the American Planning Association*, 57(1): 44–56.

Checkland, P. B. (1981) *Systems Thinking, Systems Practice*, Chichester: Wiley.

——(1983) 'OR and the Systems Movement: Mapping and Conflicts', *Journal of the Operational Research Society*, 34: 661.

Checkland, P. B. and Holwell, S. (1998) *Information, Systems and Information Systems*, Chichester: Wiley.

Checkland, P. B. and Scholes, P. (1990) *Soft Systems Methodology in Action*, Chichester: Wiley.

Churchman, C. West (1968) *The Systems Approach*, New York: Delacorte Press.

——(1970) *The Systems Approach and Its Enemies*, New York: Basic Books.

Clark, T. and Mangham, I. (2004) 'From Dramaturgy to Theatre as Technology: The Case of Corporate Theatre', *Journal of Management Studies*, 41(1): 37–59.

Clark, T. and Mangham, L. (2004) 'Stripping to the Undercoat: A Review and Reflections on a Piece of Organization Theatre', *Organization Studies*, 25(5): 841–51.

Coase, R. (1988) *The Firm, the Market, and the Law*, Chicago, IL: University of Chicago Press.

Cohen, M. D., March, J. G. and Ohlsen, J. P. (1972) 'A Garbage Can Model of Organizational Choice', *Administrative Science Quarterly*, 17: 1–25.

Commons, J. (1934) *Institutional Economics: Its Place in Political Economy*, New York: Macmillan.

——(1957) *Legal Foundations of Capitalism*, Madison, WI: University of Wisconsin Press.

Crossan, M. and Sorrenti, M. (2002) 'Making Sense of Improvisation', in Kamoche, K., Cunha, M. and Cunha, J. (eds) *Organizational Improvisation*, London: Routledge, pp. 29–51.

Dalal, F. (1998) *Taking the Group Seriously: Towards a Post-Foulkesian Group Analytic Theory*, London: Jessica Kingsley.

Davies, P. (1987) *The Cosmic Blueprint*, London: Heinemann.

DeShon, R. and Svyantek, D. (1993) 'Organizational Attractors: A Chaos Theory Explanation of Why Cultural Change Efforts Often Fail', *Public Administration Quarterly*, 17(3): 339–55.

Dewey, J. (1934) *A Common Faith*, New Haven, CT: Yale University Press.

DiMaggio, P. and Powell, W. (1983) 'The Iron Cage Revisited: Institutional Isomorphism and Collective Rationality in Organizational Fields', *American Sociological Review*, 48: 147–60.

Dreyfus, H. and Dreyfus, S. (1986) *Mind over Machine: The Power of Human Intuition and Expertise in the Era of the Computer*, New York: The Free Press.

Drucker, P. (1967) *The Practice of Management*, London: Heinemann.

——(1985) *Entrepreneurship and Innovation*, London: Heinemann.

Egidi, M. (1992) 'Organisational Learning, Problem Solving and the Division of Labour', in Simon, H., Egidi, M., Marris, R. and Viale, R. (eds) *Economics, Bounded Rationality and the Cognitive Revolution*, Aldershot: Edward Elgar.

——(1996) 'Routines, Hierarchies of Problems, Procedural Behaviour: Some Evidence from Experiments', in Arrow, K., Colombatto, E., Perlman, M. and Schmidt C. (eds) *The Rational Foundations of Economic Behaviour*, London: Macmillan.

Elias, N. (1987) *Involvement and Detachment*, Oxford: Blackwell.

——(1991) *The Society of Individuals*, Oxford: Blackwell.

——(1997) *The Germans*, Cambridge: Polity Press.

——(2000) [1939] *The Civilizing Process*, Oxford: Blackwell.

——(2008) 'Civilization', in Kilminster, R. and Mennell, S. (eds) *Essays II: On Civilising Processes, State Formation and National Identity*, Dublin: University College Dublin Press.

Elias, N. and Scotson, J. (1994) *The Established and the Outsiders*, London: Sage.

Feldman, M. (2000) 'Organisational Routines as a Source of Continuous Change', *Organization Science*, 11(6): 611–29.

Feldman, M. and Pentland, B. (2003) 'Reconceptualizing Organisational Routines as a Source of Flexibility and Change', *Administrative Science Quarterly*, 48(1): 94–118.

Fligstein, N. (1996) 'Markets and Politics: A Sociological View of Market Institutions', *American Sociological Review*, 61: 656–73.

——(2001) *The Architecture of Markets: An Economic Sociology of Twenty-First-Century Capitalist Societies*, Princeton, NJ: Princeton University Press.

Flood, R. L. (1990) 'Liberating Systems Theory: Towards Critical Systems Thinking', *Human Relations*, 43(1): 49–75.

——(1999) *Rethinking the Fifth Discipline: Learning within the Unknowable*, London: Routledge.

Flyvbjerg, B. (2001) *Making Social Science Matter: Why Social Inquiry Fails and How It Can Succeed Again*, Cambridge: Cambridge University Press.

Fonseca, J. (2002) *Complexity and Innovation in Organizations*, London: Routledge.

Foucault, M. (1977) *Discipline and Punish: The Birth of the Prison*, London: Penguin Books.

——(2004) *Society Must Be Saved*, London: Penguin Books.

——(2009) *Security, Territory, Population: Lectures at the Collège de France 1977–1978*, London: Palgrave Macmillan.

——(2010) *The Government of Self and Others: Lectures at the Collège de France 1982–1983*, London: Palgrave Macmillan.

Freeman, W. J. (1994) 'Role of Chaotic Dynamics in Neural Plasticity', in van Pelt, J., Corner, M. A., Uylings, H. B. M. and Lopes da Silva, F. H. (eds) *Progress in Brain Research*, 102, Amsterdam: Elsevier Science BV.

——(1995) *Societies of Brains: A Study in the Neuroscience of Love and Hate*, Hillsdale, NJ: Lawrence Erlbaum Associates Publishers.

Freeman, W. J. and Barrie, J. M. (1994) 'Chaotic Oscillations and the Genesis of Meaning in Cerebral Cortex', in Buzsaki, G., Llinas, R., Singer, W., Berthoz, A. and Christen, Y. (eds) *Temporal Coding in the Brain*, Berlin: Springer.

Freeman, W. J. and Schneider, W. (1982) 'Changes in the Spatial Patterns of Rabbit Olfactory EEG with Conditioning to Odors', *Psychophysiology*, 19(1): 45–56.

Gabriel, Y. (1998) 'Same Old Story or Changing Stories? Folkloric, Modern and Postmodern Mutations', in Grant, D., Keenoy, T. and Oswick, C. (eds) *Discourse and Organisation*, London: Sage.

Geertz, C. (1973) *The Interpretation of Cultures*, New York: Basic Books.

Gleick, J. (1988) *Chaos: Making a New Science*, London: Heinemann.

Goldberger, A. L. (1997) 'Fractal Variability versus Pathological Periodicity: Complexity Loss and Stereotypy in Disease', *Perspectives in Biology and Medicine*, 40(4): 553–61.

Goldstein, J. (1989) 'A Far from Equilibrium Systems Approach to Resistance to Change', *Organizational Dynamics*, 17(2): 16–26.

Goold, M. and Campbell, A. (1988) *Strategies and Styles*, Oxford: Blackwell.

Granovetter, M. (1985) 'Economic Action and Social Structure: The Problem of Embeddedness', *American Journal of Sociology*, 91(3): 481–510.

Griffin, D. (2002) *The Emergence of Leadership: Linking Self-Organization and Ethics*, London: Routledge.

Griffin, D. and Stacey, R. (eds) (2005) *Complexity and the Experience of Leading Organizations*, London: Routledge.

Grimshaw, J. M. and Eccles, M. (2004) 'Is Evidence-Based Implementation of Evidence-Based Care Possible?', *Medical Journal of Australia*, 180: 50–1.

Guastello, S. (1992) 'Population Dynamics and Workforce Productivity', conference paper, Second Annual Chaos Network Conference, Santa Cruz, CA.

Hamel, G. and Prahalad, C. (1989) 'Strategic Intent', *Harvard Business Review*, May–June.

Hersey, P. and Blanchard, K. (1977) *The Management of Organizational Behavior*, 3rd edn, Upper Saddle River, NJ: Prentice-Hall.

Hodgson, G. (2006) 'What Are Institutions?', *Journal of Economic Issues*, XL(1): 1–25.

Holmes, J. and Stubbe, M. (2003) *Power and Politeness in the Workplace*, Harlow: Pearson Education.

Honneth, A. (2007) 'Recognition as Ideology', in van den Brink, B. and Owen, D. (eds) *Recognition and Power: Axel Honneth and the Tradition of Critical Social Theory*, Cambridge: Cambridge University Press.

Hsieh, D. (1989) 'Testing for Nonlinear Dependence in Daily Foreign Exchange Returns', *Journal of Business*, 62(3): 339–68.

Jackson, M. C. (2000) *Systems Approaches to Management*, New York: Kluwer.

Jensen, M. C. and Meckling, W. H. (1976) 'Theory of the Firm: Managerial Behavior, Agency Costs, and Ownership Structure', *Journal of Financial Economics*, 3(4): 305–60.

Joas, H. (2000) *The Genesis of Values*, Cambridge: Polity Press.

Johnson, G., Whittington, R. and Scholes, K. (2011) *Exploring Corporate Strategy*, Harlow: FT Prentice-Hall.

Johnstone, K. (1979) *Improvisation and the Theatre*, London: Methuen.

——(1999) *Impro for Storytellers*, London: Faber & Faber Ltd.

Kauffman, S. A. (1995) *At Home in the Universe*, New York: Oxford University Press.

Keefe, J. A. (2003) *Improve Yourself – Business Spontaneity at the Speed of Thought*, New Jersey: John Wiley & Sons.

Khurana, R. (2007) *From Higher Aims to Hired Hands: The Social Transformation of Business Schools and the Unfulfilled Promise of Management as a Profession*, Princeton, NJ: Princeton University Press.

Klein, M. (1975) *The Writings of Melanie Klein*, London: Hogarth Press.

Kolb, A. and Kolb, D. (2005) 'Learning Styles and Learning Spaces: Enhancing Experiential Learning in Higher Education', *Academy of Management Learning and Education*, 4(2): 193–212.

Kuhn, T. (1970) *The Structure of Scientific Revolutions*, Chicago, IL: University of Chicago Press.

Larsen, H. and Friis, P. (2006) 'Theatre, Improvisation and Social Change', in Shaw, P. and Stacey, R. (eds) *Experiencing Risk, Spontaneity and Improvisation in Organizational Change: Working Live*, London: Routledge.

Lawson, T. (2003) *Reorienting Economics*, London: Routledge.

Levy, D. (1994) 'Chaos Theory and Strategy: Theory, Application, and Managerial Implications', *Strategic Management Journal*, 15(S2): 167–78.

Lindblom, L. (1959) 'The Science of Muddling Through', *Public Administration Review*, 19(2): 79–88.

Lorenz, E. (1963) 'Deterministic Non Periodic Flow', *Journal of the Atmospheric Sciences*, 20(2): 130–41.

McDonald, L. and Robinson, P. (2009) *A Colossal Failure of Common Sense: The Inside Story of the Collapse of Lehman Brothers*, London: Ebury Press.

MacIntyre, A. (1998) 'Social Science Methodology as the Ideology of Bureaucratic Authority', in Knight, K. (ed.) *The MacIntyre Reader*, Cambridge: Polity Press.

McKeown, T. (2001) 'Plans and Routines, Bureaucratic Bargaining, and the Cuban Missile Crisis', *Journal of Politics*, 63(4): 1163–90.

Maguire, S. and McKelvey, B. (1999) 'Complexity and Management: Moving from Fad to Firm Foundations', *Emergence*, 1(2): 19–61.

Mandelbrot, B. (1982) *The Fractal Geometry of Nature*, New York: Freeman and Company.

Mead, G. H. (1914) 'The Psychological Bases of Internationalism', *Survey*, XXIII: 604–7.

——(1923) 'Scientific Method and the Moral Sciences', *International Journal of Ethics*, XXXIII(3): 229–47.

——(1934) *Mind, Self, and Society: From the Standpoint of a Social Behaviourist*, Chicago, IL: University of Chicago Press.

——(1938) *The Philosophy of the Act*, Chicago, IL: University of Chicago Press.

——(1964) 'Social Consciousness and the Consciousness of Meaning', in Reck, A. J. (ed.) *Selected Writings*, Indianapolis, IN: Library of the Liberal Arts.

Meisiek, S. (2002) 'Situation Drama in Change Management: Types and Effects of a New Managerial Tool', *International Journal of Arts Management*, 4(3): 48–55.

Mezrich, B. (2009) *The Accidental Billionaires: The Founding of Facebook. A Tale of Sex, Money, Genius and Betrayal*, New York: Doubleday.

Midgley, G. (2000) *Systemic Intervention: Philosophy, Methodology, and Practice*, New York: Kluwer.

Miller, E. J. and Rice, A. K. (1967) *Systems of Organization: The Control of Task and Sentient Boundaries*, London: Tavistock.

Mintzberg, H., Theoret, A. and Raisinghani, D. (1976) 'The Structure of the Unstructured Decision Making Process', *Administrative Science Quarterly*, 21(2): 246–75.

Mitchell, W. (1937) *The Backward Art of Spending Money and Other Essays*, New York: Augustus M. Kelley, Inc.

Moss Kanter, R. (1985) *The Change Masters*, New York: Simon & Schuster.

Mowles, C. (2011) *Rethinking Management: Radical Insights from the Complexity Sciences*, London: Palgrave Macmillan.

Nee, N. (2003) 'The New Institutionalism in Economics and Sociology', in Smelser, N. and Swedberg, R. (eds) *New Institutionalism, Economic and Sociological: Handbook for Economic Sociology*, Princeton, NJ: Princeton University Press.

Nelson, R. and Winter, S. (1982) *An Evolutionary Theory of Economic Change*, Cambridge: Cambridge University Press.

Nonaka, I. (1988) 'Creating Organizational Order out of Chaos: Self Renewal in Japanese Firms', *California Management Review*, Spring: 57–73.

North, D. (1981) *Structure and Change in Economic History*, New York: Norton.

——(1990) *Institutions, Institutional Change and Economic Performance*, Cambridge: Cambridge University Press.

——(1991) 'Institutions', *Journal of Economic Perspectives*, 5: 97–112.

Ofshe, R. (2000) 'Coercive Persuasion and Attitude Change', in Borgatta, E. and Montgomery, R. (eds) *Encyclopaedia of Sociology, Volume 1*, New York: Macmillan.

Ohmae, K. (1990) *The Borderless World*, London: Harper Business.

Orwell, G. (1949) *Nineteen Eighty-Four*, London: Secker & Warburg.

Oswick, C., Keenoy, T. and Grant, D. (2001) 'Dramatizing and Organizing: Acting and Being', *Journal of Organizational Change Management*, 14(3): 218–24.

Pascale, R. (1988) 'The Honda Effect', in Quinn, J., Mintzberg, H. and James, R. (eds) *The Strategy Process*, London: Prentice-Hall.

Penrose, R. (1988) *The Emperor's New Mind*, Oxford: Oxford University Press.

Pentland, B. and Feldman, M. (2007) 'Narrative Networks: Patterns of Technology and Organization', *Organization Science*, 18(5): 781–95.

Peters, T. J. and Waterman, R. H. (1982) *In Search of Excellence*, New York: Harper & Row.

Pettigrew, A. (1973) *The Politics of Organizational Decision Making*, London: Tavistock Publications.

Pfeffer, J. (1981) *Power in Organizations*, London: Pitman.

Porter, M. (1980) *Competitive Strategy: Techniques for Analyzing Industries and Competitors*, New York: The Free Press.

——(1985) *Competitive Advantage: Creating and Sustaining Superior Performance*, New York: The Free Press.

Priesmeyer, H. (1992) *Organizations and Chaos: Defining the Methods of Nonlinear Management*, Westport, CT: Quorum Books.

Priesmeyer, H. and Baik, K. (1989) 'Discovering the Patterns of Chaos', *Planning Review*, 17(6): 14–21.

Prigogine, I. and Stengers, I. (1984) *Order out of Chaos: Man's New Dialogue with Nature*, New York: Bantam Books.

Quinn, J., Mintzberg, H. and James, R. (eds) (1988) *The Strategy Process*, London: Prentice-Hall.

Rasmussen, D. and Mosekilde, E. (1988) 'Bifurcations and Chaos in a Generic Management Model', *European Journal of Operational Research*, 35(1): 80–8.

Richards, D. (1990) 'Is Strategic Decision-Making Chaotic?', *Behavioral Science*, 35(3): 219–32.

Schein, E. H. (1961) *Coercive Persuasion*, New York: Norton.

——(1985) *Organizational Culture and Leadership*, San Francisco, CA: Jossey-Bass.

——(1999) 'Empowerment, Coercive Persuasion and Organizational Learning: Do They Connect?', *The Learning Organization*, 6(4): 163–72.

Schön, D. (1983) *The Reflective Practitioner*, New York: Basic Books.

——(1987) *Educating the Reflective Practitioner*, San Francisco, CA: Jossey-Bass.

Scott, J. C. (1990) *Domination and the Arts of Resistance: Hidden Transcripts*, New Haven, CT: Yale University Press.

——(1998) *Seeing Like a State: How Certain Schemes to Improve the Human Condition Have Failed*, New Haven, CT: Yale University Press.

Searle, J. (2005) 'What Is an Institution?', *Journal of Economic Foundation*, 1(1): 1–22.

Senge, P. M. (1990) *The Fifth Discipline: The Art and Practice of the Learning Organization*, New York: Doubleday.

Shaw, P. (2002) *Changing Conversations in Organizations: A Complexity Approach to Change*, London: Routledge.

Shaw, P. and Stacey, R. (2006) *Experiencing Risk, Spontaneity and Improvisation in Organizational Change: Working Live*, London: Routledge.

Shenkman, J. and Le Baron, J. (1989) 'Nonlinear Dynamic and Stock Returns', *Journal of Business*, 62(3): 311–37.

Shotter, J. (1993) *Conversational Realities: Constructing Life through Language*, Thousand Oaks, CA: Sage.

Simon, H. (1970) *The New Science of Management Decision*, New York: Harper & Rowe.

Smith, C. (1986) 'Transformation and Regeneration in Social Systems: A Dissipative Structure Perspective', *Systems Research*, 3(4): 203–13.

Snowden, D. (2000) 'Cynefin: A Sense of Time and Space, the Social Ecology of Knowledge Management', in Despres, C. and Chauvel, D. (eds) *Knowledge Horizons: The Present and the Promise of Knowledge Management*, Oxford: Butterworth-Heinemann.

Stacey, R. (1966) 'Some Observations on the Economic Implications of Territorial Segregation in South Africa', *South African Journal of Economics*, 34(1): 50–67.

——(1968) 'The Accuracy of the Stellenbosch Bureau Forecasts', *South African Journal of Economics*, 36(3): 198–210.

——(1969) 'Uniformity in Output Growth Patterns in the Manufacturing Sector', *South African Journal of Economics*, 37(1): 55–75.

——(1990) *Dynamic Strategic Management for the 1990s*, London: Kogan Page.

——(1991) *The Chaos Frontier: Creative Strategic Control for Business*, Oxford: Butterworth-Heinemann.

——(1992) *Managing the Unknowable: Strategic Boundaries between Order and Chaos in Organizations*, San Francisco, CA: Jossey-Bass. Also published in the UK as *Managing Chaos*, London: Kogan Page.

——(1993) *Strategic Management and Organisational Dynamics*, London: Pitman.

——(1995) 'The Science of Complexity: An Alternative Perspective for Strategic Change Processes', *Strategic Management Journal*, 16(6): 477–95.

——(1996) *Complexity and Creativity in Organizations*, San Francisco, CA: Berret-Koehler.

——(2001) *Complex Responsive Processes in Organizations: Learning and Knowledge Creation*, London: Routledge.

——(2003) *Complexity and Group Processes: A Radically Social Understanding of Individuals*, London: Brunner-Routledge.

——(ed.) (2005) *Experiencing Emergence in Organizations: Local Interaction and the Emergence of Global Pattern*, London: Routledge.

——(2010) *Complexity and Organizational Reality: Uncertainty and the Need to Rethink Management after the Collapse of Investment Capitalism*, London: Routledge.

——(2011) *Strategic Management and Organisational Dynamics: The Challenge of Complexity to Ways of Thinking about Organisations*, London: Pearson Education (6th edn).

Stacey, R. and Griffin, D. (eds) (2005a) *A Complexity Perspective on Researching Organizations: Taking Experience Seriously*, London: Routledge.

——(2005b) *Complexity and the Experience of Managing in the Public Sector*, London: Routledge.

——(2008) *Complexity and the Experience of Values, Conflict and Compromise in Organizations*, London: Routledge.

Stacey, R., Griffin, D. and Shaw, P. (1998) 'Speaking of Complexity in Management Theory and Practice', *Organization*, 5(3): 315–38.

——(1999) 'Knowing and Acting in Conditions of Uncertainty: A Complexity Perspective', *Systemic Practice and Action Research*, 12(3): 295–309.

——(2000) *Complexity and Management: Fad or Radical Challenge to Systems Thinking?*, London: Routledge.

Stewart, I. (1989) *Does God Play Dice? The Mathematics of Chaos*, Oxford: Blackwell.

Streatfield, P. (2001) *The Paradox of Control in Organizations*, London: Routledge.

Swedberg, R. (1994) 'Markets as Social Structures', in Smelser, N. and Swedberg, R. (eds) *The Handbook of Economic Sociology*, Princeton, NJ: Princeton University Press.

——(1998) *Max Weber and the Idea of Economic Sociology*, Princeton, NJ: Princeton University Press.

——(2003) *Principles of Economic Sociology*, Princeton, NJ: Princeton University Press.

Taylor, C. (1997) *Philosophical Arguments*, Cambridge, MA, and London: Harvard University Press.

Taylor, J. (2005a) 'The Leader: An Emergent, Participative Role', unpublished thesis, University of Hertfordshire.

——(2005b) 'Leadership and Cult Values: Moving from the Idealized to the Experienced', in Griffin, D. and Stacey, R. (eds) *Complexity and the Experience of Leading Organizations*, London: Routledge.

Tobin, J. (2005a) 'The Practical Side of Complexity: Implications for Leaders', unpublished thesis, University of Hertfordshire.

——(2005b) 'The Role of Leader and the Paradox of Detached Involvement', in Griffin, D. and Stacey, R. (eds) *Complexity and the Experience of Leading Organizations*, London: Routledge.

Veblen, T. (1909) 'The Limitations of Marginal Utility', *Journal of Political Economy*, 17(9): 620–36.

——(1989 [1934]) *The Theory of the Leisure Class: An Economic Study in the Evolution of Institutions*, New York: The Modern Library.

Waldrop, M. (1992) *Complexity: The Emerging Science at the Edge of Order and Chaos*, London: Viking.

Weick, K. (1979) *The Social Psychology of Organizing*, Reading, MA: Addison-Wesley.

Wheatley, M. J. (1992) *Leadership and the New Science*, revised edn, San Francisco, CA: Berrett-Koehler.

Williamson, O. (1975) *Markets and Hierarchies: Analysis and Antitrust Implications*, New York: The Free Press.

——(1981) 'The Economics of Organization: The Transaction Cost Approach', *American Journal of Sociology*, 87(3): 548–77.

——(1985) *The Economic Institutions of Capitalism*, New York: The Free Press.

——(1994) 'Transaction Cost Economics and Organization Theory', in Smelser, N. and Swedberg, R. (eds) *The Handbook of Economic Sociology*, Princeton, NJ: Princeton University Press.

——(2000) 'The New Institutional Economics: Taking Stock, Looking Ahead', *Journal of Economic Literature*, XXXVIII(3): 595–613.

Winnicott, D. (1971) *Playing and Reality*, London: Tavistock.

Young, T. R. (1992) 'Chaos Theory and Human Agency', *Humanity and Society*, 16(4): 441–60.

Zaleznik, A. (1977) 'Managers and Leaders: Are They Different?', *Harvard Business Review*, 70(2): 126–35.

Zaleznik, A. and Kets de Vries, M. (1985) *Power and the Corporate Mind*, Chicago, IL: Bonus books.

Zimmerman, B. (1990) 'Nonequilibrium: The Flipside of Strategic Process', working paper, North York, Canada, Faculty of Administrative Studies, York University.

——(1992) 'The Inherent Drive towards Chaos', in Lorange, P., Chakravarty, B., Van de Ven, A. and Roos, J. (eds) *Implementing Strategic Processes: Change, Learning and Cooperation*, London: Blackwell.

INDEX